ON

THE ORIGIN, NATURE,

PROGRESS AND INFLUENCE

OF

CONSULAR ESTABLISHMENTS,

BY D. B. WARDEN,

CONSUL GENERAL OF THE UNITED STATES OF AMERICA, AT PARIS; D.r MED. COLL. NOV. EBOR.; MEMBER OF THE PHILOSOPHICAL SOCIETY OF PHILADELPHIA; OF THE PHILOMATIC SOCIETY, AND OF THE SOCIETY FOR THE ENCOURAGEMENT OF ARTS AND MANUFACTURES, AT PARIS; OF THE BELFAST LITERARY SOCIETY, ETC. ETC. ETC.

With a new introduction by William E. Butler

John Edward Fowler Distinguished Professor of Law,
Pennsylvania State University;
Academician, National Academy of Sciences of Ukraine and
Russian Academy of Natural Sciences

THE LAWBOOK EXCHANGE, LTD.
Clark, New Jersey

ISBN 9781616190668 (hardcover)
ISBN 9781616191160 (paperback)

Lawbook Exchange edition 2011

The quality of this reprint is equivalent to the quality of the original work.

THE LAWBOOK EXCHANGE, LTD.
33 Terminal Avenue
Clark, New Jersey 07066-1321

Please see our website for a selection of our other publications and fine facsimile reprints of classic works of legal history:
www.lawbookexchange.com

Library of Congress Cataloging-in-Publication Data

Warden, David Bailie, 1772-1845.
On the origin, nature, progress, and influence of consular establishments / by D.B. Warden.
p. cm.
Originally published: Paris : Printed and sold by Smith, 1813.
With a new introduction by William E. Butler.
Includes bibliographical references.
ISBN 978-1-61619-066-8 (hardcover : alk. paper) --
ISBN 978-1-61619-116-0 (pbk. : alk. paper)
1. Consular law. 2. Diplomatic privileges and immunities.
I. Title.
K3201.W37 2010
341.3'5--dc22 2010039007

Printed in the United States of America on acid-free paper

DAVID BAILIE WARDEN AND THE DEVELOPMENT OF CONSULAR LAW

William E. Butler

In the formative days of the United States of America, just as in the formation of the centralized Muscovite State and eventual emergence of the Russian Empire, it was the diplomatic corps that played the major role in articulating concepts and rules of the law of nations in the course of the performance of their duties. Some, such as P. P. Shafirov in Russia,[1] or David Bailie Warden in the United States, were the authors of pioneering treatises on aspects of the law of nations. In this capacity they advanced the emergence of doctrinal views and a specialist literature on international law. As Grabar expressed the position with reference to Russian diplomats, they were "diplomat-jurists, ambassadorial secretaries" – these, he said, "… are our 'legists'".[2] The same applies to diplomats of the United

[1] See P. P. Shafirov, Рассуждение, какие законные прийины Петр I, царь и повелитель всероссийский, к начатию войны против Карла XII, короля шведского, в 1700 году имел [Discourse on the Legal Reasons of Peter I, Tsar and Ruler of All the Russias, to Commence War Against Charles XII, King of Sweden, in 1700], intro. W. E. Butler (2008). For the most recent version of my essay on Shafirov, see W. E. Butler, "P. P. Shafirov and the Law of Nations", in Butler, *Russia and the Law of Nations in Historical Perspective* (2009), pp. 207-250.

[2] V. E. Grabar, *The History of International Law in Russia 1647-1917: A Bio-Bibliographical Study*, transl. & ed. by W. E. Butler (1990). A revised Russian-language edition has been issued which incorporates the editorial emendations drawn from my English translation: id, Материалы к истории международного права в России (1647-1917) [Materials on the History of International Law in Russia (1647-1917)], ed. W. E. Butler (2005).

States in the early years of the American Republic. It was they who were learned in the law of nations.

Consular law, it is widely believed, is among the most venerable of the institutes of the law of nations and an early example, in State practice and doctrinal form, of the comparative investigation and analysis of State practice in the form of treaties, national legislation, and judicial application.

The Author

David Bailie Warden was born in 1772, precise date unknown, in Ballycastle, County Down, Ireland. His father (Robert Warden; m. Elizabeth Bailie) held a tenancy on the estates of the Stewarts, the Londonderry family that produced Robert Stewart, Lord Castlereagh (1769-1822), in due course Secretary of War and then Foreign Secretary of the United Kingdom. Warden attended Bangor Academy and then the University of Glasgow. At Glasgow he was awarded the Master of Arts degree in 1797, a prize for natural philosophy, and a certificate in midwifery.[3] His interest in medicine, or "physick" as the discipline was widely known at the time, endured throughout his life. For the moment, however, he resolved to pursue a career in the Presbyterian ministry. The Presbytery of Bangor issued Warden a provisional license to preach, but almost immediately Warden found himself among the group behind the Irish uprising led by Theobald Wolfe Tone (1763-1798). Warden accepted a commission of colonel

---

[3] The diploma (Glasgow University), prize certificate, and midwifery certificate (Glasgow College) are held among the Warden Papers at the Maryland Historical Society (hereinafter: MdHS). See Reel 1, Warden Papers, MdHS.

and aide-de-camp to the Lisburn draper, General Henry Munro[e] (d. 1798).

The uprising went badly. Warden was among those captured by British forces. Imprisoned under desperate conditions on a prison ship, Warden was eventually given the choice through the intercession of influential friends of exile from Britain forever or of standing trial and risking execution.[4] America was his choice. He set sail in 1799. His relations with the Wolfe Tone family endured, both with the widow and her son, William Theobald Wolfe Tone (1791-1828).[5]

Once in the United States he enjoyed the assistance of Peter Wilson (1746-1825), the Professor of Latin and Greek at Columbia College in New York City, in seeking employment. Wilson wrote after an interview with him that Warden was well-grounded in medicine, civil law, elocution, and the French language.[6] Warden accepted an appointment as Principal of a seminary at Kinderhook, New York, where he taught a vast range of subjects and devoted himself to sundry agricultural, meteorological, chemical, and medical research. The surviving notebooks show Warden to be an alert and knowledgeable student of natural phenomena.[7] His duly recorded observations and samples of plants, rocks, minerals, and relics sent to his

---

[4] Warden's experience in the Irish uprising became the subject of public comment in the United States some years later. See a biographical article on Warden written with his approval by William Sinclair, *Whig* [Baltimore], 9 July 1808, and related correspondence between Sinclair and Warden, 18 September 1808. Warden Papers, MdHS. Also see Rev. W. T. Latimer, "David Bailie Warden, Patriot 1798", *Ulster Journal of Archaeology*, XIII (1907), pp. 29-38.

[5] A number of letters to Warden survive from the Wolfe Tone family period in France and later in Washington D. C.

[6] Wilson to Isaac Labagh, 20 June 1799. Warden Papers, MdHS.

[7] Some of the notebooks survive in the Warden Papers, Manuscript Division, DLC.

friend, Dr. Samuel Martin Stephenson (1742-1833) in Belfast, Ireland, secured election to the Literary Society of Belfast.[8]

In 1801 Warden accepted an appointment as principal tutor in the Kingston Academy in Ulster County, New York. The range of subjects for which he was personally responsible was formidable: as enumerated in his contract,[9] for the sum of $450 per annum (raised to $500 on 28 October 1802) he taught some fifty students Greek, Latin, elementary and practical geometry, mathematics, logic, moral and natural philosophy, ancient history, geography, the history and government of the United States, and the French language if required. A fragment from the local press in Kingston recorded: "The students of Kingston Academy were yesterday examined by the Trustees of this seminary. In the presence of several literary gentlemen – The progress of the students in the different sciences was highly flattering to their parents, and did honor to the genius and ability of the principal".[10]

The removal to Kingston proved to be greatly in Warden's interest. There he preached in the local churches from time to time and mixed with leading figures in the local community.[11] Soon he attracted the attention of General John Armstrong, Jr. (1758-1843), who had relocated to New York following a celebrated political

---

[8] The Certificate of election is held in the Warden Papers, MdHS.

[9] The contract is held in the Warden Papers, MdHS. Also see D. B. Warden, *The Frame of the Material World Manifests, that There Must be a God: A Discourse on the Ensuing Words of the Book of Psalms: Delivered before the Students in Kingston Academy* ([1804]).

[10] The date is obscured but ca. 2 October 1802. See Reel 7, Warden Papers, MdHS.

[11] See D. B. Warden, *A Sermon on the Advantages of Education: Preached in the Reformed Dutch Protestant Church, Kingston, on the 30th of April, 1802* (1802).

career in Carlisle, Pennsylvania, where he was born.[12] Armstrong persuaded Warden to join his household as tutor for his children, an appointment that enhanced Warden's social status and provided opportunities to extend what proved to be in later life a useful range of contacts. In Kingston, Warden continued to pursue his investigations into local physical geography, developing an enduring interest in Indian artifacts. The abrupt appointment of his employer to be the United States Minister to France in replacement of his brother-in-law, Robert Livingston (1746-1813), changed his life completely and forever. Armstrong resolved to have Warden accompany him to Paris as secretary of the Legation.

This was an appointment that could entail serious risks for Warden, he having undertaken to never set foot on British territory for the remainder of his life. Any ship sailing from the United States to France was likely to put into a British port. General Armstrong had two suggestions for reducing, if not eliminating, the dangers: Warden should take United States citizenship and carry with him documents confirming his appointment as secretary of the Legation, at the same time keeping his presence on the ship and his Irish past as confidential as possible.[13] Warden accepted the appointment and followed Armstrong's advice. It required some time to complete the citizenship formalities, but on 23 October 1804 Warden became a

---

[12] On Armstrong, see C. E. Skeen, *John Armstrong, Jr., 1758-1843: A Biography* (1982).

[13] "There is no difficulty in acquiring citizenship … With regard to the passports you will have no difficulty … I shall leave with Gen. Bailey a certificate of your being my Secretary, upon which you will obtain them at once. With these, you will have nothing to fear, observing the ordinary prudence of keeping your own secret. We sail on Tuesday … Loose [sic] no time in following me". Armstrong to Warden at Kingston Academy, 24 August 1804. Reel 1, Warden Papers, MdHS.

United States citizen, obtained his passport, and followed Armstrong to Paris without further incident.

Whether in Paris Warden continued to act as tutor to the Armstrong children – as Armstrong's political opponents in the United States were later to charge in the American press – while employed as secretary to the Legation is unclear but unproved. Assuredly, he did help the Armstrongs integrate into French life and society, his fluency in the French language being of inestimable help to them and to himself. Plainly his duties as secretary left Warden with time to continue his medical studies at the elite École de Médecine de Paris.[14]

Medicine competed with chemistry in Warden's career ambitions, so much so that at one point he was prepared to abandon medicine completely in favor of chemistry. His medical friends advised against this course of action, which Warden evidently accepted. Although the documentation is not complete, it would appear that Warden passed the examinations for a medical degree at Paris in 1808. He is identified as "M.D." on the title page of his treatise on consular law. For Warden, however, medicine was merely one point of access to the pursuit of science. There is no evidence that Warden ever practiced, or intended to practice, as a physician.

The potent combination of career path and aspirations, intellectual curiosity and ability, social and linguistic skills, and an engaging personality enabled Warden to secure an unrivalled niche for himself in Paris for the remainder of his life. As secretary of the United States Legation, he encountered virtually every United States citizen passing

[14] For the list of his courses and instructors, see an anonymous obituary whose facts are not always correct: "Some Lie Far Off Beyond the Wave", *Northern Whig* [Belfast], 12 May 1846. Available in the Warden Papers, MdHS.

through the capital of France in whatever capacity. His rank and his pursuit of scientific studies brought him into useful contact with the elite of the French intellectual community. He befriended all effortlessly, rapidly making himself indispensable as principal and intermediary between the two cultures and gradually positioning himself as an original contributor to both intellectual communities.

In this he exceeded the abilities of his superiors and colleagues, most of whom were disadvantaged linguistically or intellectually, or both, in comparison with Warden. They were perforce dependent upon him in so many ways, factors that promoted his prospects and, on occasion, generated destructive envy and rivalry. The Warden archives collectively document the exceptional role that Warden came to play in promoting intellectual, cultural, commercial, and diplomatic contacts for the United States at governmental and interpersonal levels. The outlines of these have been well documented by Haber[15] and need not detain us here other than to note that Warden's role was seen, and rightly so, as innovative for the post of Legation secretary and later Consul. It came, as we shall see below, to dominate his understanding of what functions the consul should perform.

The services which Warden came to routinely perform included a massive correspondence with Americans, whether they had or intended to visit Paris or not, who wished to be kept apprised of European scientific achievements or who wished to have their own accomplishments and ideas brought to the attention of European colleagues. This meant letters, of course, and the

---

[15] See Francis C. Haber, *David Bailie Warden, A Bibliographical Sketch of America's Cultural Ambassador in France, 1804-1845* (1954).

exchange and circulation of publications.[16] Being close to the Legation meant that Warden knew the movements of most ships in and out of France; he was well positioned to move letters and packages for people.

Correspondent of International Lawyers

Although Warden was trained principally in the natural sciences and philosophy, his legal acumen was noted when he interviewed for his first teaching appointment in the United States. He impressed his interlocutor with his command of civil law, perhaps not surprising for a graduate of a Scottish university. Even a passing background in natural law philosophy and civil law will have made Warden more comfortable with the law of nations in his day.

Warden was in frequent contact with several international lawyers before and after the publication of his work on consular law. We consider the more important and interesting of these relationships below.

Peter Stephen Du Ponceau (1760-1844). Warden and Du Ponceau evidently first met in the Spring of 1811 when Warden visited Philadelphia during his return to the United States in order to secure support for his appointment as Consul in Paris. Their friendship endured until Du Ponceau's death a year or so prior to Warden's. Du Ponceau presented Warden with a copy of his recently published translation of Bynkershoek[17] "which I have been fortunate enough to find myself yet possessed of, when I

[16] In March 1838 Warden distributed 27 copies of Du Ponceau's prize-winning work on Chinese writing and a further 35 copies to M. Eyres. Reel 6, Warden Papers, MdHS.

[17] See P. S. Du Ponceau, *A Treatise on the Law of War*, intro. W. E. Butler (1810; Lawbook Exchange ed., 2008).

thought I had disposed of all".[18] Warden had offered Du Ponceau a copy of his translation of Marcus Aurelius to be collected from the Philadelphia printer and publisher, Mathew Carey. Unfortunately, Carey had exhausted his stock, and Du Ponceau was obliged to seek a copy directly from Warden.[19]

Du Ponceau frequently referred fellow Americans to Warden with letters of introduction and a request that the bearer be shown about Paris. These included students wishing to pursue the science of chemistry, medical doctors, and jurists investigating the prison system.[20] In the course of time Du Ponceau and Warden discovered a mutual interest in the production of silk. Du Ponceau labored assiduously for several years and invested considerable funds in introducing silkworms to the United States and developing domestic American silk production. He failed, but not for want of trying. In 1837 Du Ponceau prepared and arranged the printing of a pamphlet on the history of the Silk bill in the form of a letter to Warden so that Warden might report to the Agricultural Society of Paris on the state of silk culture in the United States.[21] In

---

[18] Du Ponceau to Warden, 14 May 1811. Reel 1, Warden Papers, MdHS. See W. E. Butler, "Cornelius van Bynkershoek and P. S. du Ponceau: A Likely Pair", in Butler, note 1 above, pp. 306-334.

[19] Du Ponceau to Warden, 28 June 1811. Reel 1, Warden Papers, MdHS.

[20] See Du Ponceau to Warden, 10 May 1828, 23 July 1829, 1 April 1831, 13 May 1833, and 12 December 1835. Reels 3 and 4, Warden Papers, MdHS; Du Ponceau to Warden, 21 April 1821 and 27 February 1831. Warden Papers, DLC.

[21] P. S. Du Ponceau, *The History of the Silk Bill, in a Letter from Peter S. Duponceau to David B. Warden* (1837). 12 p. The Society to which Du Ponceau referred was presumably the Société d'Agriculture, Sciences et Arts du Département de l'Eure, to which Warden was elected on 5 July 1827.

his letter accompanying a supply of the pamphlet Du Ponceau wrote:

> According to my promise, I send you the History of the Silk Bill, with the number of the American Quarterly Review for December 1831, in which there is an article on silk, which, with the other pamphlet, will, I hope, enable you to make a full communication to the Agricultural Society of Paris, on the state of the silk culture in this country.
>
> I beg you will present a copy of the "Silk Bill" to the Geographical Society, of which I have the honor to be a Corresponding Member; a few are marked with the names of persons to whom I beg you will deliver and forward them in my name with my respects. The remainder you will dispose of as you shall think proper.[22]

It was Warden, moreover, who acquired on behalf of Du Ponceau from the translator a supply of the French version of Du Ponceau's work on the United States Constitution:

> I received yesterday your favor of the 24th of May, in which you are pleased to inform me that Mr d'Homerque has put into your hands some copies of his translation of my little work on the Constitution of the U.S. & that you distribute them among the different learned societies. I have not yet seen this translation; I presume Mr. d'Homerque sent it to me, but it miscarried. I have not heard from him for quite a while, & do not know whether he is yet in France, or when he will return to this country.[23]

---

[22] Du Ponceau to Warden, 9 July 1837. Warden Papers, DLC. On 12 September 1837 Du Ponceau sent a List to Warden of individuals who should receive a copy of the pamphlet, among them: Mr. Eyres, Robert Walsh, and Baron Pichon. Reel 6, Warden Papers, MdHS.

[23] Du Ponceau to Warden, 28 July 1837. Warden Papers, DLC. Du Ponceau refers to Mr. John d'Homerque, who published Du Ponceau, *Exposé sommaire de la Constitution des États-Unis d'Amérique* (1837).

When du Ponceau was awarded the Volney Prize for his seminal work on language, Warden collected and dispatched the diploma to him on 29 August 1839.[24]

Late in life Du Ponceau complained of failing eyesight but continued to exchange books with Warden[25] and from time to time expounded at length on his linguistic research, world politics, and the politics of the day.[26]

Henry Wheaton (1785-1848). Wheaton initially produced a treatise on the law of nations[27] and was later inspired to devote a substantial work specifically to the history of international law by a prize competition arranged by the Academy of Moral and Political Sciences in the Institute of France on the subject: "Quels sont les progress qu'a fait le droit des gens en Europe depuis la Paix de Westphalie?".[28]

---

[24] Warden to Du Ponceau, Reel 6, Warden Papers, MdHS. See P. S. Du Ponceau, *Mémoire sur le systéme grammatical des langues de quelques nations indiennes de l'Amerique du Nord* (1838). The English-language version was published in the same year by the American Philosophical Society.

[25] "I am now in my 84th year and it is time I should extinguish myself at least as a writer. But I am fond of reading and conversation, but I can only enjoy the first in broad day light and when the sky is not overcast". Du Ponceau to Warden, 6 August 1842 and 10 August 1843. Reel 5, Warden Papers, MdHS.

[26] Du Ponceau to Warden, 17 November 1843. Warden Papers, DLC.

[27] H. Wheaton, *Elements of International Law with A Sketch of the History of the Science* (1836), 2 vols.. The "Sketch" is brief indeed, although many years earlier Wheaton had produced a "rapid view" of the history of the science of "Public or International Law" upon which he drew for his later studies. See Wheaton, *An Anniversary Discourse, Delivered Before the New-York Historical Society, on Thursday, December 28, 1820* ([1821]).

[28] Wheaton, *History of the Law of Nations in Europe and America; From the Earliest Times to the Treaty of Washington, 1842* (1845). A French edition, however, appeared several years earlier and the Harvard Law School Library records a "Memoire" which may or may not be related to this work, undated but ascribed to ca. 1838. Wheaton's entry

Not unlike Warden, Henry Wheaton spent long periods abroad in diplomatic service and published his major works on international law in European countries.

Wheaton approached Warden, however, by reason of the latter's membership in that most prestigious of learned academies, the Institute of France, also known as the French Institute.[29] Wheaton initially sought Warden's support for election in a letter of 15 February 1838,[30] which he apparently was given. Thereafter Wheaton lobbied vigorously, seeking information on the number of vacancies, support from other academicians, including Alexander von Humboldt (1769-1859), instructions to persist with his candidacy, and constant updates on the state of play in the Institute.[31] In passing he reported on his own intellectual achievements which he hoped would buttress his election to the Institute. On 15 January 1840 Wheaton wrote to Warden that his work on the historical view of the progress of international law would be published at Paris "in the course of the Winter or Spring", though in fact it was delayed until 1841, and added that "I have prefixed a sketch of the history of the law of Nations before the Peace of Westphalia so as to make it a complete history of the

---

in the competition was awarded Honorable Mention. For the French edition, see H. Wheaton, *Histoire des progrès du droit des gens en Europe, depuis la paix de Westphalie jusqu'au Congrès de Vienne, avec un précis historique du droit des gens Européen avant la paix de Westphalie* (1841).

[29] Founded in 1795, the Institut de France combined five academies, of which the Académie des sciences morales et politiques was the relevant body for Warden and Wheaton. There was a fixed quota of places in the Institute, which meant that elections were possible when vacancies occurred, usually by reason of death of a member.

[30] Wheaton to Warden, Reel 4, Warden Papers, MdHS.

[31] Wheaton to Warden, Letters of 16 October 1838, 13 December 1838, 26 February 1839, 26 March 1839, 24 April 1839, 15 January 1840, and others. Reels 4 and 5, Warden Papers, MdHS.

Science". In a passage that must have struck terror into the heart of Warden, who spoke from time to time of revising his work on consuls, but might have been intended as encouragement, Wheaton said: "Baron Miltitz has not yet done his interminable work on Consuls, which will still leave room (as it appears to me) for a compendium in one volume containing in a succinct form all that is most useful & necessary & to serve as a ready book of reference for Consuls".[32]

Wheaton was elected to the Institute of France in 1843.

Joseph Story (1779-1845). Henry Wheaton was not the only American seeking election to the Institute of France. Story's protégé and colleague, Charles Sumner (1811-1874), wrote to Warden inquiring about the procedures and practices for election:

> I now trouble you again with regard to this matter, to request that you would explain the rule and practice with regard to the candidate's addressing a letter to the Academy. Is this absolutely required? Are not persons chosen, who do not do this? I think that Dr. Bowditch was on the eve of being elected at the time of his death, & he certainly never addressed any such letter to the Academy. I fear that Judge S. would be unwilling to do this.
>
> I feel ashamed of myself for troubling you so much about this affair; but I love Story as a personal friend, and I think him the first jurist – not simply of America – but of an age.[33]

Robert von Mohl (1799-1875). The then young German legal scholar, Robert von Mohl, presented his first (of many

---

[32] Wheaton to Warden, 15 January 1840, Reel 5, Warden Papers, MdHS. Wheaton is referring to the massive treatise by Alexandre de Miltitz, *Manuel des Consuls* (1837-41), published in parts over a five-year period.

[33] Sumner to Warden, 31 March 1840. Reel 5, Warden Papers, MdHS.

to come) work on United States constitutional law to Warden.[34] In his accompanying letter Mohl explained that he had relied upon Warden's historical account of the United States. Although there may be inaccuracies in his own work, Mohl said that the book was intended for compatriots in Prussia who needed the necessary knowledge to govern themselves with a federative constitution. Mohl subsequently became a member of the Frankfort Parliament of 1848 and Minister of Justice. So far as is known, Warden did not have a command of the German language and did not use German sources in his own researches.

Warden as Bibliophile and Bibliographer

Books were a central part of Warden's life. He must have been the darling of the French book trade, new and antiquarian, for he filled massive requests to acquire particular titles or even shop generally on certain subject-matter. He routinely advanced monies of his own to acquire books for others (Thomas Jefferson[35] was a frequent and long-term debtor, who did, however, ultimately settle his accounts) or accepted substantial sums on deposit for others to be used for book purchases. His "clientele" ranged from the United States Department of State (especially expensive atlases and European accounts of geographical or boundary

---

[34] R. von Mohl, *Das Bundes-staatsrecht der Vereinigten Staaten von Nord-Amerika* (1824). See Mohl to Warden, 10 March 1824. Warden Papers, DLC.

[35] The Library of Congress was given Jefferson's copy of *Mémoires de Louis XIV écrits par lui-même*, edited by J. L. M. Gain-Montagnac (1806) inscribed by David B. Warden. The Library noted that Warden had dedicated his translation of Antoine Thomas, *Eulogium on Marcus Aurelius* (1807) to Jefferson, "The Marcus Aurelius of the United States".

"discoveries" in the New World),[36] to American lawyers forming a personal library of comparative and international law,[37] to learned institutions such as the American Philosophical Society[38] or Columbia University,[39] to American tourists passing through. For himself and fellow Europeans he solicited the assistance of American

---

[36] On 8 March 1811 the Department of State sent Warden the sum of $250 to purchase publications useful to the Secretary of State and an atlas. In responding to a price inquiry from John Graham, Clerk of the Department of State, about the price of G. F. Martens, *Traité de paix*, Warden replied in November 1811: "The Traité de paix by Martens has become rare, which is the cause of the high price as the bookseller had great difficulty to procure a copy". Reels 1 and 7, Warden Papers, MdHS.

[37] John Rodman wrote from New York to Warden on 3 December 1815 with a lengthy, priced request for books, even recommending the bookshop in Paris where they might best be obtained (chez Madame Veuve Dufresne Librairie). Among the titles sought were: the Elsevier edition of the "Code et novelles de Justinian"; the Consulat de la Mer in the Boucher translation; the Cours elementaire du droit civil by Vasscher; the Droit de la guerre et de la paix by Grotius ($10); Droit de la nature et des Gens, of Pufendorf translated by Barbeyrac ($12), Elemens de droit natural by Burlamaqui ($5); Us et coutumes de la mer ($10), and Code des prises maritime by Guichard ($6). In all the requests exceeded US$1,000. Later correspondence indicates that Rodman experienced difficulties in paying for the books, which he duly received in 1816. See Warden Papers, DLC.

[38] Warden was elected to the American Philosophical Society on 1 April 1809. His first, of many, gift of books to the APS was 18 August 1809. Throughout the remainder of his life he was a major source of books for the APS, the archives being especially rich in communications from the Librarians, John Vaughan and then George Ord, thanking Warden for materials supplied and/or requesting others. Some APS members, for example, Peter Du Ponceau, used the Society as a convenient center for items to be delivered to them.

[39] Among Warden's friends at Columbia was Samuel L. Mitchill (1764-1831), for whom Warden acquired 55 volumes of the *Annales de Chimie* and other journals. See Warden to Mitchill, 1 August 1807. Warden Papers, MdHS.

correspondents to acquire items published in the United States. The Warden archives are rich in documentation for such transactions, but can only represent a small percentage of the actual trade. Warden will single-handedly have accounted for many tens of thousands of volumes making their way across the Atlantic Ocean in both directions to enrich personal and institutional libraries.[40]

So far as is known, Warden did not have a personal bookplate. His manuscript ex-libris is found on individual volumes from time to time. But Warden was a major bibliophile of his era. Twice in his lifetime he formed truly remarkable personal libraries devoted primarily to Americana. Both were catalogued and sold, the first for $5,000 to Samuel Atkins Eliot (1798-1862) who presented the books to Harvard University; the second for $4,000 to the State of New York.

"Catalogued" in this case means not a private handlist in his own hand, although he filled notebooks with his own collection inventory. Although most entries were handwritten, he did preserve small clippings from newspapers or book catalogues and paste these in. The notebooks are organized by subject.[41] Ultimately, each notebook presumably served him as a reminder of what he already had and as copy for the printer. Warden arranged to have his catalogues printed and circulated among friends, acquaintances, and institutions in the hope that sooner or later someone would purchase the collections en bloc. Whether he intended this as a form of business or merely

---

[40] This is a dimension of the Atlantic book trade mostly neglected in recent systematic studies of the flow of books, which have necessarily concentrated upon exports and imports flowing directly from one publisher and/or bookseller to another. Whatever these statistics show, materials such as the Warden Archives will suggest that they represent merely a fraction of the true figures.

[41] Several examples are to be found in the Warden Papers, DLC.

an act of desperation to augment his slender revenues cannot be determined with certainty. To his friends he constantly emphasized the last, although he routinely rejected offers to acquire individual volumes.

The first catalogue appeared in 1820, printed in Paris by Imprimerie Nouzou.[42] It is widely respected as one of the early examples of American subject-based bibliography.[43] The collection comprised some 1,200 volumes and a number of maps. Although formed with the passion and skills of a committed bibliophile, the collection was plainly used as a working library to assist especially with Warden's well-received *A Statistical, Political, and Historical Account of the United States of North America: from the Period of Their First Colonization to the Present Day* (Edinburgh, 1819). It is unlikely to be coincidental that he decided to part with the reference collection used to write this three-volume work (in English; five volumes in French) upon completion.

By May 1820 the catalogue was in the hands of potential purchasers or those who might influence a potential purchase. Byerley wrote to thank Warden for the catalogue of his library but cautioned: "I fear you will

---

[42] See D. B. Warden, *Bibliotheca americo-septentrionalis: Being a Choice Collection of Books in Various Languages, Relating to the History, Climate, Geography, Produce, Population, Agriculture, Commerce, Arts, Sciences, Etc. of North America, from its First Discovery to its Present Existing Government ... with all the Important Official Documents Published ... by the Authority of Congress* (1820). 147 p.

[43] Harisse described Warden as the "first notable bibliographer of Americana from the United States" and author of a work which "evinces methodical habits, and a competent knowledge of the subject". See [Henry Harisse], *A Description of Works Relating to America Published Between the Years 1492 and 1551: Bibliotheca Americana Vetustissima* (1866), pp. xxv-xxvi.

experience great difficulty in disposing of it in one lot".[44] William Wolfe Tone expressed the same view writing from Washington D. C.: "... General Mason says and I believe with truth that there is no possibility of disposing of your books here. Economy is so much the order of the day at headquarters. But there is no possibility of disposing of them to the Government and they would go for little or nothing at a Sale from the glut of the markets".[45] Both were excessively pessimistic, as the course of events proved.

By the early 1830s Warden found himself in a similar financial position. A catalogue published in 1831 offered 1,790 volumes, twelve atlases, 121 separate maps, charts, and plans, nine medals, and two prints, "many of them are rare and valuable".[46] On this occasion a sale proved more difficult. The Warden Collection substantially duplicated that which he had previously sold to Harvard. Apparently Warden used every opportunity to distribute the catalogue. A distribution list drawn up in ca. May 1831 gives names for 152 copies, including one to Peter S. Du Ponceau.[47] As

---

[44] J. Byerley to Warden, 24 May 1820. Reel 3, Warden Papers, MdHS. There were offers to purchase selected volumes from the collection. David James McCord (1797-1855) wrote to Warden and, in his capacity as a trustee for South Carolina College, expressed interest in buying volumes. See McCord to Warden, 29 June 1831. 1996 Manuscripts Collections, South Caroliniana Library.

[45] William Theobald Wolfe Tone, 7 January 1823, writing from Georgetown. Reel 3, Warden Papers, MdHS.

[46] [D. B. Warden], *Bibliotheca Americana, Being a Choice Collection of Books Relating to North and South America and the West-Indies, Including Voyages to the Southern Hemisphere, Maps, Engravings and Medals* (1840). Printed by Paul Renouard. Catalogues have their risks too. The Marquis de La Fayette, having received this catalogue, wrote on 7 July 1831 to say that one volume listed therein he had lent to Warden and never received back. Warden said that the Marquis was mistaken and that he had never borrowed the book. Reel 4, Warden Papers, MdHS.

[47] The List is found on Reel 6, Warden Papers, MdHS.

late as 1838 his friend Joseph Cabell wrote Warden to express his regrets at his inability to sell the library.[48]

The library did not increase markedly in size during the 1830s while it was on the market. Perhaps this reflected Warden's financial difficulties and an inability to add to the collection, or perhaps advanced age and the completion of a number of writing projects. Whatever the reason, Warden decided to print a new catalogue and endeavor once again to dispose of his library en bloc. The 1840 catalogue contained 1,978 volumes, with no change in the numbers of maps, charts, plans, medals, or prints.[49] Warden wrote to Isaiah Townsend that he wanted $11,000 for the library payable in two yearly installments.[50] Townsend lobbied assiduously on Warden's behalf, as did others. The State of New York Library was a promising prospect. In late February 1844 Townsend advised Warden that a report on the Warden Collection was pending in the New York legislature.[51] That Report was forthcoming in May 1844, having been prepared jointly by George Bancroft (1800-1891), the noted historian and statesman, and Jared Sparks (1789-1866), the historian and educator. It is appropriate to quote their observations at length:

---

[48] Joseph C. Cabell to Warden, 18 May 1838. Reel 4, Warden Papers, MdHS. Cabell played a leading role in founding the University of Virginia.

[49] [D. B. Warden], *Bibliotheca Americana, Being a Choice Collection of Books Relating to North and South America and the West-Indies, Including Voyages to the Southern Hemisphere, Maps, Engravings and Medals* (1840). Printed by Fain and Thunot. A manuscript version of this catalogue is in Reel 6, Warden Papers, MdHS, and on Reel 7 there is a manuscript copy of "Books Relating to the United States" with locations and/or prices marked.

[50] Warden to Townsend, 12 February 1843. Reel 6, Warden Papers, MdHS.

[51] Townsend to Warden, 26 February 1844. Reel 5, Warden Papers, MdHS.

[Bancroft]: I hope you will be able to secure to your New York State Library Warden's American collection. I have not his catalogue and can therefore form no judgment of its pecuniary value: but since experience leads me to know the difficulty of getting together books in American History. Wardens position in Paris has been extremely favorable for that end; and the next eighteen years of diligence could achieve less than the last. Every year enhances the cost and difficulty of making these collections ...

As to the cost of old books, Rich sent me last steamer five volumes, three of them very small: the cost was more than $15. Besides: of these, one little one cost £1.10 or more that is, delivered here, more than $8. So the price of Wardens library is moderate enough if his books are rare, but I have not his catalogue at hand, which I regret the less as Sparks is enough on that head.

[Sparks continues]: I have received your letter asking my opinion of the character and value of the collection of books offered for sale by Mr. Warden. After a partial examination of the books themselves in Paris, and a careful inspection of the catalogue, I cannot hesitate to say that I think they would make an extremely important addition to any public library in the United States, which does not already possess them. I know from my own experience that books on America are constantly becoming more and more scarce in Europe, because the demand of them is increasing and very few of them are printed. It is moreover a rare chance to find any considerable number of these books on sale at one time. It would take years to make such a collection as that of Mr. Warden; and if the works were ordered separately, the average cost would be much larger than the price at which he will sell them, because it would be swelled by booksellers commissions and other charges. In my opinion therefore, the expediency of procuring such a collection by any institution which has the means cannot for a moment be doubted. There is scarcely a probability that an opportunity of this kind will recur in a number of years. …

The maps and charts, the titles of which are contained in Mr Warden's catalogue, are many of them peculiarly valuable and of some of them, particularly those relating to the military movements of the Revolution, I know of no copies in the United States. And in fact, it is by mere accident that they can now be

> found anywhere. It is only necessary to run one's eye over the titles to be convinced of their historical importance.[52]

In the end the State of New York was convinced by the quality of the collection and prepared to spend $4,000, with cost of carriage to the seller.[53] Warden's financial condition had so worsened that he had little choice but to accept, which he did, but not happily. Packing, freight to Havre, New York and Albany, plus insurance was quoted as not exceeding $200. A book firm in New York City offered to furnish a like collection in writing for $3,000 (Bartlett and Welford). Townsend wrote, in urging that Warden accept the terms: "I am grieved that the terms should not have given you satisfaction. Better it was impossible for me to obtain ... It has cost me a great deal of time and labor during the better part of three years to secure the purchase ... I was supported and encouraged by the thought that it would be extremely gratifying to you and some amends for the flagrant injustice you once experienced. Sorry indeed should I therefore be, if you found it inexpedient to avail yourself of the occasion".[54]

---

[52] Bancroft and Sparks to Townsend, 10-11 May 1844, Reel 5, Warden Papers, MdHS.

[53] New York did not rely solely on the catalogue. Robert Walsh (1784-1859), then United States Consul in Paris, was asked to view the library, which he duly did and must have given a positive report. Walsh reported to Warden on the proposed sale. See Reel 6, Warden Papers, MdHS.

[54] Townsend to Warden, 29 April 1845. Reel 5, Warden Papers, MdHS. The State of New York by an "Act relative to the State Library" passed 24 April 1845 appropriated the sum of $4,000 for the purchase of the Library of David B. Warden of Paris to be posited in the State Library provided the said Library be delivered for that sum without any charge for transportation of any other expenses of any description. The Collection was placed in a separate locale within the Library. Its loss in a tragic fire of 1911 was inestimable.

Warden as Consul

In April 1808 the United States Consul in Paris, Fulwar Skipwith (1765-1839) resigned his post and returned to his home country to pursue interests in Florida and Louisiana.[55] Warden moved swiftly to be considered for the position, writing both to his superior General Armstrong and to President Jefferson. On 24 August 1808 Armstrong advised Warden of his appointment as Consul and Agent of Prize Causes, but two days later wrote to clarify the situation:

> "... I omitted informing you in my last letter that this appointment made of you as Consul is only provisional & until the President shall make another appointment. I now copy that part of my orders which relate to this subject "The President requests that you will appoint a fit person to discharge the business of the office held by M. Skipworth until a regular appointment be made. It will be advisable to let the individual selected understand, that the arrangement being purely provisional, forms no lien which is to control the choice of the President. The temporary functionary will be entitled, of course, to the official emoluments during the term of his service".[56]

So delighted was Warden that he advised Jefferson of his determination to abandon any thoughts of a medical career in favor of being a civil servant.[57] Jefferson's own term as President of the United States was coming to an end, and he cautioned Warden against assuming there would be a permanent appointment as Consul. In a letter of

[55] A distant cousin of President Thomas Jefferson, Skipwith had served as Consul in Martinique and later was elected to the Louisiana Senate. See H. B. Cox, *The Parisian American: Fulwar Skipwith of Virginia* (1964).

[56] Armstrong to Warden, 26 August 1808. Reel 1, Warden Papers, MdHS.

[57] See Warden to Jefferson, 2 September 1808. Jefferson Papers, DLC.

25 February 1809, Jefferson advised that the general expectation in Washington D. C. was that war would soon be undertaken: "So certainly is this expected that we have deemed it improper to propose to the Senate this Session any new appointments of consuls to France or England lest it should excite false doubts in those nations whether we mean to meet their edicts with war if they are not repealed". Jefferson informed Warden that a competitor had made himself known of such standing in the United States and peculiar qualifications for the office that he would command a majority in the Senate. Had war not been imminent, Jefferson said, this candidature would have prevented Warden's nomination. And, Jefferson concluded, he would not be in office when the state of affairs would be proper to renew the appointment of the Consul.

The politics of Warden's provisional appointment, his falling out with Armstrong and subsequent dismissal, his restoration to office on a permanent basis, and his ultimate removal from the position in 1814 have been ably summarized by Haber.[58] Overlooked in these summary accounts are the international legal aspects of what transpired and the legal justifications adduced by those in dispute. It is helpful in this connection to consider Warden's consular status in two phases: first, his provisional appointment, and second, his permanent appointment.

Provisional appointment

Warden, just as his predecessor Skipwith, was wearing two hats simultaneously. The first was consul; the second was agent of prize causes, which Armstrong had indicated should bring as much as $3,000 per year in personal

---

[58] Haber, note 15 above, pp. 11-19.

revenue unless Warden employed someone to assist him. The precise scope of prize agent jurisdiction was not clearly defined in either United States legislation or internal practice. In France, since Warden was the only American official designated as agent for prize causes, he not unreasonably assumed that he had jurisdiction over all American prizes in French ports. When he sought to take charge of prize causes in ports outside Paris, he came into immediate conflict with a political opponent of General Armstrong who resented Warden's assertion of expansive jurisdiction. This was Isaac Cox Barnet (17?-1833), who seemed to specialize in placing obstacles in Warden's path. Warden for his part was soon caught up in the petty bickering and competition among consuls and prize lawyers and easily took offense at the slightest affront to his dignity, real or imagined.

The relationship between the Minister and the Agent for Prize Causes was made clear from the outset by General Armstrong. In his letter to Warden announcing Warden's appointment as Consul *pro tempore*, Armstrong addressed the activities of Warden's predecessor, Mr. Skipwith: "... you will also inform Mr. Skipwith that I am authorized to disapprove his conduct in the settlement he has made with the agent of Mrs. Millar and that I hereby expressly forbid you, as his successor, to relinquish any part of the claims of the United States to the said agent by way of compromise ...".[59]

Warden's association with General Armstrong carried political liabilities. A favorite target for criticism in the Federalist press, Armstrong was accused (falsely) of charging inflated fees for issuing United States passports at the Legation in Paris or refusing to assist destitute

[59] Armstrong to Warden, 26 August 1808. Reel 1, Warden Papers, MdHS.

American seamen stranded in France. Warden was untutored enough in American politics to come to his patron's rescue by writing to the Editor of the *New York Evening Post* in support of Armstrong and promptly became a target himself. Alarmed at being portrayed as Armstrong's puppet, Warden actually wrote to President James Madison to deny that he was in any way a tool of the Minister.[60] For his part, Armstrong was annoyed that a young man who had started his career as his domestic servant was receiving praise, however faintly, in the Federalist press while he was being savaged. He wondered whether Warden was actually conspiring to undermine him.

From that time forward, relations between Armstrong and Warden worsened. Warden was flourishing in French social circles and among the Parisian savants. Armstrong, not by nature especially sociable in the French language, was so morose and uncommunicative that Napoleon actually requested his recall.[61] Matters came to a head in early September 1810. Armstrong had probably made his decision to remove Warden as Consul when he wrote an angry letter as follows:

> I have been informed that in speaking of Mr Russell's character & appointment as chargé d'affaires of the U.S. you have at different times and to different persons permitted yourself to use the following language viz: "That it was a matter of surprise that a mere Supercargo should have been selected for such an official, that it was a disgrace to the U.S. that your studies & occupation had been of the Diplomatic Kind, and that your pretentions were better than those of Mr. Russell that you had therefore expected to have been the person chosen but that I had deceived you, & lastly that you had been set aside to make room

---

[60] Warden to Madison, 26 January 1810. Warden Papers, Register C, MdHS.

[61] Haber, note 15 above, p. 13.

for a Damned Yankey and that an Irishman had nothing to expect from the present Administration.

I am also informed that the night before Seth Hunt left Paris, you went to his lodging, at a very late hour, and even when he was in bed, and after many apologies for not having furnished him with an instance or materials you had prepared for a future attack upon me in the U.S. you added that if any person other than yourself was appointed to the Consulate & Agency of Prize Causes in Paris, you would, in that case, bind yourself to his (Hunt's) object, most cordially and entirely. As these reports may be untrue, I offer you an opportunity of denying them openly, solemnly and in writing. And if on the other hand, they are well founded it becomes you to justify them in the best way you can, & as promptly as possible. In particular, if I have deceived you, you will not be at a loss to detail the circumstances of the case, the time, the occasion, and the mode of deception employed by me, as well as the deception itself, and if in the eight years acquaintance & intimacy in which we have been, you have, at any time, or on any occasion found my conduct inconsistent either with private morals or public duty, I invite you to specify and declare the offense, or offences which I may have committed. At the same time, I release you from every obligation to silence, and to secrecy, and from every tie both of discretion and of gratitude.[62]

Warden replied at length on 9 September 1810, denying the allegations as challenged by Armstrong to do so. Armstrong in essence rejected Warden's explanation in a reply of 10 September 1810, to which Warden in turn responded on the same date. On the day of his own resignation as Minister on 13 September 1810, Armstrong appointed Alexander MacRae (also spelled McRae) as

[62] Armstrong to Warden, 6 September 1810. Reel 7, Warden Papers, MdHS. Notwithstanding his protestations, Armstrong has come down in history as an individual given to intrigue and indolence. See Henry Adams, *History of the United States of America during the Administrations of James Madison* (1986), p. 593.

Warden's successor.[63] In fact, Armstrong had informed Warden several months earlier that he had recommended to President Madison against the permanent appointment of Warden as Consul. Warden did not accept that the Minister was empowered to replace him as Consul and promptly returned to the United States in order to contest his dismissal.

Permanent appointment

The details of Warden's successful campaign to be permanently appointed United States Consul at Paris need not detain us here, having been admirably recounted by Haber, as noted above. Suffice it to note that Warden arrived back in the United States before General Armstrong and had mobilized his friends up and down the Eastern seaboard to support his campaign for appointment. He was able to rely upon the immense good will accumulated during his six years in Paris as secretary of the legation and provisional consul. Former comrades in the Irish uprising of 1798 had come to America and risen to positions of prominence and power; they supported him. So did Thomas Jefferson and the man eventually appointed to succeed General Armstrong as Minister – Joel Barlow (1754-

---

[63] Armstrong's appointment is recorded in a register copy: "I have this day given notice to the Minister of Exterior Relation that Mr. Alexandre McRae is appointed to the office provisionally held by you. You will accordingly deliver to Mr. McRae all books and other documents belonging to the said office". See Reels 1 and 7, Warden Papers, MdHS. On 24 September 1810 the same register records a letter from Warden to a Mr. Cromie seeking an explanation of the critical remarks made about and to Armstrong and attributed to Warden. On the same day McRae requested Warden to hand over papers and documents.

1812).[64] The grand-daughter of Martha Washington (1731-1802), Eliza Parke Custis (1776-1831), proved to be a vigorous supporter and lifelong correspondent with him. Armstrong had been out maneuvered, and his vituperative campaign against Warden failed. The United States Senate unanimously confirmed Warden as Consul in Paris and Agent of Prize Causes.

Barlow, the new Minister, and Warden sailed together to take up their respective posts on the *U.S.S. Constitution*, departing on 1 August 1811.[65] Barlow had achieved distinction on a number of fronts, not least poetry. His poem "Vision of Columbus" brought him fame well-known to Warden several years before Barlow's diplomatic appointment to France. On 28 July 1807 Barlow replied to Warden that the enlarged volume containing his poetry "… will be through press in about a month … It will be a quarto vol. of about 500 pages, done in a very superior stile, with 12 engravings by the first artists in England".[66] The following year Barlow, writing from his home at "Calorama", now in northwest Washington D. C. but then beyond the boundaries, recalled his earlier times in Paris: "… So much of self mingled in my sympathies that I shall write to you & think of you with more interest since I find that you occupy part of the house which sheltered me so long & in which I made & penned so many reflections. In

---

[64] On Barlow, see J. Woodress, *A Yankee's Odyssey. The Life of Joel Barlow* (1958). Barlow had been United States Consul General for Algiers, Tunis, and Tripoli from 1795 to 1797, during which time he had negotiated a Treaty with Tripoli (1796). Also see M. H. Hoeflich, *Legal Publishing in Antebellum America* (2010), p. 175.

[65] On the voyage, see D. B. Warden, "Journal of a Voyage from Annapolis to Cherbourg on Board the Frigate Constitution, 1 Aug. to 6 Sep. 1811", *Maryland Historical Magazine*, XI (1916), pp. 127-141, 204-217.

[66] Warden Papers, DLC.

the northeast corner room over the Library was the study where I wrote the greater part of the Columbiad".[67]

In his capacity of Minister, Barlow was charged by his Government with improving commercial relations between France and the United States and securing either the release of American property confiscated by the French or compensation for the value thereof. His timing was inauspicious. Napoleon Bonaparte was preparing for his invasion of Russia and disinclined to be helpful to the United States. After repeated efforts, Barlow succeeded in scheduling a personal meeting with the Emperor at Vilna and travelled there in December 1812 for that purpose. By then Napoleon was in the midst of his legendary disastrous retreat. The meeting with Barlow did not transpire. So ravaged were the lands by the retreating forces that Barlow died of starvation in the Polish village of Zarnowiec, where he is buried.

It required over two weeks for information of the Minister's death to reach the United States Legation in Paris. Barlow had not designated a chargé d'affaires in his absence. Warden was the senior diplomat on site. He took the initiative to inform the Duc de Bassano, the Minister of Foreign Affairs of France, about the situation and was accredited as the official representative of the United States.[68] Simultaneously, he informed the Department of

---

[67] Barlow to Warden, 28 April 1808. Warden Papers, DLC.

[68] Duc de Bassano to Warden, 15 January 1813. Cited in Haber, note 15 above, p. 16. Warden had written to the Duc de Bassano on the same date: "Finding myself at present the only public agent of the Government of the United States, at Paris, in my quality of Consul General, acknowledged as such, the 17th of Sept 1808, and confirmed, at my return from America, by the letter of your Excellency, dated the 18th of December, 1811, I have thought, that according to the character with which I am invested by my Government, it was my duty to state to your Excellency, that I am the only legal representative of the Government of the United States; that I wait for new instructions, and

State about his actions and undertook to act as intermediary between the French and American governments until he was given further instructions or a replacement appointed. These moves succeeded in building upon earlier antagonisms and generating new ones that shaped, indeed plagued, his status as an American diplomat and raised a number of issues of diplomatic and consular law.

The first issue had been generated immediately by and upon his return from the United States. Warden promptly submitted his papers of appointment as Consul to the French authorities, who in turn promptly agreed to his taking up office with the "character" of *Consul General* of the United States in France. The President and Senate of the United States had appointed Warden as Consul, not Consul General, leaving the question whether consular rank was to be determined by the receiving country or the sending country. Should the United States object if the consular appointee was received with greater rank than he was intended to have? Why France chose to elevate Warden's status is unknown. Warden did indeed get along with his French compatriots, but that in itself would not account for the elevation. Nor is there any indication that Warden sought such elevation in title. From that day forward, however, Warden constantly referred to himself as "Consul General". Correspondence directed to his name, especially from French sources, addresses him as such. His American colleagues, including Minister Barlow, objected strenuously. Lest there be any doubt as to the position, formal inquiry was made of the Duc de Bassano, who replied unequivocally that Warden had been recognized even in his provisional capacity from 17 September 1808 as

---

from your Excellency the Communications which you may wish to transmit". Reel 1, Warden Papers, MdHS.

Consul General of the United States and there was no intention to change the matter.[69]

To reinforce his position Warden composed and had specially printed in broadside format a "Circular" addressed "To the Consuls, and Vice Consuls of the United States of America, residing in Ports of France, or in those over which her Imperial Prize-court has jurisdiction".[70] The Circular did not work entirely to Warden's advantage as time passed. After Warden's dismissal from the post of Consul, I. Cox Barnet complained that the materials handed over to his successor were not consistent with what might be expected on the basis of the Circular:

> … there is not, that I have been yet able to discover, a single letter from the Department of State, a single line of instructions from any branch of the American Government, not a page of the

---

[69] "… il etait reconnu dans le Departement de la Seine en qualité de Consul General des États-Unis, et que depuis cette époque, aucune disposition contrarire n'avait en lieu". Barlow confirmed in his own hand that this was a true copy of the communication but added that he: "… ought to observe that the Commission to Mr Warden from the President of the United States is that of Consul for Paris and not Consul General". Warden Papers, DLC. In a later communication from I. Cox Barnet to Warden, Barnet specifically disavowed the allegation that Warden's predecessor as Consul, Mr. Skipwith, has been accredited as Consul General. See Cox to Warden, 20 November 1813, Warden Papers, DLC.

[70] See Reel 6, Warden Papers, MdHS, Warden also reproduced the Circular in the present volume, at pp. 165-167 below. Warden paid $20 for printing the Circular and as late as 20 October 1821 was still seeking reimbursement, the account then being sent to John Quincy Adams in his capacity of United States Secretary of State. Warden invoked the Circular in his correspondence with William Lee in a Letter of 13 July 1813: "By the authority of the President and Senate of the U.S. the Agency of Prize Cases is superadded to the duties of American consuls at Paris. This circumstance is known to all our consuls, for it was communicated to them in a Circular Letter, of which I inclose a copy …". Reel 7, Warden Papers, MdHS.

laws of the United States, nor a letter from any department of the French Government nor any note or statement by you of the situation or progress of any prize case with which you was charged as agent of prize causes – not even the seal of office.

Yet in your printed circular of the 1st of August 1812 you speak of having been 'authorized and directed' and of having received 'general and special instructions from the President and Secretary of Foreign Relations of the United States' &c &c. These authorizations and Instructions – all letters and notes from any government or officers of government relative to the office, the laws and the seal ought to be delivered over to me.[71]

When news arrived in Paris of Barlow's death in Poland, Warden's actions to ensure continuity in Legation administration annoyed Mrs. Barlow, who thought that the responsibilities of Minister should devolve upon her or, if not, upon Barlow's nephew, Thomas. Warden's opposition immediately seized upon the situation. Isaac Cox Barnet raised the succession issues in a letter of 16 January 1813:

On the 14th instant we received the melancholy tidings of the death of Mr. Barlow, Minister Plenipotentiary of the United States. On the same day – as I am told by M. Marcardier – you applied to him for the blank passports and certain other papers in the office of the legation – and yesterday you renewed your demand in writing.

Altho, Sir, I have not had occasion before to give you official information thereof – you have not remained ignorant of the agency confided to me by the Minister of the U. States. This agency you well know embraces in the Letter of my Instructions the delivery of passports and the care of the distressed American citizens whose liberation had been asked by the Minister. How then, forgetting the respect that is due to the memory of Mr Barlow and insensible to the anguish of his inconsolable widow – and while his mortal remains are scarcely cold – could you apply to M. Marcardier for official papers which his quality of private secretary could not authorize him to deliver to you? Have you so soon forgotten the duties of a private secretary as

[71] Barnet to Warden, 18 July 1814. Warden Papers, DLC.

> not to know that M. Marcardier has no official character in the case and could not act without the instructions of his principal?
>
> While I cannot withhold this remark as the expression of the wounded feeling of Mrs. Barlow – of her family and friends – you must permit me to inform you it is a principle admitted that a substitution of powers is annulled only by the death of the Constituent or Principal, and as in this case, the principal is the American Government, the delegation of the public duties made to me by the Minister Plenipotentiary ought to remain in full force until some other disposition of his shall be known or the Government of the United States shall give new instructions on the subject. It will remain with you as an agent of the same Government to determine how far you ought to regard the will of the person lately invested with the full confidence of the President and to whom was entrusted the most important branch of the foreign relations of the United States.[72]

Cox continued to challenge Warden's right and authority at every opportunity – and claimed tò have written instructions in support of his view. On 1 February 1813 Cox wrote to Warden:

> Finding that upon your application made since intelligence was received of the decease of Mr. Barlow, you are considered by the French Government as attending to the affairs of the American legation and are accredited as Consul General of the U. States, it becomes my duty to enquire of you whether your commission from the President or your Instructions from the Department of State go to supercede the agency left me by the late Minister?
>
> One part of that agency being under the control of the French Government, namely the delivery of passports and your being now acknowledged, it is not my present purpose to call your attention to that subject – But Mr. Barlow in his letter to me of

---

[72] Barnet to Warden, 16 January 1813. Warden Papers, DLC. On 15 January 1813 J. Marcardier wrote to Warden: ".... I will call at your lodgings with the blank passports, registers of passports, and such documents relating to American prisoners of war in France as I can get". Ibid.

> the 26th October written the day before he left Paris – gave me the following instructions, viz: 'Should our citizens now held as prisoners of war be set at liberty during my absence, you will be kind enough to advise as to the route they are to take and the means of getting employment for such as desire it and for the distressed ones a passage to their country with as little expense to the public as may be, not exceeding in any case the provisions made by law for such purposes'.[73]

The *New York Gazette* published a letter dated "Paris, 6th February 1813" from an anonymous writer who said that "The French government has chosen Mr. Warden, consul for Paris, who now stiles himself 'consul-general' of the United States" to correspond with them, which has "enraged all our countrymen who think it is a disgrace to be represented by an United Irishman, who, but a few years ago, fled his country and has not lived long enough in ours to be properly naturalized". The choice of Warden the writer attributed to the "intrigues of the Irish party here; add to this, Mr. Warden's secretary is a Scotchman". Whether the stinging rebuff to this letter repaired any damage done is a matter of speculation.[74]

William Lee, the United States Consul at Bordeaux, took a similar position with what he regarded as Warden's arrogation of authority and suggested that the law of nations did not support Warden:

> … If you are Consul General of the United States, you ought to have notified to all the consuls your appointment and the date of your Commission as such from the President of the United States. But whether Consul General or Consul for Paris only, you cannot take upon yourself on the death of the Minister any political or diplomatic character while there exists a Secretary of Legation. He becomes of right in such an event chargé d'affaires. It is his duty to preserve intact the archives of the

[73] Barnet to Warden, 1 February 1813. Warden Papers, DLC.
[74] The clippings are preserved in the Warden Papers, MdHS.

> Legation, and to correspond with the Minister of Foreign Relations, on the current affairs of the Legation. The political interests of the United States, & the special business of the Minister, he cannot touch upon. This, sir, the least informed clerk in the Duke of Bassano's office knows to be the rule and usage of all nations. While therefore we have at Paris a Secretary of Legation regularly commissioned by the President, it would be incorrect in me to recognize you as the representative of the United States at this Court and of course I cannot correspond with you as such.
>
> But, Sir, I have another reason more potent than the usages of nations for refusing to sanction your Measures.
>
> In the year 1798-9 when our Envoys Messrs. Pinkney, Marshall & Gerry left Paris, the Government of the United States was without a representative here – The then Consul of the United States in union with a very respectable citizen undertook to carry on a correspondence with the Directory, for which they were highly censured by all parties in America and in consequence of which Congress passed a Law interdicting all our citizens at home or abroad from holding any unauthorized correspondence with a foreign Government touching the interests of the United States under the penalty of Five Thousand Dollars and an imprisonment of three years.
>
> Thus you will find, Sir, that were you as conversant with the annals of diplomacy and the Laws of the United States, as you profess and ought to be, you would not have taken such an untenable & unprecedented ground.
>
> How far the dignity, honor & interests of the United States will be maintained by the Duke of Bassano's having acknowledged you 'as Consul General of the United States, and as the only commissioned agent and organ of our Government to supply the vacancy left by the death of out late Minister' time will disclose.[75]

The United States Minister to Russia, John Quincy Adams (1767-1848), had no difficulties with Warden's

[75] Lee to Warden, 18 February 1813. Reel 2, Warden Papers, MdHS. Lee graduated from Phillips Academy in 1785, served as United States Consul in Bordeaux for some fifteen years, and then became Auditor-General of the United States Treasury, 1817-1829.

assumption of authority. Making clear that he was familiar with the situation in Paris, Adams directed Warden to perform certain tasks on his behalf:

> On receiving information of Mr. Barlow's decease, I addressed two letters to the Chargé d'Affaires of the United States at Paris and sent by Mr. John C. Delprat, an American Gentleman for whom I procured a Couriers passport, and who left this City on the 14th of last month intending to go by the way of Vienna. Since his departure I have been informed that Mr. Barlow left no Chargé d'Affaires and that you are the only acknowledged public officer of the United States at Paris. I therefore authorize and request you to receive from Mr. Delprat the two letters that I have him addressed to the Chargé d'Affaires and will thank you to inform them, as soon as convenient, particularly with regard to certain papers concerning which the letters contain inquiries.[76]

In the meantime relations had worsened with William Lee, the United States Consul at Bordeaux, over the disposition of the good ship *Maria*, captured by Commodore John Rodgers (1772-1838) in June 1813 and brought in as prize. Rodgers had secured Warden's assistance in obtaining his prize money. In his capacity as Consul, Lee proceeded to arrange the auction of the ship and its cargo and offered to share his commission with Warden. Warden in reply challenged Lee's authority to act simultaneously as judge, agent, and merchant. The lengthy and harsh correspondence contained a number of references to the legal powers of consuls and commercial agents under the law of nations:

[76] Adams to Warden from St. Petersburg, 5 March 1813. Reel 2, Warden Papers, MdHS. An equally formidable winter journey, but without lethal results, was made by John Quincy Adams' wife and son in the winter of 1815. See M. O'Brien, *Mrs. Adams in Winter: A Journey in the Last Days of Napoleon* (2010).

… I now come to another point of your letter in which you say 'If I was neither Consul general nor general agent in prize causes You have no right to dispose of property for the Sales and proceeds of which I am accountable' thus minuting that you are Consul General and confirming what you have written to a Gentleman in this town, that you are 'General agent in all prize cases by an extension of your powers from the Department of State'.

I recollect that when you left Washington in March 1811 to embark at Newport, you caused to be inserted in the newspapers as you progressed north, that you had been appointed by the President and unanimous vote of the Senate, Consul General and agent for all prize cases, to reside at Paris – This article appeared so often in the newspapers that the Department of State thought proper to correct it by causing to be inserted in the National Intelligencer a paragraph informing the public, that you were not appointed Consul General as had been announced to them but Consul for Paris only & agent for prizes – Now, Sir, as there is a wide difference between being Consul for Paris, and Consul General for this vast Empire, and a still wider difference between being simply agent for all prizes made on the commerce of the United States by French cruisers and brought before the Imperial Court of Prizes, and being agent general for all prizes sent into the ports of France by American cruisers, and as I find notwithstanding this declaration in the National Intelligencer, that you still persist in announcing you are both Consul General and General Agent for all prize causes, I have for my instruction and on account of the public Service requested my friend I. C. Barnet Esq. Consul at Havre, now at Paris, to call on you and request of you in my name an exhibition of your Commission and powers from the President of the United States, as Consul General and general agent for all prize causes in the Empire and to demand of you a copy of the same which I have begged him to transmit to me –

If you have received such additional powers from the Department of State, You will find me ready, not only to assist but to support you in the exercise of the duties arising out of them –

If you have not received those powers, you have no right whatever, to interfere with my district for in the standing instructions to Consuls of the United States we are told the

Consul of one district is totally independent of the Consul of another.[77]

Warden's reply to the position taken by William Lee was set out in a communication to the Department of State and is itself an exercise in comparative consular law. As for Lee's behavior, Warden said:

> ... there are two points to be distinguished: its real object, and the animosity which it occasioned; The first is the most important. Concerning the authority and privileges claimed by Mr. Lee, in the management of the prizes sent, by the President frigate, into the ports of France, and the pretension of constituting himself judge in these cases, founded on a communication said to emanate from the Director of the French custom house at Bayonne, which he invoked as a justification of his conduct, Mr. Lee appeared to me to act contrary to the principles of the Government of which he is an agent. In the first place, the Laws of the United States, as far as I knew, did not grant to American consuls the right of judging prizes. This attribution appeared to me to be in direct opposition to the Laws, and Constitution of the United States. The French consuls residing in our country have long claimed a similar jurisdiction which was constantly opposed by the American authorities, and I was informed that our Government had determined not to respect the adjudication of American prizes pronounced by French or by Spanish consuls. I observed that the Section of the act of the 26th June 1812 relative to the circumstance of a prize conducted to a friendly port supposes that it will be there adjudged by a competent tribunal. The terms of this law did not permit me to believe that there was question of an American consul. I have carefully examined the French legislation on this subject, and had ascertained from the Reglement, or Decree of the 27th September 1778, Concerning prizes brought to the ports of France, by American corsairs, that, even in this war, in which two nations were allied against the common enemy, the right of judging prizes by the respective consuls was not acknowledged by either Government.

---

[77] Lee to Warden, 12 July 1813. Reel 2, Warden Papers, MdHS.

> [With regard to Lee] … I only observed 'that he had no authority except that derived from acts of Congress, which might authorize him to act as protector and perhaps as judge'. I was far from denying that Mr Lee had certain appraisal functions to fulfill, … but I did assert that he had no right to constitute himself agent, or Consignee of the prize, without the approbation of the Captor (Letter of 19 July 1813).
>
> [Mr Lee] … constituted himself effectively the agent, the Consignee, of his property; and consequently he was determined to retain a commission on the Sales; he already proposes to share it with me …
>
> I had made several personal applications to the Duke of Bassano on this subject, and I requested him, in my note of the 22nd of April last, to inform me what powers and privileges our Nation and its Consuls were to enjoy with respect to prizes conducted by American corsairs to the ports of France. In his answer of the 3d of May, nothing more is said concerning the jurisdiction of our consuls 'that they shall exercise, in prize matters, the same jurisdiction as the French consuls exercise in countries where they are the most favored'.[78]

The replacement for Joel Barlow as Minister to France was William Harris Crawford (1772-1834).[79] Crawford was decidedly reserved towards Warden from the moment of his arrival in France, and that coolness deteriorated into hostility. On 31 May 1814 Crawford removed Warden from the office of Consul and replaced the vacancy with a temporary appointment. Crawford informed Warden that "… from the official letter of the Secretary of State, it appears that your assumption of the title of Consul General of the United States, and having sought, and exercised, the functions of Chargé d'affaires, upon the death of the late Minister, without having received the authority or

[78] Warden to Department of State, 31 August 1813. Reel 6, Warden Papers, MdHS.

[79] See P. Green, *The Life of William Crawford* (1965); C. Mooney, *William H. Crawford 1772-1834* (1974).

permission of the President, are among the causes of your removal".[80]

Warden disputed his dismissal and sought reinstatement and/or reappointment for most of the remainder of his life. Friends intervened on his behalf, but to no avail. In 1828 the United States Minister to France, James Brown (1766-1835), reviewed the Warden affair and concluded that Warden had dealt with unusual circumstances about which there could be genuine differences of opinion without prejudice to the quality of his record of performance.[81] Some saw the hand of General Armstrong behind Warden's fate, insofar as Armstrong failed to persuade President Madison not to appoint Warden but succeeded in prejudicing Crawford against Warden.[82]

Nor did matters rest there. The election of Andrew Jackson (1767-1845) as seventh President of the United States raised the hopes of Warden and his supporters that the consulship in Paris might once more be his. A campaign was undertaken on Warden's behalf. He entered the lists in Paris by replying to an article in a French journal devoted to the differences between France and the United States.[83] The author had written that "the death of M. Barlow in December 1812 had momentarily left the Government of the United States without representation".

Not so, replied Warden. "The following facts will, I believe, prove the inaccuracy of this assertion". In a lengthy communication setting out the entire affair of

---

[80] Crawford to Warden, 31 May 1814. Reel 2, Warden Papers, MdHS.

[81] Brown to Warden, 8 November 1828, Warden Papers, DLC.

[82] Such was the speculation of Correia de Serra (1750-1823), who wrote to Warden to that effect on 26 November 1814. See José Francisco Correia de Serra to Warden, Warden Papers, DLC.

[83] "Des Différends de la France avec les États-Unis", *Revue des Deux Mondes* (September 1830), p. 256 (my translation).

seventeen years previous Warden reiterated: "I was the only secretary at the American Legation in Paris, since I had been named, without any solicitation on my part, consul and prize agent, by President Jefferson and confirmed in this post in 1812 by the unanimous vote of the United States Senate. The death of M. Barlow left me the sole accredited agent to the French Government, which recognized me, inter alia, in the quality of Consul General, which is proved by the letter of M. le Duc de Bassano of 13 January 1813 … and I had custody of the archives of the Embassy of Russia at the request made of me by Ambassador Prince Kourakin".[84]

Although Warden's name continued to come up as a potential consul in France thereafter, there was no serious expectation that this would happen. Jackson, as it happened, was not inclined to favor Warden and that was effectively the end of the matter.

After having been relieved of his consular post and having made rudimentary efforts to make a living through commerce, Warden decided to devote half his time for service to American citizens and interests and the other half for his own scholarly research and writing. He turned first to the description of the District of Columbia (1816),[85] particularly well received in France where people were genuinely interested in the New World. He followed in 1819 with a massive and comprehensive account of the United States as a whole, factual with brief bibliographies

---

[84] Printed copies of the Letter appear in the Warden Papers at MdHS and DLC.

[85] Warden, *A Chorographical and Statistical Description of the District of Columbia: The Seat of the General Government of the United States* (Paris, 1816).

for each section.[86] One reviewer said that Warden's work "… contains more information about the United States of America than is to be found in any other work, and is very deserving of our attention".[87]

This work too excited the admiration of the French and secured his election to the Institute of France on 3 April 1826 (Academie des Sciences, Section de Geographie et navigation). A six-volume French edition appeared in 1820. He later wrote on Mexican antiquities. He was also commissioned to prepare the article on America for the Supplement to the fourth edition of the *Encyclopedia Britannica* and entries on individual Americans. For the *Revue encyclopédique* Warden compiled a section summarizing recent American publications, the activities of learned societies and universities, and the work of American scientists and literary figures. In 1821 he was retained to prepare the New World sections of the monumental *L'Art de verifier les dates*, a project underway since 1743. Between 1826 and 1844 he published ten volumes and had readied an eleventh for press when the project folded. In his later years he suffered from intense migraines. Warden died at Paris on 9 October 1845.

The Book

Warden produced the first treatise in the English language on consular law; it ranks among the early works

---

[86] Warden, *A Statistical, Political, and Historical Account of the United States of North America; from the Period of Their First Colonization to the Present Day* (Edinburgh, 1819).

[87] Edward Everett (1794-1865), in the *North American Review*, XIII (July 1821), p. 62.

on the subject.[88] Warden's surviving papers give no indication as to why he undertook to write the book. One must therefore take the author at his word, as set out in his Preface, that he wished to draw the attention of the United States Government to certain shortcomings in the consular system that might be easily remedied (p. 5). His searches in the public libraries of Paris for comparative materials illustrating the improvements adopted by other nations turned up nothing, he said, so he turned to treaties and diplomatic documents for assistance. The War of 1812 between England and the United States gave him "hours of leisure from public business" which he devoted to preparing the book.

When his "task was nearly finished", he was informed by a Parisian friend that a Leipzig bookseller was offering a copy of Borel's *De l'origine et des fonctions des consuls*, published in the French language at St. Petersburg by an Italian in Russian service. This statement is perhaps disingenuous, for Borel's study had been available for nearly six years prior to the appearance of Warden's treatise and has plainly been used to advantage by Warden. Moreover, for reasons to be discussed below, Warden was aware of Borel's existence personally, although he seems not to have known that Borel produced two volumes, and not one.

One suspects that Warden had a larger grand design in producing his work. First, the book helped establish his academic and professional credentials as an experienced and knowledgeable consul and diplomat familiar more than most with how other countries arranged their consular

---

[88]D. B. Warden, *On the Origin, Nature, Progress and Influence of Consular Establishments* (Paris, 1813). Warden was aware of and did use Jean Toubeau, *Les Institutes du droit consulaire* (2d ed.; 1700), although in the book Toubeau was misspelled as "Loubeau".

affairs. He will surely have expected the appearance of the book to strengthen his case for reappointment as consul and perhaps elevation to a more senior diplomatic assignment. Notwithstanding the matter of Borel, the paucity of doctrinal writings on consular law by individuals with actual experience was real, the more so for those who had no knowledge of the German or other European languages.[89]

Second, Warden used his book to articulate his own conception of the consul and its proper role in diplomacy. His conception was far in advance of its time, yet the book epitomized and encapsulated what Warden considered to be the shortcomings on the institution of consul, namely the preoccupation of the consul with commercial affairs to the neglect of cultural matters. Commonly, individuals appointed to consulships in the late eighteenth and nineteenth centuries were individuals with a commercial background or commercial interests, often permanently resident in the receiving country. Even on the understanding that a consul should not permit conflicts of interests with his own business affairs, such conflicts could and did arise. Warden criticized this entire approach. "To be useful to his country in arts, sciences, and manufactures, a consul must have no commercial engagements". One

[89] It does seem odd that Warden did not cite and presumably did not use J. C. W. Steck, *Essai sur les consuls. On y a joint les traités de commerce et de navigation les plus recens comme aussi l'ordonnance du roit de France pour les consulats du Levant du 3 mars 1781* (Berlin, 1781). Warden often referred to his book as an "Essai", although he did not use that word himself in the title. George Ticknor drew Warden's attention to de Steck years later. See Ticknor to Warden, 5 January 1817. Reel 2, Warden Papers, MdHS. Grabar wrote that "Borel's book was in its day the best and – if one excludes J. C. W. de Steck's work … -- the first monograph on consular law, and it long remained the sole manual in the field". Grabar, note 2 above, p. 246. Grabar was unaware of Warden.

whose mind is absorbed in the pursuits of gain, he said, cannot be expected to be useful in this way. The consul must be an intellectual, must "... not only love, but must also have time to communicate knowledge". If he has no regular salary and is obliged to "seek support as a merchant or factor", his eye must be constantly directed to his private advantage" (p. 20).

Warden expanded upon the qualities of a consul. His time and labor belong not to himself, but to his country, to the government of which the consul should communicate all that is good and useful to know concerning the laws, customs, manners, arts, commerce, and manufactures of the receiving country. The consul must be fair, of honorable reputation, and knowledgeable, mild in conduct, free from passion, not hasty in decision-making, firm in resolutions well deliberated, prudent, conciliating, the faithful depository of private communications – all qualities which Warden possessed (p. 21). Precisely how Warden reconciled these desirable features of the consul with an appointment as prize agent is not addressed in the book. But it should be noted that Warden was prepared to act in many capacities as a prize agent without cost to his client.

For the most part Warden's characterization of the ideal consul he himself personified. Both in the office of consul and out, Warden devoted his life to advancing knowledge of the United States in France and to establishing intellectual, professional, educational, cultural, and commercial contacts between Americans and the receiving country. Small wonder that in his treatise Warden extolled the role of the consul that he sought to exemplify. In this he was no doubt influenced by French models and practices. The French Government required its consuls to maintain a regular correspondence with respect to science, manufactures, and the arts: "Though this medium it was proposed to facilitate communication between the French *savans* and the learned of other countries: to disseminate new publications, accelerate the circulation of thought and discovery, and increased the fame and prosperity of France …" (p. 29).[90]

Third, Warden gives an excellent introduction to the operations of a consulate and its legal status and quite a thorough account of consular treaties in force at the time.

Finally, a careful reading of Warden's list of foreign consuls suggests that he has chosen to enumerate only those consuls who had published books or otherwise left an enduring legacy on the history of diplomacy – in other words, consuls such as himself who left something to posterity other than mere service to their governments. This will doubtless have enraged his compatriot-consuls in France, for the only American consul mentioned in this capacity was the late Joel Barlow (1754-1812), whom Warden hoped to succeed as Minister. Moreover, Warden placed Barlow first on the list among all consuls and offered no other Americans for inclusion.

Warden had indeed read widely in composing his work. The final product lacked both a Table of Contents and an Index. However, the Warden Archives contain a "List of authors and works cited in this Essay", together with page numbers.[91] The page references are correct, which suggests that for some reason, perhaps cost, or urgency in wanting the volume to appear quickly, an Index was intended. Had a Table of Contents been supplied, the errors in numbering the chapters might have been avoided (there is no Chapter III and two Chapter VI).

---

[90] Warden quotes Bishop Henri Grégoire (1750-1831), whose work he had previously translated: *An Enquiry Concerning the Intellectual and Moral Faculties, and Literature of Negroes: Followed with an Account of the Life and Works of Fifteen Negroes and Mulattoes, Distinguished in Science, Literature and the Arts* (1810).

[91] Warden Papers, DLC.

Intended to be helpful to his superiors in Washington D. C., the book, his colleagues suggested, was destined to fail in its aim. Warden's conception of consular functions was much too "enlightened" for the Department of State in 1813. Sylvanus Bourne (1761-1817), Consul at Amsterdam and previously in Haiti, observed to Warden that his principles, although excellent, faced insurmountable opposition in the United States because "the grand basis on which the American Consular System is predicated on the head of emolument is that our consuls shall cost nothing to the country … & every branch in its detailed ramifications is made subservient to that all important concern".[92]

Others were more optimistic. Alex Hammet wrote from Naples that "As you justly observe, there are so many plain and obvious reasons why consuls should not trade that I am surprised our Government have not thought to supply a better system". He did not doubt that "your work will give motive to the President to reflect on the Subject and to propose to Congress to act upon".[93]

The precise print run is unknown. On 27 September 1813 the printer, J. Smith in Paris, submitted his "Memoire d'Impression" and requested settlement. The "Memoire" would have itemized all the costs of production, but unfortunately is missing from the archives.[94] Later

---

[92] Bourne to Warden, 13 September 1813. Warden Papers, MdHS.

[93] Hammet to Warden, 13 October 1813. Reel 2, Warden Papers, MdHS.

[94] J. Smith to Warden, 27 September 1813. Warden Papers, DLC. The Warden Archives do contain a "Memoire d'Impressions" from the same printer for Warden, *A Chorographical and Statistical Description of the District of Columbia, the Seat of the General Government of the United States, with an Engraved Plan of the District, and View of the Capitol* (1816). 600 copies were printed, including six copies on "Velum paper" specially bound. The total sum was 795.15 francs and payment received on 12 April 1816. Warden Papers, DLC.

correspondence with the printer makes reference to as many as 500 copies, but also mentions 200.[95]

While the Warden archives suggest that he had always been generous with copies of books which he published, the work on consular law was in a different category altogether. Warden signed his Preface on 1 July 1813. The first recorded correspondence thanking him for sending a copy is dated 24 August 1813, suggesting that delivery of copies from the printer commenced in late August.[96] He presented copies to all of his friends and acquaintances, it is clear, including senior French and American officials and the learned societies to which he belonged. Warden's friend, John Rodman, wrote from New York: "I have read your book on Consular establishments … it is really a very valuable treatise and does you great credit …".[97] Glasgow College, where Warden received his certificate in midwifery, wrote a letter of gratitude for "… a copy of your valuable and original treatise on the Consular Office".[98] Copies continued to be in demand from fellow consuls for many years.[99] Publication was noted in the *National Intelligencer*.

---

[95] J. Smith to Warden, 19 October 1813. Reel 2, Warden Papers, MdHS.

[96] In a letter to John Graham (1774-1820), Chief Clerk to the Secretary of State, Warden wrote: "I have delivered to the Minister six copies of my Essay on Consular Establishments for the President, Secretaries of State, Treasury, and Navy, and for Yourself. I hope that it will meet your approbation". See Reel 6, Warden Papers, MdHS. The book was dedicated to the President of the United States. James Madison (1751-1836) was not mentioned by name.

[97] Rodman to Warden, 28 October 1814. Reel 2, Warden Paper, MdHS.

[98] Lockhart Muirhead to Warden, 6 February 1816. Warden Papers, MdHS.

[99] The British Consul in London sought from Warden via Reuben Gaunt Beasley, United States Consul in London, a copy of both Borel's and Warden's books on consular law. Warden was able to oblige with

By the time that Warden offered his second collection of Americana (see above), he added to his 1831 and 1840 catalogues a "Supplement" listing several works by himself as part of the collection. In the 1831 catalogue only the English language version of his work on consular law was included and described as "scarce". Both the English and French language versions were listed in the 1840 Supplement and the characterization "scarce" was removed.

In 1815 the French Consul in Corogne (Coruna), Spain, Mr. Bernard Barrère, published a translation of Warden's work. To it Barrère added his own Preface, which is essentially a summary outline of the book.[100] The Warden archives offer no materials on the translator or the translation. Warden in any event made no changes for the French translation. He continued to be listed as Consul General of the United States in Paris, as he had been on the title page of the English language edition. The errors in numbering the chapters were corrected in the 1815 version, but different mistakes made. Finally, the French edition contains three full pages of "Corrections" in the French, which makes one wonder whether Warden may have reviewed the French proofs after all.

The English-language version is uncommon. OCLC lists 40 copies in the United States and six in Europe. The French-language version is rare; OCLC lists six copies in the world. One must assume a modest print run for the French translation.

Given the relative scarcity of the book in both languages, was it influential in its day? Correspondence

---

his own, receipt being duly acknowledged on 26 August 1818. See Beasley to Warden, 18 August 1818. Warden Papers, DLC.

[100] D. B. Warden, *De L'Origine, de la nature, des progress, et de l'influence des établissemens consulaires* (1815).

suggests that other consuls read the book, both American and foreign. Whether the many individuals to whom Warden presented copies actually read it is problematic. Many later writers on consular law omit the book in their footnotes or bibliographies. Some refer to Borel; others to Warden. Rarely are both referred to in the same work (although Chitty did so). Warden had a major champion in the person of Joseph Chitty (1776-1841). Chitty devoted all of Chapter 3 of his monumental treatise on commercial law to consuls. Warden's work, described by Chitty as "an able modern treatise by an American consul", is a principal source for the chapter.[101] The book is not listed in Cohen, which includes "works on foreign, comparative, and international law if published in this country",[102] i.e. the United States. The Warden study, being an early example of comparative approaches to international law, was deemed to fall outside the parameters of Cohen even though American consular legislation was discussed at length.

Correspondence in the Warden Papers suggests that Warden contemplated a revised edition of his book, or at least his friends and colleagues so believed. Some kept him alert to new literature in the field. George Ticknor (1791-

---

[101] See Joseph Chitty, *A Treatise on the Laws of Commerce and Manufactures, and the Contracts Relating Thereto: with An Appendix of Treaties, Statutes, and Precedents* (1824), I, p. 52. Chitty has been aptly described as England's counterpart to Joseph Story in his production of authoritative treatises. His books were immensely popular in the United States, where they were published by G. & C. Merriam. In America most of Chitty's works were accompanied by notes commissioned by the Merriams. An advertisement by the Merriams of 1844 boasted that the Chitty volumes were available from "the principal law booksellers throughout the United States". See Hoeflich, note 46 above, p. 61.

[102] See M. L. Cohen, *Bibliography of Early American Law* (1998), I, p. xvii.

1871), a considerable bibliophile in his own right, sent books to Warden and recommended German works on consular law.[103] The United States Consul in Vienna, J. G. Schwarz, wrote to Warden:

> As I well know what a lively Interest you take in all that which concerns the Literature of Consular matters, I am encouraged by the present to introduce Mr. de Castilho Barreto, Portugese Vice Consul to your acquaintance. This Gent. is author of the work in 2 volumes entitled "Traité du Consulat par J. Ribeiro dos antos C. G. et le Dr. de Castilho Barreto[104] which appeared at Hambourg in 1839 and which is not only suitable for Portugese consuls but also for others of all Nations, in consequence of the variety of matter and the well chosen Forms. …
>
> Of the Work entitled "Manuel des Consuls par Miltitz" 3 volumes have already appeared, and in Naples is appeared a Work called Guide des Agents Consulaires par Bursotti (1837)[105] which is all that I know of on Consular Literature since I last had the pleasure of conversing with you.
>
> If you publish a new edition of your "Origin Nature of Consular Establishments" I beg you to acquaint me thereof, as I may perhaps be able to impart something. I have also collected some notes on the Biography of Consuls.[106]

Barreto, then acting as the Consul General of Uruguay in Denmark, did make contact with Warden in a chatty letter. He sought advice and reminiscences from Warden

[103] Ticknor to Warden, 5 January 1817. Reel 2, Warden Papers, MdHS. Ticknor spent some years in Göttingen and formed a magnificent library in his own field of Spanish and Portugese literature.

[104] Schwarz is referring to: José Ribeiro dos Santos (1798-1842) and José Feliciano de Castilho Barreto e Noronha (1810-1879) (eds.), *Traité du Consulat* (1839). 2 vols.

[105] Schwarz is referring to J. Bursotti, *Guide des agents consulaires* (1837-38). 2 vols.

[106] Schwarz to Warden, 4 September 1840. Reel 5, Warden Papers, MdHS.

for the contemplated next edition of his work, which he said would be in four or five volumes.[107]

Warden and Russo-American Consular Relations

Although the Warden archives presumably must understate the reality, apart from correspondence with his own fellow United States diplomats, occasional communications with fellow consuls such as Barreto, and, of course relations with his receiving country, Warden's diplomatic and consular contacts were confined to the foreign Government of one country alone – Russia. That Russian international legal doctrine should influence the earliest American writings on the subject is itself remarkable and unnoticed previously. This could happen only because the Russian work concerned had been published in French and was therefore accessible to a foreign readership.

F. F. Borel. The Russian influence on Warden's treatise devoted to consular law is related by Warden himself in the Preface to his own work. He said that he had nearly completed his treatise when a friend in Paris informed him that a book had been advertised in a book catalogue from Leipzig under the title "On the Origin and Functions of Consuls", by Franz Frantsevich (Frederick) Borel (1775-1832).[108] Warden allegedly obtained a copy through the bookseller and promptly acknowledged that

---

[107] Barreto to Warden, 30 September 1840. Reel 5, Warden Papers, MdHS.

[108] F. Borel, *De l'Origine et des fonctions des consuls* (St. Petersburg, Pluchart, 1807).

> the appearance of his publication would have rendered mine unnecessary, if the matter and arrangement were not essentially different. Mr. Borel has devoted eighty pages of his work to an examination of the origin and functions of Consuls, which evinces an intimate acquaintance with this subject. The remainder, consisting of two hundred and ninety pages, is made up of extracts of treaties, and other documents relative to the employment of commercial agents (p. 7).[109]

Although the books by Borel and Warden are indeed quite different, it is plain that Warden nonetheless drew upon Borel in preparing his own work.[110] Whether there was personal contact between the two has not been conclusively determined. On the title page of his St. Petersburg book, Borel was described in French "Assesseur de College de S. M. l'Empereur de toutes les Russies, et Chef de division au Ministère de Commerce", which Warden renders as "... chief of division of the Ministry of commerce, and assistant judge of the Imperial College of St. Petersburg". Because Borel dedicated his book to Count "Nicolas de Romanzoff", Warden readily concluded that Borel owed his position to the patronage of Count Nikolai Petrovich Rumiantsev (1754-1826), the State Chancellor of the Russian Empire at the time. However, Warden adds that Borel is "a native of Milan" and "now resides at the island of Madeira as Consul general of Russia". These details Warden obtained elsewhere, as they did not appear in Borel's book and were not true when Borel's book was

[109] Warden seems to have been unaware that Borel published a second volume: Borel, *Formulaire des consulats* (Paris, Pluchart, 1808). Also see Grabar, note 2 above, pp. 245-246; and Grabar, note 2 above (2005), pp. 251-253.

[110] See Warden, note 88 above, pp. 6, 7, 46-48, 50, 54, 56, 57, 62, 66, 71, 72, 74-80, 91, 96-98, 102, 104, 123, 296, 328.

published.[111] In his discussion of the Russian consular system (pp. 294-301), Warden cites Borel, but also has used the well-known History of Catherine II by William Tooke, available at the time in English and French versions. In his list of "Consuls of Russia", Warden is aware of only three: Andrei Iakovlevich Dashkov (1776-1831), who served as Russian Consul General in the United States before being appointed Minister in that country;[112] Borel; and Ia. M. Evreinov, whom, relying on Borel, he indicates was appointed by Peter the Great to be the Russian consul at Cadiz in 1723.

Thanks to a recent Russian biography,[113] we now know more about Borel, although much remains to be done by way of a full-scale examination of his career. Borel was in fact French, born in Lombardy, Italy,[114] and began his career in Poland before finding a position in Russian service in 1799. At various times he held posts for Russia in Naples, Friedrichsham, Paris, London, Madeira, Lisbon, Salvador, and, finally, Rio de Janeiro. His initial Russian posting was as an assistant to a Russian commercial agent

---

[111] In fact, Grabar believed that "as one may conclude from the preface to the book, the author was a German by nationality since the French language in which the book was written was not, in his words, either his mother tongue or the language of the country in which he lived". Grabar, note 2 above, p. 245.

[112] On Dashkov, see Русский биографический словарь [Russian Biographical Dictionary] (1905; reprint ed., 1996).

[113] See B. N. Komissarov and S. G. Bozhkova, Первый российский посланник в Бразилии Ф. Ф. Борель [First Russian Envoy to Brazil: F. F. Borel] (2000). This excellent work draws on Russian archives and certain unpublished manuscripts that mention Borel and corrects a number of minor errors in Russian Ministry of Foreign Affairs documentary volumes that publish some of Borel's official dispatches to St. Petersburg. Unless indicated otherwise, my account of Borel relies chiefly on this study.

[114] Warden, as noted above, named Milan, and Komissarov and Bozhkova consider Warden to be authoritative.

in Naples. In 1804 Borel was sent to St. Petersburg to deliver diplomatic communications and there met Count Rumiantsev, most probably in August-early September 1804.[115] On 23 September 1804 Borel was appointed to the College of Foreign Affairs and then within three months transferred through Rumiantsev's influence to the Ministry of Commerce. Following a delicate and secret mission to Naples from January to May 1805, Borel returned to St. Petersburg where he spent more than three years. He apparently did not know the Russian language; all surviving manuscripts of his making are in French. However, he did publish a book in the Russian language, which one must assume someone translated for him: a comparative table of foreign weights, measures, and exchange rates. Dedicated to the Russian merchantry, it appeared in 1807 under the auspices of the State Commercial College.[116] Emperor Alexander I was shown the manuscript before Borel had completed it by Count Rumiantsev and endorsed the project.

In his work on consular law Borel adhered basically to the approach of de Steck, whose treatise he had consulted in preparing his own volume – an approach which emphasized the diplomatic and political role of the consul. Unlike Warden, Borel did have a command of the German language and used German doctrinal writings to good purpose. One of Borel's colleagues in the Ministry of

---

[115] Here too Komissarov and Bozhkova rely upon Borel's dedication to Rumiantsev as evidence of the latter's patronage of Borel.

[116] F. F. Borel, Сравнительныя таблицы иностранных весов, мер, вещественных и курсовых монет, в отношении и сравнении к Санктпетербургской бирже [Comparative Tables of Foreign Weights, Measures, Material and Exchange Rates of Coins in Relation to and Comparison to the St. Petersburg Stock Exchange] (1807). See Сводный каталог русской книги 1801-1825 [Complete Catalog of the Russian Book 1801-1825] (2000), I, item 747.

Commerce when he was preparing his treatise was Andrei Dashkov. Dashkov cannot fail to have known about Borel's treatise. Moreover, Borel visited Paris in autumn 1808, after his book was published, as part of a Russian diplomatic mission headed by Count Rumiantsev. While there is no archival evidence discovered that Warden and Borel met on that occasion, the probabilities must be high that they did. It is suggested that Dashkov's appointment to the United States as both Consul General and Chargé d'affaires, that is, "simultaneously to consular and diplomatic posts (which thereafter was repeatedly practiced in the American representations of Russia) indirectly affirmed the correctness of the theoretical views of Borel concerning their close interlinkage".[117]

Upon his return to Russia, Borel was appointed in May 1809 to head a consular department within the Ministry of Foreign Affairs. Called an "expedition", all internal and external correspondence on consular matters passed through this body, including correspondence with foreign consuls in Russia, the compilation of instructions for Russian consuls, and much to do with trade and navigation, especially prize causes. Borel was appointed to head this Expedition by Rumiantsev with the approval of the Emperor.

His book was actively disseminated to Russian and foreign consuls by the diplomatic and consular corps. The Russian Consul in Sweden, A. K. Brun, reported in 1810 that he had been instructed by the Ministry of Foreign Affairs to distribute copies of Borel on consular law to all consuls in post and had done so. He further observed that in

[117] Komissarov and Bozhkova, note 113 above, p. 18.

Braunschweig (Brunswick), Germany, it was proposed to reissue Borel, which was apparently done.[118]

When Count Rumiantsev's star dimmed in St. Petersburg as the Emperor's "liberal period" gave way to conservative policies, so too did Borel's. Borel assisted in the formation and organization of Rumiantsev's personal library – one of the truly remarkable collections of its time. Like Warden, Borel spent time in bookshops in Paris and London acquiring titles for his patron, having a generous budget to this end. In 1825 the title of Baron Palens was conferred on Borel, he having on 26 June 1824 received the Order of St. Vladimir, 2d degree. Borel has achieved fame today in his capacity as the first Russian envoy to Brazil.[119]

Notwithstanding his few years in St. Petersburg, Borel established no roots there, left no personal correspondence or diaries, and apparently no friends or acquaintances with whom he corresponded other than Count Rumiantsev himself. That leaves the official archives, which are helpful but not that forthcoming.

A. B. Kurakin. Among the Russian diplomats who maintained contact with Warden was Prince Alexander Borisovich Kurakin (Kourakin, usually in the French transliteration) (1752-1818), the Russian Ambassador to France from 1809 to 1812. That they saw one another socially was confirmed by Kurakin's letter to Warden of 25 November 1811 regretting that illness had made it impossible to entertain him at his home. The Russian legation in Washington D. C. used American ships and

---

[118] Ibid., p. 27. Komissarov and Bozhkova cite an 1812 Brunswick edition of which I have been unable to locate a copy.

[119] One cannot fail to note, whether there were personal contacts or not, that Borel and Warden shared a deep interest in Americana and especially the southern hemisphere. If meet they did, they had much in common to talk about besides consular law.

diplomats to send diplomatic and personal correspondence.[120] On this occasion Warden delivered to Kurakin four packets from Andrei Dashkov, three for Chancellor N. P. Rumiantsev, and one for "Mr. le Conseiller Borel". Kurakin wished to know when someone was returning to the United States so that he could write to Dashkov.[121] On 15 January 1812 Kurakin wrote to Warden to thank him for a gift and a newspaper article discussing the appointment of Count Pahlen in the United States.[122] Kurakin also wrote to Warden a letter of condolence upon the death of Joel Barlow and routinely addressed Warden as "Consul General" in his correspondence. They continued to meet and dine together long after Warden's diplomatic appointment had terminated.[123]

Among the services performed by Warden at Kurakin's request was to take custody of Russian legation property and probably the Ambassador's personal effects. The nephew of the late American Minister, Thomas Barlow, wrote to Warden of Kurakin's letter "on the subject of his effects deposited in her Hotel" and that when convenient he will execute the prince's instructions.[124] The

---

[120] Russian diplomats reciprocated. Albert Gallatin (1761-1849) and William Crawford used Pierre Poletika as a reliable messenger for secret correspondence. See N. N. Bolkhovitinov, *The Beginnings of Russian-American Relations 1775-1815*, transl. Elena Levin (1975), p. 330.

[121] Kurakin to Warden, 25 November 1811. Reel 1, Warden Papers, MdHS. This letter is further confirmation that Borel's name was known to Warden well before he completed his book.

[122] Kurakin to Warden, 15 January 1812. Reel 1, Warden Papers, MdHS.

[123] See Kurakin to Warden, 6 January 1813, 10 March 1813, and 27 October 1817. Warden Papers, DLC.

[124] Thomas Barlow to Warden, 29 March 1813. Warden Papers, DLC. Thomas Barlow is referring to the hotel in which his mother resided before returning to America.

Russian Legation archives were retrieved in 1816. Henry Jackson, the secretary to the United States Minister at the time, wrote to Warden:

> I had a visit this morning from the Secretary of the Russian Legation. The object of this visit was to ascertain in whose hands the archives of the Russian Embassy left by Prince Kourakin were at present. As they were deposited with you, or transferred to you, you will oblige me by informing me that you still have them, and what they are at the orders of the Russian Ambassador. In which case, I will immediately write His Excellency Pozzo di Borgho on the subject.[125]

A. Ia. Dashkov. Andrei Dashkov, initially Consul General of Russia in the United States, later elevated to the post of Minister of the Russian Legation, dispatched letters to his friends from Philadelphia via Warden.[126] Although Warden has been described as a person who "lived in quiet bachelorhood, frugally, and simply", surviving correspondence suggests that his "idealistic intellectual,

---

[125] Jackson to Warden, 12 March 1816. Warden Papers, DLC. At the time Carlo Andrea, Count Pozzo di Borgho (1764-1842), had been appointed Ambassador to Russia following the Bourbon Restoration. The Warden Papers contain a laconic receipt for the Russian embassy archives:" Je reconnois d'avoir recu 6 Caisse pour l'Ambassadeur de Russie. Frideric Long". Dated 21 July 1814. Warden Papers, DLC. Long was Warden's secretary.

[126] Dashkov to Warden, 10 August 1809 and 16 July 1810. Warden Papers, DLC. Dashkov was accredited to the United States as Consul General and Chargé d'Affaires on 14 July 1809. His letter of credence took the form of a Letter from Emperor Alexander I to the President of the United States. For the text, see N. N. Bashkina, et al. (eds.), *The United States and Russia: The Beginning of Relations 1765-1815* (1980), Doc. 272, p. 538. Dashkov was replaced as Consul General by Nikolai Iakovlevich Kozlov, who served in Philadelphia from 1811 to 1818. On Dashkov, Pahlen, and Poletika, see the respective entries in A. Grinev, Кто есть кто в истории русской Америки [Who is Who in the History of Russian America], ed. N. N. Bolkhovitinov (2010).

sensitive, congenial, and talkative" nature conveyed considerable charm.[127] Warden met the wife of Andrei Dashkov, Princess Evgeniia Osipovna Dashkova (17?-1881), who traveled about the United States with her husband and her sister, Sofia. Evgeniia met Warden in Washington during the year 1810 when Warden had returned to pursue his reappointment in Paris. Warden must have made an impression, for she wrote to him at length from Washington D. C. on 19 February 1810 and twice while returning home via England/France from Dunkerque. The final letter is signed "votre irreconcilable".[128]

P. I. Poletika. Petr Ivanovich Poletika (1778-1848), commonly spelled as Poletica and known as Pierre Poletica in foreign lands, served as Counselor of the Legation from 1809 to 1812 prior to Sverchkov's appointment. He corresponded with Warden on various matters of current concern. On 19 November 1811 he brought Warden up to date on the "great change which took place in the Russian Legation here. The whole was appointed to Brasil, and a new set is arrived from St. Petersburg". Count Fedor Petrovich Pahlen (1780-1863), he said, "accepted his appointment for my part & declined it under pretense of bad health. Andrei Dashkov was "happy beyond every conception", but the American public "is not at all satisfied". As for American political gossip, Poletika reported that John Quincy Adams had declined appointment to the United States Supreme Court and

---

[127] Haber, note 15 above, p. 19.

[128] Evgeniia Dashkova to Warden, 19 February, 24 April, and 25 April 1810. Warden Papers, DLC. In his correspondence with Warden, Poletika routinely reported on Evgeniia Dashkova, a "most interesting Lady" who, when Poletika wrote from England "was perfectly well". See Poletika to Warden, 19 November 1811 and 9 June 1812. Warden Papers, DLC.

remained at St. Petersburg. President Madison had filled the two vacancies on the bench with Gabriel Duvall (1752-1844) and Joseph Story.[129]

A. V. Sverchkov. Aleksei Vasilevich Sverchkov (1788-1828), commonly rendered Svertchkoff at the time and interpreter at the Russian Mission in Philadelphia from 1809 to 1811, was appointed Counselor of the Legation when Dashkov was elevated to become Minister. He was obliged for Warden's role in passing on Legation correspondence and a grateful recipient of Warden's book on consular law.[130]

Concluding Observations

Looking back two centuries, it is plain that David Bailie Warden was an exceptional United States consul and remarkable representative of the United States abroad in his personal capacity.[131] These personal qualities carried over

[129] Poletika to Warden, 19 November 1811. Warden Papers, DLC.

[130] Sverchkov to Warden, 21 January 1813. Warden Papers, DLC; 29 November 1814. Reel 2, Warden Papers, MdHS.

[131] Haber gives an excellent précis of the individuals in France with whom Warden mixed and/or corresponded. See Haber, note 15 above, pp. 26-27. The impressions offered by General John R. Fenwick (1780-18?) are apt: "I knew him esteemed by Men of the first political worth – by persons of high distinction in the Literary World, those who were admired by the emperor, and received his patronage resorted to the humble roof of Mr. Warden. They went there not to seek political informations for they knew his virtue could not be entrameled, but they became his intimate that they might discuss subjects of science and to rebuke him for not affording them more of his amiable society, and devoted more time to their far famed 'Institute' …". Fenwick to E. P. Custis, 15 June 1811. Warden Papers, MdHS. Warden's social diaries from 1817 to early 1824 and from 1829 to 1835 inclusive indicate he was a person with exceptional contacts. See Warden Papers, DLC.

to his conceptualization of the proper role of a consul abroad and have been substantially incorporated into modern consular law. Warden's view that consuls should not pursue business interests while in office has been consolidated in the 1963 Vienna Convention on Consular Relations (Article 57).[132]

The role of consuls in promoting cultural and scientific relations between the receiving and sending country has been recognized in the 1963 Convention. Article 5 enumerates among the "Consular Functions": "furthering the development of commercial, economic, cultural and scientific relations between the sending State and the receiving State ..." and "ascertaining by all lawful means conditions and developments in the commercial, economic, cultural and scientific life of the receiving State, reporting thereon to the Government of the sending State and giving information to persons interested ...". These are precisely the functions which Warden excelled at performing, whether officially or unofficially.

The practice of a receiving State granting a consul higher status than is indicated by or requested by the sending State seems not to have been definitively resolved. Stewart wrote that "Of more importance in the determination of the public character of a consul is the law of the state which receives him ... [a state] may grant privileges beyond those which international law

---

[132] See I. Roberts (ed.), *Satow's Diplomatic Practice* (6th ed.; 2009), p. 253. This approach later won supporters in the United States Government, when consuls were appropriated an annual salary in lieu of being expected to rely upon consular fees and commissions for services performed. See Wilbur J. Carr, "The American Consular Service", *American Journal of International Law*, I (1907), pp. 891-913.

requires".[133] France was among those countries which was ready to extend broad privileges even in the absence of treaty stipulations, as it would appear was done with respect to Warden in accepting his credentials at the level of Consul General, rather than Consul. The French would have found support in Borel:

> If the prerogatives of consuls have not been specified in the modern treaties which have been negotiated between the sovereigns of Europe, it is because they are too well-known for it to be thought necessary to give them an ulterior designation. For, these same princes have taken care to express them in the conventions they have made with the less enlightened powers, as with the Barbary States and with the Ottoman Porte.[134]

Modern doctrine, looking back, suggests that "historically, the classification of consuls by rank has been a matter of discretion for the sending State".[135] Although that may have come to be the case, French practice in the late eighteenth and early nineteenth centuries was otherwise in the absence of a treaty provision to the contrary. The French practice would not have been

---

[133] See I. Stewart, *Consular Privileges and Immunities* (1926), p. 9. If privileges for these purposes is understood to encompass a higher status without a requirement of reciprocity, French practice would seem to have been in accord with international law. The 1963 Vienna Convention does not expressly require that the request of the sending State to accept a person as consul precludes the receiving State from offering more than is requested. This view would mean that Article 11 of the 1963 Vienna Convention sets a minimum standard for an appointment, rather than an absolute standard.

[134] Borel, note 108 above, p. 12.

[135] L. T. Lee and J. B. Quigley, Jr., *Consular Law and Practice* (3d ed.; 2008), p. 32. Both Warden and Borel are unknown to all three editions of this treatise, and the problem of French practice and Warden's status are not discussed. Garbesi cited Warden in his bibliography but not in the text. See George C. Garbesi, *Consular Authority Over Seamen from the United States Point of View* (1968), p. 223.

inconsistent with the modern requirements that the designation of consular ranks be consistent with the categories set out in the 1963 Vienna Convention.

Warden's view that the origins of consular law lie in remote Antiquity has been widely (though not universally) accepted in modern international legal doctrine and practice. The Preamble to the 1963 Vienna Convention begins by "recalling that consular relations have been established between peoples since ancient time". This is true of civilizations in Europe and the Near East predating Greek and Roman times and of Chinese civilization.[136] As Sir Paul Vinogradoff (1854-1925) concluded, "… in every stage of civilization we are met with characteristic features of international law".[137] Judge Roberto Ago (1907-1995) was more emphatic:

> It is too often overlooked, in flagrant contradiction to historical reality, that in fact the emergence and progressive development of law occurred in parallel within human groupings of quite different types, composition and dimensions. And no less disregard of history is implied by failure to grasp the fact that international law is a phenomenon which has always emerged and developed among a group of distinct and sovereign political

---

[136] "… the treaty system, which gleamed so new in the eyes of British consuls, was actually from the Chinese point of view little more than a refurbishing of the traditional tribute system, a variation on ancient and well-tested themes … The consuls merely represented the ancient principle that a community of foreign merchants in China should be superintended by a head man who would take responsibility for his countrymen". See J. K. Fairbank, "The Early Treaty System in the Chinese World Order", in Fairbank (ed.), *The Chinese World Order* (1968), pp. 259-260.

[137] P. G. Vinogradoff, "Historical Types of International Law", in W. E. Butler (ed.), *On the History of International Law and International Organization: Collected Papers of Sir Paul Vinogradoff* (2009), p. 67.

entities whenever sustained and organized relations have come to exist between them.[138]

A Note on Sources

The best single work on Warden remains Francis C. Haber, *David Bailie Warden: A Bibliographical Sketch of America's Cultural Ambassador in France, 1804-1845* ([Washington D. C.], Institut de francais de Washington, 1954). There is an excellent sketch in C. Edward Skeen, "Warden, David Bailie", *American National Biography, XX* (1999), pp. 656-657. On Warden's early life, also see Skeen, *John Armstrong, Jr., 1758-1843: A Biography* (1981).

The Warden Papers exist principally at two sites: the Maryland Historical Society (MdHS), which has placed its collection of more than 4,000 letters, seven registers and letterbooks, and boxes of notes and memoranda on seven reels of microfilm. The Finding Aid which accompanies the microfilm by Bayly Ellen Marks, *Guide to the Microfilm Edition of the David Bailie Warden Papers* (Baltimore, Maryland Historical Society, 1970) provides an admirable overview of the Maryland holdings.

The second site of Warden Papers is the Manuscript Division of the Library of Congress (DLC). It comprises more than 5,000 items in twenty-two volumes and six boxes. There is a local Finding Aid.

Scattered Warden correspondence exists in many other archives, including the Townsend Family Papers at the New York Public Library, the American Philosophical

---

[138] See R. Ago, "The First International Communities in the Mediterranean World", *British Year Book of International Law*, LIII (1982), p. 213.

Society, the Clements Library at the University of Michigan, University of South Carolina, among others.

On 29 October 2009 a group of manuscript reports, lists, and bibliographies on American subjects was sold, about 385 pages in total, from the English Library of Archibald, 5th Earl of Roseberry and Midlothian, for £3,500, including buyer's premium, at Sotheby's, Sale L09794, Lot 123.

The Warden title reprinted herein was obtained from the Rutgers School of Law – Newark, received there by donation from the Prudential Insurance Company. The Prudential had purchased in the 1890s the large law collection by Joseph P. Bradley (1813-1892), Associate Justice of the United States Supreme Court. One may only speculate why Justice Bradley should have a copy of Warden's treatise on consular law, but it may be worth observing that Bradley published in 1875 a Memorial to the life and character of William Lewis Dayton (1807-1864), late United States Minister to France.

CONTENTS
(added by William E. Butler)

ON

THE ORIGIN, NATURE,

PROGRESS AND INFLUENCE

OF

CONSULAR ESTABLISHMENTS,

BY D. B. WARDEN,

CONSUL GENERAL OF THE UNITED STATES OF AMERICA, AT PARIS; D.r MED. COLL. NOV. EBOR.; MEMBER OF THE PHILOSOPHICAL SOCIETY OF PHILADELPHIA; OF THE PHILOMATIC SOCIETY, AND OF THE SOCIETY FOR THE ENCOURAGEMENT OF ARTS AND MANUFACTURES, AT PARIS; OF THE BELFAST LITERARY SOCIETY, ETC. ETC. ETC.

PARIS:

PRINTED AND SOLD BY SMITH, RUE MONTMORENCY, n.° 16.

1813.

ON THE ORIGIN,

NATURE, PROGRESS AND INFLUENCE

OF

CONSULAR ESTABLISHMENTS.

TO THE PRESIDENT

AND SENATE

OF THE UNITED-STATES,

The following Essay is dedicated as a public memorial of the respect and gratitude of the author,

DAVID BAILIE WARDEN.

PREFACE.

Nothing was more remote from my thoughts than to write a volume when I first turned my attention to consular establishments. I had only proposed to point out, to my Government, some defects in our consular system, which, by a wise interposition, might be easily remedied. For this purpose, I wished to avail myself of the improvements adopted by other nations in relation to their foreign commercial agents, and was surprised at not finding in any of the public libraries of Paris even a simple memoir written professedly upon this subject. This circumstance induced me to seek information in collections of national treaties, and other documents of a diplomatic nature. In this research, I was insensibly conducted to ancient classic ground, where an ideal picture presented itself to the imagination, the subject of which was, *The origin, progress and influence of consular establishments for the protection of commerce.* I wished to be able to embody this picture, but not only canvass and other materials were wanting, but also skill to adapt them to a happy execution. I therefore resolved to confine my plan to a mere profile, which has been sketched during hours of leisure from public business, since the late rupture between England and the United States. When my task was nearly finished, I was informed by one of the *literati* of Paris, that in the book-catalogue of *Leipsic,* for the present year, a volume is announced, *On the origin and functions of Consuls,*[1] and he was pleased to procure

[1] *De l'origine et des fonctions des consuls,* par

it for me through a German bookseller. The appearance of this publication would have rendered mine unnecessary, if the matter and arrangement were not essentially different. This is evident from a simple inspection of the analytical table of the contents of each. Mr. Borel has devoted eighty pages of his work to an examination of the origin and functions of Consuls, which evinces an intimate acquaintance with this subject. The remainder, consisting of two hundred and ninety pages, is made up of extracts of treaties, and other documents relative to the employment of commercial agents.

It may not be improper here to observe, that although I am decidedly of

F. Borel. This gentleman is a native of Milan, whose talents and conduct procured him the friendship of Count Nicholas de Romanzoff, by whose recommendation he was appointed chief of division of the *Ministry of commerce*, and assistant judge of the Imperial college of St. Petersburg. He now resides at the island of Madeira as Consul general of Russia.

opinion, that a Consul, for reasons which shall hereafter be mentioned, ought to have no interest in trade, yet I am, nevertheless, the friend and advocate of liberal commerce; which, if founded on the principles of justice, honor, and reciprocity, would form, between nations and climates, a chain of communication highly favorable to the improvement of arts, industry, and political economy. Commerce might then, with some propriety, be defined the art of rendering a people happy; but unfortunately it has been the engine of wickedness, the source of division and discord, both foreign and domestic. Instead of softening national animosity, it has almost always served to renew those fierce resentments which it is the province of civilisation to extinguish. At the shrine of commerce, the ruling powers of different countries have sacrificed the most solemn principles, and individuals, by a sort of *Circean* enchantment, have been transformed into monsters divested of every thing which constitutes the social man. Nothing can be conceived more mean, selfish, or contracted, than the mind of a person whose sentiments and thoughts are regulated by the simple balance of profit and loss. Still, however, there are merchants who love their country more than their coffers; men of noble and enlightened minds, who do honor to patriotism and to virtue, by exemplary conduct, elevated conceptions, and the liberal and useful employment of a portion of their capital; between whom and a mere speculator or projector there is as much difference as between the greatest and meanest, the most enlightened and most stupid of mankind.

The insatiable and indiscriminate pursuit of objects of traffic in which something may be gained, has tarnished abroad the lustre of our republican character; for, unfortunately, the opinion, however ill-founded, is almost universal, that every American is more or less engaged in foreign or domestic trade, or barter; and the noble and independent spirit of the country is believed to be truly avaricious and commercial.

Should this essay happen to fall under the inspection of critics, I have only to alledge that it was not prepared for rigid examination. It is a mere skeleton, whose usefulness might have been injured by any attempt to give it flesh and coloring. If it be acceptable to the government and country of which I am the agent, my object is attained, and my leisure hours will not have been uselessly employed. The volume, however, may not be altogether uninstructive to diplomatic agents, magistrates, lawyers, and merchants; and it may attract, by its novelty, other classes of readers, to whom the subject is of less importance. In speaking of myself it is well to recollect the observation of an ancient philosopher, "That self-praise is as vain as "self-accusation is mean."[1]

[1] Aristotle

Paris, July 1, 1813.

ON THE ORIGIN,

NATURE, PROGRESS AND INFLUENCE

OF

CONSULAR ESTABLISHMENTS.

CHAPTER I.

The commercial advantages of Consular Establishments.

THE advantages of consular establishments for the protection of mercantile concerns, were obvious to those who first ventured their property in a foreign land. Though confided to the care of an intelligent factor, the laws of equity were often disregarded. Civilized, as well as barbarous nations, among whom no foreign public agent resided, from some pretended infraction of rules, or non-observance of customs or usages, but little if at all known, seized, with unblushing rapacity, property which they had invited to their shores and acknowledged as sacred. Even the Greeks and Romans, whose civilisation is still the theme of eloquence, in their commerce with foreigners, considered the law of expediency as superior to and more profitable than that of justice. Such was their jealousy of other nations, that they had adopted as synonimous the terms *enemy* and *foreigner;* and though he arrived on their shores with friendly intentions, with smiles and with presents, he was nevertheless suspected of treacherous designs. The invention of the trader was employed to frame regulations for reciprocal commerce, for the sale and exchange of productions, and government felt a deep interest in having them adopted and enforced. The figures and inscriptions of medals, which were intended as emblems of national faith and existing compacts, made but slight impressions on minds, whose sole occupation was gain. To facilitate commerce, and the more effectually to protect persons and property, recourse was had to commercial treaties; and in a variety of cases, growing out of mercantile jealousy and prejudice, these too were found ineffectual. From commerce, in its progress and growth, a thousand disputes originated, which rendered necessary the presence of an agent, clothed with legal authority, and acting for his country in the smallest as well as greatest affairs; in the trifling disputes of seamen, as well as in those on which depended the friendship or hatred of governments.

Vessels were plundered on the high seas by pirates, or sea-rovers, who entered ports with impunity, to share and enjoy the spoil with the partners and abettors of their depredations. The active hand of justice was required to bring to condign punishment those enemies of the human race.

The quantity and quality of articles, the variable duties to which they were liable, the prices of the market, and the rights and privileges of traders, became the subject of frequent dispute. An authority, always at hand, was necessary to maintain probity, and prevent fraud and prevarication.

Merchant vessels, forced by pirates, by

stress of weather or the dangers of the sea, to seek shelter in ports or havens where they expected kindness and protection, were searched and molested; and though they broke no bulk, and paid strict attention to municipal laws, duties were imposed as the condition of their departure.

Sovereign princes and republics, when preparing a warlike expedition, from motives of utility or of expediency, seized goods and merchandises,[1] and obliged foreign vessels, in their ports, to carry to certain places, troops, victuals and ammunition, which circumstance often retarded, and sometimes consumed the profits of the voyage.

Effects saved from shipwreck were pillaged or confiscated, because there was no person authorised to claim them in the name of his nation.

The *Droit d'aubaine*[2] was applied to the moveable, as well as immoveable property of merchants dying intestate.

[1] *Anguria navium,* from *ango,* personal or forced services.

[2] From *alibi natus,* a stranger.

Religious worship different from that of the established church, the *Jupiter peregrinus*, was a pretext for depriving foreigners of decent sepulture.

In time of war, captains and capers employed cruelty and bribes to extort confessions to legalize their prize; and the captured, in their appeal to humanity and justice, vainly sought satisfaction for injuries and wrongs.

Shipwrecked seamen lost their freedom with their goods, and were thus without the means, and even without the hope of return to their native land.

The debts and disputes of seamen, when in port, required frequent and prompt attention. Accustomed to privations and to slavish treatment, this brave and generous, though turbulent race of men, were guilty of gross excesses. Among the earliest commercial nations, undisciplined seamen [1] were the same as in the present times. They have still some resemblance with their portrait by *Hecuba* "An incorrigible race, whose fury is more difficult to quench than a

[1] ναυτικη τ'αναρχια.

violent conflagration. Hardened by crimes, they consider him as wicked who has not been guilty of some marked atrocity."[1]

A jurisdiction over seamen, vessels, and merchandise became necessary, not only for the purpose of protecting the rights of merchants, but also to prevent the merchants themselves from endangering the general interests of the nation; and this jurisdiction could not be established without a national agent, invested with proper attributions; for experience showed, that the nautical code of the Rhodians, the wisdom and equity of which has been praised by Cicero,[2] and the still more perfect laws of Oleron[3] and of Wisby,[4] without magistrates to see

[1] *Euripides* in *Hecuba*, verse 507, 8. The unfortunate captive thus exclaimed to the messenger of Agamemnon, whom she sent to drive away the crowd, and not to suffer unhallowed hands to touch the body of her beloved daughter.

[2] *In Orat: pro lege Manilia.*

[3] The isle of *Oleron*, celebrated for its commerce and excellent seamen, is situated near the coast of France, about two leagues from La Rochelle. The population is about twelve thousand.

[4] Wisby is the capital of the island of Gothland, in the Baltic Sea.

them enforced, were but feeble barriers against pride, ambition, or the love of gain.

It became necessary to establish, in the place where foreign commerce was transacted, a person authorised, by a commission, to watch over the preservation of the rights and privileges of seamen and merchants; to determine their disputes, and to direct the political and commercial administration of the affairs of his nation.

CHAPTER II.

The political and economical advantages of Consular Establishments.

To be useful to his country in arts, sciences, and manufactures, a consul must have no commercial engagements. Services of this kind cannot be expected from, as they cannot be performed by him, whose mind is absorbed in the pursuits of gain. The consul must not only love, but must also have time to communicate knowledge. His conduct and usefulness will always be influenced by the circumstances in which he is placed. If he have not a regular salary, and be obliged to seek support as a merchant or factor, his eye must be constantly directed to his private advantage; and, in this position, he insensibly adopts the fundamental doctrine of the trader, "Every man for himself, and God Almighty for us all."[1]

[1] Millar's View of the English Government, vol. IV, p. 249. London edition.

There are many reasons why a consul ought not to be permitted to have an interest in trade; and, therefore, his salary ought to be commensurate with his situation. His time and labor are not his own but those of his country, to the government of which, like the philosophic traveller of *Anacharsis,* he ought to communicate all that is good and useful to know, concerning the laws, customs, manners, arts, commerce and manufactures of the country of his residence. It is not enough to have leisure for the performance of this task: other qualities are requisite. The consul must have a fair character, an honorable reputation, and a mind stored with knowledge. He ought to be mild in conduct, and free from passion; not hasty in decision on subjects which admit of doubt; but firm in resolutions well deliberated: prudent, and conciliating; communicative on subjects which require publicity more than concealment; the faithful depository of private communications, and free from that ridiculous affectation, that air of mystery, which makes secrets even of newspaper articles, and thus destroys all friendship and all confidence.

The portrait, which the Roman orator has drawn of the first magistrate of his country, might serve, though it certainly could never have been intended, as a model for an officer of commerce, whom the proud Romans placed under the protection of *Mercury*, the tutelar deity of thieves and of robbers: "*Animo consulem esse opportet, consilio, fide, gravitate, vigilantiâ, curâ, toto denique munere consulatus omni officio tuendo, maximeque id quod vis nominis præscribit Reipublicæ consulendo.*"[1]

How important to a government is the knowledge of this fact, that a consul of an elevated character, in the midst of strangers, has it in his power to make almost whatever impression he pleases concerning his country, and the administration of its government. In enlightened society, he is obliged to answer a thousand questions concerning the nation he represents. One person inquires concerning its constitution and government; another wishes to be informed

[1] Oratio in Pisonem, cap. 10.

of the character of the chief magistrate, and heads of the civil and military administration; a third of the soil and its productions; and a fourth of the pursuits, habits and amusements of the people. The replies of the consul are treasured up for future conversations, repeated in different circles, communicated to persons in authority, and sometimes employed by editors and authors to support a favorite opinion or theory. Wo be to the country of the consul, if his observations have been those of ignorance, prejudice or self-interest; for it is natural to believe, and to adopt the opinions of a foreign agent, who is not supposed to be ignorant of the soil from which he sprung; of the temperature of the air which he long breathed; the nature and views of the government of which he is the agent; and the character of the people among whom he lived till after the usual term for the developement of mind.

The true employment of a minister is diplomacy, or the art of conducting public affairs with the view of attaining a great national object; and he cannot, without injury to his private and public character, go aside from this path, and occupy himself with the details of consular, or commercial business. He is not even permitted to visit or correspond directly with the secretaries of courts or of bureaux, whose duty it is to furnish the consul with verbal, or written information on maritime and commercial subjects. Whatever is contrary to diplomatic usage, becomes the subject of diplomatic ridicule. Every step of a minister is watched with *Argus'* eyes. All his words and actions are minutely scrutinized. His ministerial influence in private business naturally excites suspicion and jealousy; and he cannot, without great danger to himself and to his country, deviate from the diplomatic path.

The functions of a consul are quite distinct from those of a minister, even in places where the latter resides. The former is charged with the individual commercial concerns of his country; with the prosecution of private claims, with the business of seamen, and cases of vessels seized or captured. It is his special duty, to establish, in a civil point of view, births, marriages and deaths: to grant certificates of life; and to, decide, upon testimony, cases of doubtful or disputed citizenship. He is often appointed, by the courts of his country, to act as commissioner in receiving evidence in important cases pending before them. He is generally charged with the formalities of this business, and may do great injury to individuals, by corruption, negligence, or interested friendship. He is often requested to examine and verify affairs conducted by agents, who have not satisfied the views of their constituents. In this respect, he acts like an attorney-general, and is obliged to communicate to the party the result of his inquiry.

It is his duty to be as useful, as time and circumstances may permit, to scientific or literary travellers of his nation; and, at their arrival, to procure them information in the line of their profession; to facilitate their correspondence, and to communicate to them the passing events of their country, in which they express an interest.

The consul, if he be not a merchant, is often consulted in secret, concerning the moral and pecuniary character of his countrymen, whose object is credit, or an interest in a mercantile or manufacturing association. He is also consulted by foreigners, concerning the nature and value of the lands and stocks of his country; the best mode of remitting monies, and the means of procuring passages for their respective countries.

In almost all cases of injustice, or of bad faith, experienced by foreigners from his countrymen, he is appealed to as mediator or umpire.

He is also requested yearly to correct the statistical table of the state to which he belongs, inserted in *Commercial Almanacks,* and other similar publications; with the exception of the list of consuls which is regularly submitted to the revision of the minister.

Documents of various kinds are deposited in the chancery of the consulate, of which, when required, he gives extracts. He legalizes signatures and declarations, executes and registers letters of attorney, bonds, mortgages, and other instruments of writing. He corresponds with his government on every subject which he considers of sufficient importance to occupy its attention.

In the course of a few years, what a variety of useful information may a consul communicate to his country, if he have an acquaintance with the directors and professors of public establishments. Books, maps, pamphlets, models and drawings of machines, seeds and plants, are gladly offered in exchange for similar articles.

How important the services which a consul might render to his country, by the communication of inventions and improvements in manufactures, husbandry, and the useful arts. In a late work,[1] it is observed, that among the events which render illustrious the reign of a prince, are voyages of discovery, of which he is the protector and supporter; and there is allusion to that of the celebrated *Cook*, and to the generous enterprise of *Sir Joseph Banks*, " by which the limits of science have been extended, and the globe traversed without any motive of lucre or of conquest."

The discovery, however, of a new country is valuable only in the advantages which result from it to civilized man; and those advantages are best and soonest acquired

[1] Macartney's travels in China, vol. I, pag. 219.—French translation by *Castera*.

by the labors and researches of commissioned and enlightened agents, protected by the authorities where they reside, and enabled, by time and by particular privileges, to furnish a complete account of every invention and improvement useful to their country. From this source, more than from any other, important information may be derived. In all places where literature and science are cherished, their votaries are welcome guests: they mingle with private society, and become intimately acquainted with its spirit, manners and opinions: they find easy access to manufactures and establishments, whether the property of the government or of individuals; and they are thus enabled to examine, with their own eyes, a thousand objects concealed from, or unknown to the passing traveller. From enlightened agents of this description, less occupied with the gains of commerce than with statistical knowledge, France has drawn, from various countries, treasures of useful information, which she has promptly and wisely employed to increase her manufactures and strength. In the midst of revolution this great object was not forgotten.

At the request of the French Committee of Public Instruction, the Department of Foreign affairs enjoined the consuls to keep up a regular correspondence on subjects of science, manufactures and arts. Through this medium it was proposed to facilitate communication between the French *savans* and the learned of other countries: to disseminate new publications, accelerate the circulation of thought and discovery, and increase the fame and prosperity of France; by uniting the fruits of her genius with those of other philanthropic nations.[1]

French consuls, at the request of the National Institute, and agricultural and other societies, have furnished interesting accounts of the countries in which they resided. The academy of sciences, by addressing a series of questions to *M. de Guignes*, resident consul in China, obtained new and accurate information concerning a country whose productions have been so carefully concealed from the eye of strangers.[2]

[1] Speech of the senator and bishop Gregoire.

[2] *Voyage à Pékin, etc. etc. par M. de Guignes*, 1808. 3 vol. Paris.

Most of the French commercial consuls have distinguished themselves in science or literature.

The former missionaries of Portugal, Spain, Italy, and particularly of France, who travelled or resided in the Indies and in the East, were ministers, agents and consuls of their government. Their great object was to propagate religion, but a portion of their time was devoted to other pursuits; and they furnished Europe with a mass of important information in natural history, commerce and the arts. The *Lettres Édifiantes*, of which there are more than twenty volumes, and the *Mémoires sur la Chine*, fifteen in number, with dictionaries, grammars and other works, published by the *propaganda* congregation, are immortal monuments of their zeal and labor. Their influence with the natives of the country, procured great advantage to their mercantile compatriots. What efforts were made by the celebrated bishop of *Adran*[1] for France and Cochinchina. In the time of the Constituent Assembly, *Cossigny* and

[1] *Pigneaux.*

other writers published memoirs to show the importance of such missions, in a commercial as well as religious point of view.

It would add much to the growth of civilisation throughout the world, if consuls and agents were permitted to communicate the discoveries of their compatriots, in exchange for those of the country where they reside. In the United-States, where nothing is concealed, where manufactures, dock-yards, inventions and improvements of every kind may be examined by strangers from every region, civilisation has made more progress, in a given time, than in any other country.

An ancient law of Iceland obliged all its inhabitants, who travelled abroad, to appear before the magistrate at their return, and to communicate to him the improvements of other countries which might be usefully adopted in theirs.

Between countries which have no commercial relations, the only convenient mode of communication is that of the consul.

A learned friend, to whom I am often indebted for information, observed to me that *Job Ludolph* and *Jos. Scaliger* had formerly certain relations with the Samaritans of *Naplouse;*[1] that Marshall, professor of Oxford, afterwards corresponded with them through Huntington, chaplain of the English factory at *Aleppo;* that all communication between Europe and this colony had ceased for more than a century, and was renewed by the gentleman to whom I allude, through the French consuls at Tripoli, Syria, Saint-Jean-d'Acre and Aleppo.

The Ionian academy of Corfu proposes to publish researches concerning the civilisation and literature of the Greeks, from the fall of the Eastern Empire; and have claimed and obtained, from the French government, the means of corresponding on this subject, through its consuls at Janina, Patras, and Constantinople.

[1] Or *Nablous*, a town of Asia, formed of the ruins of the ancient *Neapolis.*

CHAPTER IV.

The Origin of Consular Jurisdiction.

The fate of *Lucretia* inspired the Romans with vengeance against the Tarquins and royalty; and the sovereign authority was confided to two magistrates, who were first named prætors, and afterwards consuls.[1] The latter term was derived from their office; for they were the counsellors, not the sovereigns of the republic. "Let there be two in the regal empire, and let them be called prætors, judges, consuls, à *prœundo, judicando, consulendo.*"[2] If the consul remained at his post, after the expiration of the annual consulate, he was designated by the name of *proconsul.*[3] This form of government,

B. C. 516.

[1] Initio prætores erant, qui nunc consules. *Festus.*

[2] Cicero, I, 3, *de Legibus.* Quia reipublicæ plurimum consulunt. The word Consul is derived from *Consulendo* or *Consulo.*

[3] *Pro consule,* acting for the consul.

introduced by the elder *Brutus*, was of short duration; but the title of *consul*, consecrated to liberty, was long considered as a synonimous term, and was preserved, by several emperors, during the first years of their reign. When it no longer served to distinguish the first magistrate of Rome, it was applied, by the government of *Marseilles*, to agents (*inviati* [1]) commissioned to reside in ports of the Levant and of Barbary, for the protection of its citizens and commerce, and the regulation of all affairs which became the subject of litigation or dispute.

It appears, that among different nations of antiquity there existed a species of magistracy, similar to that of consuls of modern times, authorised by governments to protect their foreign commercial interests.

The Greeks had an officer of this description, named προξενος, [2] who was instructed, by a decree of the people, to

[1] From this term was derived *envoy*, or minister of the second order.

[2] From ξενος, *hospes*. — *Hospes publicus civitatis*. Arist. lib. V.

receive and entertain strangers, and to act as a judge and conciliator of the disputes of foreign merchants. His functions, in some respects, resembled those of a modern consul,[1] though he was a native of the country where he exercised his jurisdiction, and not of that of the foreign merchant. At Sparta, this honor was the price of signal services rendered by the person on whom it was conferred,[2] and was attended with various privileges and immunities. He received ambassadors,[3] assisted at the national assemblies, and presided at religious ceremonies and public *fêtes*.[4] *Alcibiades* acted as the public host of the Lacedemonians; and, in this quality, had charge of the Spartans who were made prisoners at Sylos. At Sparta he availed himelf of the privi-

[1] Keiste, Index græcitatis Demosthenæ, n. 646, t. IV.

[2] Eustath. ad Homerum, lib. III, p. 307. See also Thucydides, lib. III, n.° 70.

[3] Jul. Poll. lex III, c. 4, § 59.

[4] *Paciaudi*, in his *Monumenta Peloponesia*, mentions an inscription of the Lacedemonian republic, in which a person is styled *δ́μόν ξενον και ενεργετον*, t. II, pag. 131.

leges attached to this quality, to satiate his vengeance against the Athenians.[1]

At Athens, the affairs of the Προξενια could not be judged but by the *Polemarch*,[2] or third *Archos*.[3] The Delians decreed them grants of lands, the first places at sacrifices and public *fêtes*, and free entry into the senate and assembly of the people.[4] Like the consuls of modern times, the Προξενοι affixed above the outer door, or entrance into the house, the arms of the town of which they were the agents.[5]

Besides this mutual public hospitality, established by all the Grecian towns, maritime commerce gave rise to a particular jurisdiction, exercised, at Athens and other places, by certain magistrates, named Ναυτο-

[1] Plut. Vit. Alcib. tom. XI.

[2] From Πολέμαρχος.

[3] From Αρχος, a ruler or chief magistrate.

[4] Delior. Decret. ap. Reines, clasi. 7; n. 23.

[5] Antigonus Carystias, ch. XV, p. 25. Éd. de Beckman. The learned hellenist, *Villoison*, has left extracts from different authors, concerning the signification of the word Προξενοι, which we were permitted to examine at the National Library. From these it appears that its true meaning was such as we have described.

διχαι,[1] who went on board of vessels in the ports, and decided the disputes of seamen in a summary manner, according to their own confessions and the testimony of witnesses. Another class of officers, named Παντοδιχυς, were sovereign judges of all mercantile disputes.[2]

The Epidamnians, a colony of Corcyrians established in Macedonia,[3] on the Adriatic Gulf, appointed a magistrate, named *Polites*, to regulate their commerce with the Illyrians, a neighbouring nation, whose influence they dreaded.[4]

B. C. 600.

Teos, the birth place of Anacreon, and other towns of great antiquity, had magistrates, named *Timuques*,[5] whose employment was to superintend commercial affairs.[6]

B. C. 500.

[1] *Jus dicentes nautis.*

[2] Demosthenes against *Apatourion*, and against *Phormion*. See also *Xenophon*.

[3] Now Albania.

[4] Plut. quœst. Græc. tom. II, pag. 297. See also l'*Histoire de Marseille*, par Antoine *De Ruffi*; in folio. Marseille, 1699, p. 12.

[5] From τιμυχοσ, men highly honored.

[6] Herod. tom. XI, c. 168.

From a number of facts, recorded in history, we are led to infer, that most of the earliest maritime nations were ignorant of or hostile to the principles of maritime justice.

The Phenicians, who owed their glory to commerce, knew no law but that of force. Those who refused their gainful offers of traffic were the victims of their insatiable avarice.[1]

The Carthaginians owed their superiority
B. C. 536. over other nations to their marine and commerce; and yet they seem to have adopted no other principle than that of exercising against rivals, as well as enemies, an avaricious cruelty infinitely more terrible than the despotism of political ambition. When in possession of *Sardinia*, no Roman sailor was permitted to touch the soil of that island; and the only privilege acquired by treaty, was that of permitting a vessel, driven by storm into one of its ports, to remain a few days for the purpose of repair.[2] All foreign navi-

[1] Arist. de Mirab. tom. I. Opera, p. 711.

[2] Apud Polyb. L. III; tom. I, p. 285.

gators, whom they caught in their roads or bays, were thrown into the sea;[1] and if, struggling for their life, they regained and clung to the vessel, they were instantly dispatched. Such was the commercial avidity of the Phenicians, that they derided the name of honor, virtue, friendship; and stifled those common feelings of our nature which sway the breast even of the wandering savage.

The Tyrians, their rivals in commercial navigation, were not less cruel towards those whose power or influence they had no reason to dread. Poverty they considered as the most formidable of evils, and riches as the source of every enjoyment.[2]

The Rhodians seem to have been the only maritime commercial people of the ancient world, who, in the plenitude of naval dominion, conducted themselves, in their relations with other nations, on the great principles of neutrality, national justice, and freedom of the seas. Their Code of

[1] Strabo, tom. XVII, p. 802. Ed. Lut.

[2] Per mare pauperiem fugiens, per saxa, per ignes. *Horat.*

maritime legislation was adopted by the Roman emperors, by Augustus and by the Antoninus, for the decision of naval and commercial disputes.[1] The ports of Rhodes were open to all trading nations, who equally enjoyed the protection of a wise and humane legislation.[2]

The Romans, who despised the profession of a merchant, considered naval officers or magistrates,[3] as unconnected with the republic. They were charged with the construction and equipment of vessels, with the inspection of grain, or other merchandise that came up the Tiber; and it was their constant duty to chase pirates from the upper and lower sea, as far as the gulf of *Venice* and the port of *Marseilles*.[4] At Rome, provisions were introduced by the *Sacarii*,[5] at a price fixed by the government, after having

[1] Digest. de Lege Rhodia, leg. IX, tit. 11, lib. XIV.

[2] Strabo, lib. XIV, p. 449.

[3] *Duumviri navales.*

[4] Jorio Storia del Comm. e della navig. tom. IV' p. 202.

[5] From σαχχεφόρος, or *sack bearer.*

undergone the inspection of the *Comes portus.*[1]

The origin and improvement of courts for foreign commerce, though they must have had considerable influence over civilisation, revolutions, and important events, have been scarcely noticed by the best historians. The subject is, therefore, obscure, and cannot be explained without having recourse to a great number of volumes, from which we shall present extracts; and we regret that neither our limits nor leisure permit us to discuss and combine the facts which we have collected.

The *Prætor*[2] *mercatorum* of the Romans, like the commercial magistrate of the Greeks, decided the disputes of sailors in the cabin of the vessel to which they belonged.

The *Prætor*[3] *peregrinus* was the agent for strangers, and it was his duty to examine and to judge in a prompt manner, the litigations of foreign merchants. This magistrate was appointed by the republic; and,

[1] Cassiodorus, tom. I, de Saccar. port. Romæ.

[2] Extra ordinem.

[3] From *præire*, or *præesse*.

like the *Prætor urbanus,* was chosen from among the order of senators, knights, or Roman citizens.

When Sicily and Sardinia became provinces of the Roman empire, they were governed by *prætors.* Spain, after its subjugation, was also governed by a magistrate of the same description.[1]

Polybius mentions a treaty concluded between the Carthaginians and Romans, which, on one hand, defended the latter from trading with Sardinia and Africa, and, on the other, secured their commercial rights and privileges in Latium.

B. C. 368.

The emperor Claudius granted to the merchants of Cadix certain exclusive privileges, and exemption from the jurisdiction of tribunals established by Cesar in *Betica.*

During the reigns of Honorius and Theodosius, judges were appointed to decide cases of submerged vessels, with the curtain raised.[2] This curtain was suspended at the entrance of the

A. D. 400.

[1] Livy, lib. II, decad. 4. *Sex prætores illo anno,* etc.

[2] Levato velo.

court, and was drawn during some species of pleadings. It appears from a law of the Visigoths, that a commercial tribunal of this description continued to exist even after the fall of the Western Empire, which crushed and almost annihilated commerce.[1]

The judges of these establishments for the use of foreign merchants, had different titles, such as *Telonarii*,[2] *Bajuli*,[3] *Præpositi*,[4] *Seneschalli*, *Seniores* and *Priores mercatuum*. The term *Bajulus* was employed by the Venitians; *Consul*, by the Pisans; the *Telonarii mercati Palatii*, in France, were the directors of customs and commercial affairs, who distributed justice in the name of the king.

The historian Varro had given a detailed account of the commerce of the Romans, but his works have been unfortunately lost; and succeeding writers have treated this subject in a vague and imperfect manner.

[1] Dum transmarini negotiatores inter se causam habuerent, nullus de sedibus nostris eos audire præsumat, nisi tantummodo suis legibus audiantur apud Telonarios suos. Lib. XI, tit. III, § 2.

[2] From τελων, a collector of customs.

[3] From βαστάζω, to carry.

[4] From προστάτης, a provost, or warden.

Marseilles, when allied with Rome, carried on a very extensive commerce with Asia and with Italy. Founded by the Phocians, more than a century before the christian era, its celebrated navigators had established laws for the regulation of commerce. Their senate was composed of six hundred members, named *Timuques,* fifteen of whom were elected to judge affairs in a summary way; and, of this last number, three had powers more extensive than the rest.[1]

In the beginning of the ninth century, the republic of *Amalphi,* established on the gulf of Salernum, framed a regular maritime code, under the title of *Laws of Amalphi;* which all, who navigated the Mediterranean, were forced to obey. Hume, in his account of Richard the third, observes, that perhaps there was no event which tended farther to the improvements of the age, than one which has not been much remarked, the accidental finding of a copy of Justinian's Pandects, about the year 1130, in the town of Amalphi in Italy. An au-

[1] Strabo, t. IV, p. 124.

thor,[1] often cited as authority, observes that from the tables of *Amalphi* are derived all our laws on navigation; and he is of opinion, that they partly originated from the naval experience of this people, and were partly borrowed from the emperors of the East, with whom they carried on a constant traffic. We are informed by another authority, that the liberal principles of the Amalphian Code were derived from a copy of the Pandects, found in this town; which, three hundred years afterwards, was carried to Pisa by its victorious warriors.[2]

It appears from the chronicle of Pisa, that, in the tenth century, a species of supreme magistracy was established in this republic, under the denomination of consuls of

[1] Giannone, *Storia civile del Regno di Napoli,* t. I, l. VII, p. 492, who cites Freccia, de subfeud. de offi. admirat. num. 7. Hinc in regno non lege Rhodia maritima decernuntur sed tabula, quam amalfitanam vocant; omnes controversiæ, omnes lites, ac omnia maris discrimina, eâ lege, ac sanctione, jusque ad hæc tempora finiuntur.

[2] Brencmannus, Dissertatio II, de Amalphi a Pisanis diruta. C. XXIV et seq. ad calcem histor. Pandectarum. Cited by *Sismondi,* Hist. des Rép. Ital. vol. I, p. 264 et suiv.

navigation, and that this court was afterwards sanctioned by Gregory VII.[1] The
A. D. 1075. Pisans, offended with Alexis, avenged themselves by keeping his son a prisoner; and the price of his redemption were certain religious rights, a counting-house, and consular jurisdiction, for the protection of ships, citizens and commerce; which privileges were stipulated in a treaty of peace, and afterwards confirmed by Frederic the first and his successor.[2] The word *consulate* is expressed in a statute of Pisa, enacted in the year 1161; and the laws and ordonnances of this town, entitled *Breve maris consulum Pisæ,* are said to resemble those of the *Consulat de la mer.*

Baluzio[3] informs us, that the first consulate of the middle age was established in the town of Messina, by Roger I. king of Sicily;

[1] Azuni, Système du Droit maritime, tom. I, p. 103, sect. Pisa.

[2] *Codin curopalata* de mensâ Imperatoris, cap. VII, n. 9.

[3] Brev. hist. liberat Missanæ, tom. VI, p. [174. Miscellanorum.

who referred all maritime and mercantile affairs and negociations to the direction of two consuls, whose decisions were solemn, and enforced by authority.

Guy de Lusignan, who had preserved some possessions in Palestine, granted to the *Marsellese,* the faculty of choosing, at Accon, viscounts or consuls, for the purpose of representing the community and deciding all contestations between them and strangers.[1] About the same time Lucca and Modena had reciprocal consular establishments.[2] William, son of Emerigarde, on his return from the Holy-Land, formed similar courts for the regulation of every subject of commercial litigation.[3]

It is probable, that the naval usages and customs, which formed the materials of the *Consolato del mar,* did not all originate with the Pisans, but that many of them were common to and borrowed from less maritime nations. The origin of this celebrated

[1] See Capmany.—Memorias histor. sobre la marina, comercio, y artes de la ciudad di Barcelona.

[2] *Idem.*

[3] Aigrefeuille, Hist. de Montpellier, p. 13.

work, like that of the mariner's compass, is still a subject of doubt and discussion; and this is not to be wondered at, for it sprung from the bosom of anarchy, when the voice of the legislator was almost every where stifled by the ferocious cry of avarice or ambition. Azuni and other writers attribute it to the Pisans, whose maritime commerce during the middle ages was very extensive. *Boucher*[1] conjectures that it had its origin among the merchants of Barcelona. *Bouchaud,*[2] on the other hand, seems to be of opinion that it was composed of the customs and usages observed by foreign nations in the maritime towns of Spain, situated on the Mediterranean, which was afterwards adopted by other European nations, by the ports and commercial places of Italy and the Archipelago.

Giovanne observes, that the Catalans, Arragonese, Pisans and Genoese were about the same time powerful at sea, and not less celebrated than the Amalphians, by their com-

[1] Le Consulat de la mer.—Translated into French, in 1808, from the Catalan language.

[2] Théorie des Trait. de Com. ch. 4.

merce with the east; and that a new code of statutes and usages was then formed, known by the title of *Consolato del mare*, for the solution of all difficulties experienced by those engaged in naval commerce. The utility of this work induced princes to confirm its regulations, and to adopt them as laws. The Romans, Pisans, Lewis king of France, the count of Toulouse, and other princes and lords, also approved this work, to which additions were made by the kings of Arragon and counts of Barcelona.[1] It was printed in Venice, by Jean Baptisto Pedrezano, under the title of *Il libro del consolato de marinari*, and dedicated to Thomas Zarmora, then consul at Venice, for the emperor Charles V. Another edition was given in the same town in the year 1567, which was employed, for the decision of difficulties, by the tribunal

[1] Ceterum omnium fere gentium leges et consuetudines maritimas collectas videre licet in elegantissimo libro, qui vocatur consulatus maris, in materiis maritimis tanquam universalis consuetudo habens vim legis, inviolabiliter attendenda apud omnes provincias et nationes. *Casaregis*, dicto, n°. 12.

of the grand admiral of the kingdom of Naples

De Steck[2] and other writers have conjectured that the crusades gave birth to consular institutions; and this opinion has derived considerable weight from various facts and circumstances connected with the former. The consulate of Pisa

A. D. 1075.

was created nearly about the time of the first crusade, in the year 1095; and it is certain that the Pisans, Venetians, and Genoese, from motives of gain, supplied the crusaders with ships and provisions: from these they obtained charters, which secured to them great privileges and immunities, the right of forming establishments in maritime towns, as well as on the borders of rivers; and of governing themselves, within their own precincts, by laws and ordonnances of their own creation.[3] The first crusade consisted of three hundred

[1] Hist. Civile du Royaume de Naples, liv. XI, chap. 6, by Giovanne.

[2] Obs. Subs. X, de Consulum in emporiis Asiæ Minoris origine.—Cited by Borel.

[3] Muratori, Antiq. Ital. medii œvi. t. II, p. 906.

thousand persons, who forsook their homes and the charms of private life, to contribute towards the conquest of the Holy Land. The vessels for their transportation, which were French or Italian, the provisions for consumption, and ammunition for defence, must have given birth to maritime regulations, at the different places and ports where the supplies were disembarked. Genoa, which so powerfully aided the crusades of the twelfth and thirteenth centuries, had then formed treaties with Moorish and African princes, and had extended her commerce to Constantinople, Syria, Egypt and the Levant.

The whole army of Richard *Cœur de lion* was transported to the Holy Land by the vessels of Marseilles. A. D. 1196.

The Venetians freighted their vessels for the same purpose, furnished regular supplies, and, after the fourth crusade, which occasioned the dismemberment of the Grecian empire, they established consular jurisdictions in Dalmatia, Albany, Candia and Cephalonia. A. D. 1204.

The Venetians, in a treaty with the sultan

of Aleppo, secured the privilege of establishing in that town, a church, a counting-house and a national magistracy[1] The merchants of Venice, residing at Constantinople, assembled in the church of *St. Sophia,* for the purpose of acknowledging the *Consolato del mare* as their legal maritime code; and of having it translated from the Catalan language into that of their country.[2]

A. D. 1229.

A. D. 1255.

A late writer[3] on maritime jurisprudence, states, that this code was acknowledged as law at the following places and respective periods.

At Rome in	1075.
Acre	1111.
Majorca	1112.
Pisa	1118.
Marseilles	1162.
Almoria	1174.
Genoa	1186.
Rhodes	1190.
Morea	1200.
Venice	1215.

1 Marin, t. IV, p. 246.

2 Storia, etc. par Marin, lib. IV, p. 66 et 67.

3 Piantanida, vol. I, tit. 1, p. 1.

In Germany, in......... 1224.
At Messina............. 1225.
Nantes.............. 1250.
Constantinople....... 1262.

This statement may be tolerably correct; but the author does not cite the proofs by which it is supported.

In the Charter of Guy, king of Jerusalem, power was given to the people of *Accon* to elect viscounts or consuls of their nation, to take cognisance of disputes, and also of crimes, except theft, homicide, treason, forgery, and rape.[1] A. D. 1198.

During the twelfth century, the Italians, then known by the name of Lombards, created a number of consulates for the decision of commercial disputes, and the execu-

[1] Damus etiam vobis curiam in *Accon*, et ut vice-comites et consules de hominibus vestræ gentis habeatis, itaquæ si aliquis extraneus contra quemlibet de vestris querelam moverit, ante vice-comites vestros debeat devenire, et ibidem judicium recipere, excepto furto, homicidio, tradimento, falsamento monetæ, violatione mulierum, quod rapt vulgariter dicet, quæ omnia curiæ nostræ reservamus. Annales, par Guesnay, p. 335. Lyons, 1662.

tion of treaties and conventions with foreigners.[1]

In the same century, the Venetians had consuls at Jerusalem, Aleppo, and Alexandria, whose duty it was to support the rights, and privileges granted to the republic by the kings of Jerusalem, the sultans of Egypt, and emperors of the East.[2] The historian of the government of Venice informs us, that this republic had always an ambassador at Constantinople, with the title of *Baillo*, a word which, in the language of the Lombards, signifies judge, consul; that this embassy yielded a revenue of more than a hundred thousand crowns in the course of three years, besides the amount of considerable duties, paid by vessels which carried the flag of St. Mark. Venice had two similar establishments in the states of the grand Seignior, and another at Aleppo, the great mart of Asiatic commerce; and a fourth at Alexandria, the storehouse of Egypt and Africa. The consuls were generally selected

[1] Muratori, Antiquitates Italicæ dissertato. XXX.

[2] Amelot de la Houssaye, tom. I, p. 144. Histoire du Gouvernement de Venise.—Paris, 1676.

from the class of poor, though enlightened nobles, whom the senate allowed to remain in office during life. The consulates of Cyprus, Chios, Rosetta, Ancona, and Genoa, had always been filled by Venetian citizens. [1]

The chief judge of commercial tribunals received the title of consul, not from motives of vanity, as observed by a modern civilian, [2] but from the importance of his office, and the royal authority by which it was bestowed. The Greek emperors conferred on the dukes of Venice and of Naples, the title of υπατος,[3] or consul, and appointed agents of Athenian origin at the port of Marseilles, for the superintendence of commercial affairs. [4]

The Franks, who, at an early period, carried on an extensive commerce, had consuls in the Levant, whose decisions were

[1] De la Houssaye, Hist. du Gouv. de Venise, p. 127.

[2] Brown, Elements of civil Law, etc.

[3] From ὕπατον, which signifies high and elevated. Υπατεια was the name for the consulship. Plin. I, 14, cap. 15.

[4] Gibbon's Roman Empire, note to page 494, vol. VI. Dublin edition.

subject to the revision of a superior tribunal.

Thomas, count of Savoy, vicar of the emperor Frederick, granted by treaty to the commonalty of Marseilles, the privilege of establishing consuls at Acre, Syria, Sicily and Pouille, who had complete jurisdiction over their countrymen. [1]

A. D. 1226.

In a treaty between Frederick the first, king of Sicily, and Alburiac, a Sarazin prince, it was stipulated, that a consul, or Mahometan prefect, should be appointed to render justice to the Mahometans who trafficked in the island of Corsica. [2]

A. D. 1230.

In a treaty with the king of Tunis, the Pisans secured the right of establishing a factory and con-

A. D. 1230.

[1] Liceat habere consulatum et exercere jurisdictionem, in dictis regnis, in homines Marsiliæ.

[2] Code dipl. de Leibnitz, t. I, n.° 3, p. 13. Ut non habeant Christiani in insula Corsica jurisdictionem super ullum Mahometanum missum à rege Siciliæ, nomine suo, ad regendos, tantummodo populos unitatis, et sit occupatus in negotiis, populi unitatis quem Deus honorificet.

sul in that town. The same privilege was afterwards granted to the Genoese.[1]

The exemptions and privileges bestowed upon the consuls of Genoa by the Norman princes, were confirmed by Mainfroy of Savoy, and afterwards by king Frederick.

James the first, king of Arragon, granted by charter to the municipal magistracy of Barcelona, free powers to appoint consuls in countries beyond the sea, in Syria and in Egypt, who took an oath of office and were accountable to this council.[2]

Two years afterwards, this sovereign granted another charter to the municipal magistracy of Barce- A. D. 1268.

[1] Marin, tom. IV, p. 277.

[2] " Qui consules habeant plenam jurisdictionem ordinandi, gubernandi, compellandi, ministrandi, puniendi, et omnia alia faciendi super omnes personas de terris nostris ad ipsas partes ultramarinas navigantes, et in ipsa terra residentiam facientes; et super omnes naves et alia ligna de terris nostris illuc navigantia, sive portum facientia, et super res earundem personarum quæ illuc fuerint, tam in terra quam in mari, sicut habent in illis partibus consules de aliis provinciis, ibi positi sive constituti super personas et navigia et alias res hominum earum provinciarum. *Capmany*, Memorias historicas sobre la Marina, etc. T. II, p. 32.

lona, by which it was authorised to name consuls in the ports of the Archipelago, of Greece and the Levant.[1]

James the first, king of Sicily, granted
A. D. 1285. many exemptions to Catalan consuls, residing within his territory, and having jurisdiction over their compatriot merchants and navigators.[2]

Other privileges and immunities were also
A. D. 1299. granted to the Catalan consuls, by Charles II, king of Jerusalem and of Sicily.

It is stated by Senac, that similar consular

[1] Concedimus et donamus integram licentiam et potestatem vobis consiliariis et probis hominibus Barchinonæ, tam presentibus quam futuris, quod possitis ponere et eligere consulem vel consules, quem et quos volueritis, in partibus ultramarinis et in terra de Romania, et in quibus libet aliis partibus, in quibus naves vel ligna Barchinonæ navigaverint. *Capmany*, tom. II, p. 34.

[2] Qui consul quæstiones et causas civiles quas inter eos moveri contigeret, vel ipsos ab aliis conveniri, audiat, examinet, et debito fine decidat; et quæ sententialiter decreverit appelatione ad nos post posita observet, et faciat observari. Ita tamen quod de quæstionibus criminalibus se nullatenus intromittat, et ad easdem quæstiones criminales manus suas aliquatenus non extendat.

establishments were formed in *Armenia, Tunis* and the *Morea*. *Genoa*, about the middle of the thirteenth century, had four consulships for the management of commercial affairs.[1]

The Venetians, in the beginning of the fourteenth century, established consuls in Naples, Egypt and Syria, and also in the territory of the grand Seignior, after the termination of their wars with the Eastern powers.[2]

A. D. 1301.

It appears that there exists, in the archives of Barcelona, a work entitled, *Bolsa del cancels, ordinacions y letres*, dated in the year 1301, which contains the form of the oath taken by the consuls, *Consules maris*, of that city.[3]

[1] Soglita. Annal. Gent., p. 90. See also Foglietta, tit 5, p. 90.

[2] Gallorum venetorum, aliorumque consules, quos et *Ballivos*, et *Bajulos* appellant, qui sunt judices controversiarum, inter mercatores in Oriente, Tripoli, Halepi, Alexandria, et in Africa, Angerii et Carthagine. *Reinesias*, epit. 23.

[3] Qui juraveruntin præsentia conciliariorum per Deum, ejus sancta quatuor Evangelia manibus eorum corporaliter tacta, bene et legaliter se habere in ipso consulatu, non inspecto honore, amore, vel timore alicujus.

The Hanseatic league, composed of nearly a hundred consulates, which extended from the Baltic to the Rhine, was formed for the purpose of exchanging the productions of the North for those of the South, and protecting commerce against the piracies in the Baltic, committed by the rude nations who inhabited its borders. This celebrated association had consular establishments in Moscovy, Norway, Russia, England and Flanders.[1] The magistracy of Lubeck, with whom this great project seems to have originated, established in Russia a council of commerce, under the direction of persons named Ancients, who elected a president, judges and interpreters, all united by mutual interests and mutual wants. Their system of commercial jurisprudence was suited to the character of those rude times, and was singularly calculated to promote the views of the establishment. The fervor of religion was communicated from heart to heart, and united all its members in perfect harmony and obedience to the written statutes and regulations. A Bible, discourses

[1] Koch, Tableau des Révol., t. II, p. 344.

on the Evangelists, and the Catechism of Luther, were purchased at the expense of the merchants, from which the secretary read passages, during one hour daily, to the whole assembly, until the establishment of a Lutheran minister.

The Ancients had absolute power over all the merchants. He who refused to obey them, forfeited all his commercial rights throughout the extent of the Hanseatic towns. A *proces-verbal* of capital crimes was sent to the chief magistrate of Lubeck, whose decision was final. Improper behaviour was punished by a pecuniary fine. There was no appeal to any other tribunal.

No stranger was admitted into the assembly. Those who dissipated the property of their masters in gaming or otherwise, were excluded from the administration; and they were questioned upon oath concerning the truth of the fact alledged against them. A grocer, manufacturer, associate, or the domestic of a merchant, could not be received by another of the same profession. No foreign factory could be established. New merchants were obliged to inscribe their names on the book of commerce, and to pay for such inscription the sum of five marks. Commercial fraud was punished by expulsion. Those who forsook their master were obliged to return to Lubeck. A particular dress, neat and simple, was required. The whole company dined in the same hall, in which were three tables, the first for the ancient and his assessor, the second for the merchants, and the third for servants. Drunkenness, play, debauchery, and want of cleanliness, were punished by fine. Before the court of the company there was a night guard to prevent accidents from fire or theft. Russians and strangers, not protected by the Hanseatic league, were not received into the court in the evening. Correspondence was sacred. Every merchant was bound, by a solemn oath, to a strict observance of the statutes.

Capmany[1] has inserted in his valuable work on the maritime commerce of the ancient city of Barcelona, a copy of the instructions of the municipal magistrate of that city, for the consulate of the Catalans at

[1] Memorias historicas sobre la Marina, Comercio, y Artes della antiqùa ciudad de Barcelona, par *Capmany*. Tom. II, p. 156.

Alexandria in Egypt, dated in November, 1381. From this document it appears, that these instructions were drawn up, according to the deliberations of the maritime consuls and other merchants and enlightened persons of Barcelona. The person who was appointed to the consulate, took a solemn oath before two merchants, in the name of the honorable *Baillo* of that city, faithfully to observe all the articles and regulations prescribed for the good and honor of the office, and the advantage of the Catalans and other subjects of the king of Arragon. The consul was elected for the term of three years. No person of bad reputation, who had been expelled from Barcelona or other places for debt, could be candidate for or be employed under the consulship. The consul was authorised to sell wine in wholesale but not in retail. He was not permitted to let or lend storehouses, in any case whatever, to a Moor or a Jew, or to any other person, provided the merchants required the use of them. He was bound to assist at the inspection of goods. When he visited the exchange or the governor, he was accompanied by two gentlemen ushers in livery.

In the same work,[1] we find regulations for the consulate of Syria, drawn up by the maritime consul and body of merchants at Barcelona; and approved by the consul appointed for the city of Damascus, for the term of three years. Before his departure for Barcelona, this officer took the oath of office, before the honorable *Baillo* of that city, and engaged :—

1.° Not to sell, nor permit wine to be sold, on his own account, or for that of any other person belonging to his house.

2.° To assist personally at the payment of duties on merchandise.

3.° If goods were seized belonging to a subject of the king, and liable for the payment of consular fees, the consul, if requested by the proprietors of the said effects, was bound to exercise his authority for their restoration; and, if necessary, to carry his complaint before the governor-general.

4.° The consul was to have two gentlemen ushers (*ecuyers*) to accompany him in his visits of ceremony; and a man or

[1] Tom. II, p. 174.

woman servant, for the management of the kitchen.

5.° He was to have a priest to say mass, that he might not be obliged to hear it at the house of another consul; and the priest was to be lodged with the assembly of the faithful.

6.° If any dispute arose between the honorable consul and a merchant, the former named one Catalan merchant and the adverse party another, to terminate the difference.

Venice, in a treaty with the sultan of Egypt, obtained entire liberty of commerce in the ports of Syria and Egypt, and permission to have a consul at Alexandria and Damas.[1] The same year the consulate of Majorca was created by Peter IV. A. D. 1343.

Henry IV granted by charter to his mercantile subjects, established in the Hanseatic ports, power to select a certain number of persons, named *Gubernatores mercatorum,* to exercise, in his name, a judiciary authority. A. D. 1404.

[1] Murator, tom. XII, p. 418.

A similar privilege was granted to the English residing in the Netherlands, and to those established in Norway, Sweden and Denmark.
A. D. 1408.

Marquardus [1] informs us, that the king of England had a consul at Smyrna and at Hamburg: *in eminente dignitate constitutus.*

In Rymer's *Fœdera,* mention is made of a treaty, ratified by king Edward IV, and the *consuls* and *proconsuls* of *Lubeck, Hamburg, and Dantzick,* in the name of the Hanseatic league.[2] This work contains the substance of a charter, granted by the said king to the grandees (*gretemanis*), *consuls, proconsuls,* etc. of the county of Friesland;[3] and also the outlines of another treaty between king Henry VII of England and the *arch-prefect, proconsuls, consuls,* etc. of the city and territory of Riga.[4]
A. D. 1474.
A. D. 1478.
A. D. 1498.

[1] De Jure Mercatorum.

[2] Vol. XI, p. 792.

[3] Vol. XII, p. 51.

[4] *Idem.* p. 701. See likewise Anderson, in his History of Commerce, vol. I, p. 661, 667 and 730. Dublin edition, 1790.

After the fall of the last emperor of the East, Venice, in a treaty with Mahomet II, reserved the right of keeping a *Bailo* at Constantinople for the protection of commerce and of merchants.[1]

A. D. 1454.

In the fifteenth century, the office of consul was sought by the first families of Genoa and of Florence.

In the year 1555, Iwan Wassiliwitch, emperor of Russia and grand-duke of Novogorod and of Moscovy, granted by charter to the English, through the mediation of Richard Chancellor,[2] free permission to trade throughout the whole extent of the Russian dominions, under the direction and safeguard of their own governors, consuls and factors, who had full power and authority over their countrymen, to hear complaints, to execute justice, and to imprison and punish offenders according to the exigency of the case. In instances of

A. D. 1555.

[1] Hist. de la Rép. de Venise, tom. VII, p. 100.

[2] Chancellor commanded one of the vessels of Sebastian Cabot, in search of a North-East passage to China and the Indies. The commercial negotiation was the result of a second voyage.

revolt, the chief factor was authorised to call to his aid the local municipal officers.

In a treaty between Francis I and Solyman,
A. D. 1534. it was decided that consuls in future should be elected and considered as officers of the king. This year
A. D. 1572. resided, at Constantinople, consuls from the French, Venetians, Genoese and Florentines, but none from England.[1] The inviolability and indepen-
A. D. 1604. dence of public ministers and consuls, nominated by his majesty, were acknowledged in a treaty between Henry IV and the sultan *Amat.* They were to be received and honored with that attention which is due to public faith; and this principle was confirmed and extended by Louis XIV.

The cautious Hollanders stipulated, at an
A. D. 1679. early period of their republic, in their treaties of peace and commerce, that neither the persons nor property of consuls should be molested. The Dutch government, for its support of Albert, king

[1] Hakluyt, Vol. II, cited by Macpherson in his Annals of Commerce, p. 154. London, 1805.

of Sweden, against the tyrant *Magnus*, obtained, after his fall, certain privileges in the island of *Schowen;* among others, that of depending on the consul for protection and justice.[1] Permission was also given to establish consuls, with extensive powers, in the ports of Portugal.[2] A. D. 1661.

In a treaty between England and Portugal, it was agreed, that the consuls of the former should freely exercise their functions in the latter country, although they did not profess the Romish religion. A. D. 1642.

In a treaty between England and Spain, it was stipulated that consuls should be named by the British king, for the aid and protection of his subjects. A. D. 1667. Their powers were regulated by the convention of *Bardo*. A. D. 1679.

Spain, in imitation of France, ceased to

[1] Consules qui federatis Belgis, per ditionem Lusitanam, negotiantibus, habitantibus ve præsideo dabantur a Fœderati Belgii ordinibus creandi sint, ac constituantur. Art 9.

[2] Ducange.

employ consuls as factors or commissioners; because in this situation they were found to be incapable of executing the orders and instructions of their sovereign, as judges of captains and merchants.[1] In a treaty with the emperor of Germany, consuls were to enjoy the rights, authority, immunities and freedom of the most favored nations; and to settle the disputes of their merchants and seamen. No appeal could be made to the local judges, but only to those of the prince of which they were subjects.

A. D. 1725.

During the ministry of *Vergennes,* four consuls general were appointed for the protection of commerce; one at Smyrna, another in the Morea, a third in Syria and Palestine, a fourth in Egypt, and four subordinate consuls at Salonica, Crimea, Cyprus and Aleppo, whose decisions were to be regulated by instructions, customs, and the unerring principles of natural law. The Gallic ordonnances of 1687, 1689 and 1728, obliged all captains,

A. D. 1776.

[1] Theorica y Pratica de Comercio y de Marina, por *Ustariz.* Madrid, 1707, fol. p. 398.

seamen and other citizens, domiciliated and non-domiciliated, to submit their disputes to the local consul; and the formidable punishment of excommunication was reserved for those who refused to acknowledge his magisterial authority.

In consequence of an application by the consul of the Venetian merchants at Bruges and an English merchant, the king now took all the merchants of Venice trading to England, Ireland, and his other dominions, under his protection during one year.[1]

A. D. 1346.

Macpherson, in his Annals of Commerce,[2] observes that, "If he mistakes not, this is the "earliest notice of the office of a consul of "merchants in any English record; and "adds, that long before this time, the com-"mercial states in the Mediterranean had "consuls in every considerable port to "which they traded."

In the year 1437, a treaty was signed between king Henry VI and Paul *Rusdorfe,* master general of the Teutonic knights of Russia, and the *proconsuls* and *consuls* of

[1] Fœdera, vol. V, p. 558.

[2] Vol. I, p. 536, *note.*

the communities and cities of the Teutonic Hans: "being a renewal of all the privi-"leges granted by either contracting party "for one hundred years backwards, in com-"mercial and nautical concerns."[1]

A. D. 1438. "The Genoese, beside their great emporium at *Caffa,* had magistrates and *consuls* at Sumatra, Tunis, De Topoca, *Bosphori*, *Bimbali*, *Sebastopolis, ad Capitaneatum Gothiæ*, some of which places are not now known by these names."[2]

A. D. 1485. Richard the third, being assured of the fidelity and probity of *Lorenzo Strozzi*, a merchant of Florence, at the request of the English merchants at Pisa, and ports adjacent, appointed him their consul, and allowed him for his trouble the fourth part of one *per cent* on all goods of Englishmen, either imported or exported."[3]

A. D. 1495. By the treaty of peace, commerce, and alliance concluded between king Henry VII of England, and the

[1] Fœdera Rymeri, vol. X, p. 66.

[2] *Petrus Baptista Burgus,* De Dominio Genuensis Reipublica, in mari Ligustico, cap. 13. Cited by Anderson, vol. I, p. 605.

[3] *Fœdera,* vol. XII, p. 261.

archduke Philip, governor of the Netherlands, called the *Intercursus magnus*, sundry lords, therein named, were appointed on the part of England to be the *conservators* or consuls of this peace and intercourse.

The *Scots*, by an act of parliament, appointed a *conservator*, or *consul*, to reside in the Netherlands, A. D. 1503. "who had jurisdiction to do justice between the said merchants, being the king's liege subjects in the parts beyond the sea. But the said *conservator* shall have six, or at least four Scottish merchants to sit and determine all matters jointly with him; and that no Scottish merchant beyond sea shall sue another Scottish merchant there before any other judge than this *conservator*," who was obliged to furnish his government with a yearly report, "touching his conduct and his office beyond sea."

Comio de Balthazari, a merchant of Lucca, residing in the island of Crete, or Candia, was appointed by A. D. 1522. king Henry VIII to be "for life, governor, master, protector, or consul, of the English nation there, with the usual powers and emoluments which any consul formerly enjoyed there, or any where else, either from the said king or any of his predecessors." [1]

King Henry VIII also appointed a person, named *Justiniano*, to be governor or consul of all the merchants or other English subjects in the port and island of *Scio* or *Chios*, in the Archipelago, with power to govern them, and to receive the profits of his said office.[2]

Dionysius Harris, of London, merchant, was also appointed by king Henry VIII, to be consul of the English merchants, at Candia, during life.[3] The following year, a foreigner was appointed, by the said king, to be consul, at Scio, or Chios, and parts adjacent in the Archipelago, during the king's pleasure only; whereas till now all foreign consuls had been constituted such during life.[4]

A. D. 1530.

[1] *Fœdera Rymeri,* vol. XV, p. 766.

[2] *Idem,* vol. XIII, p. 353.

[3] *Idem.* vol. XIV, p. 389.

[4] Anderson's Hist. of Com. vol. II, p. 71.

Small traders were prohibited, by an act of parliament, from going beyond sea to France and Flanders, with less than half a *last*[1] of merchandise; and the names of those who infringed this act, were transmitted by the conservator to his government.[2]

A. D 1553.

King James granted letters patent to Thomas Glover (the first English minister who resided in Turkey) to be his envoy and agent in the dominions of *Sultan Achmet*, who was authorised to appoint *consuls* for the good government of the English in the other ports.[3]

A. D. 1606.

In a treaty between Henry IV of France and James I of England, it was stipulated, that disputes between the merchants of either country were to be submitted to the decision of two English merchants, named *Conservateurs du commerce*, nominated for that purpose, at the city of Rouen, by the English

A. D. 1606.

[1] Anderson's Hist. of Com., vol. II, p. 71.

[2] 10½ English barrels, of eight bushels each.

[3] *Fœdera*, vol. XVI, p. 659.

ambassadors; and that knotty questions, beyond their mental reach, were to be submitted to the discussion of judges, conversant with the principles of jurisprudence.

Sir John Eyre, who was appointed by king
A. D. 1619. James to be his minister at Constantinople, had power to appoint consuls "in suitable proper places in Turkey."[1]

"In the catalogue of the offices bestowed in
A. D. 1653. this year, by king Charles, we find that John Stave is appointed consul general in the kingdom of Portugal, which is the first instance of that office in Portugal to be found in the *Fœdera*."[2]

In the "*Merchant's map of commerce*," by
A. D. 1638. Lewis Roberts, esquire, published at London, in 1638, we find the following information.

"The third sort of *merchants* I account the christians of Europe, as principally the *French* and *Venetians*, who have here (*Cairo, in Egypt*) their *consuls* and *vice-*

[1] *Fœdera*, vol. XVII, p. 178.

[2] Anderson, vol. II, p. 470.

consuls, for the preservation of their trade and protection of their nation."[1]

"Here (at *Alexandria, Damietta* and *Egypt*) are found *consuls* for both the *Venetian* and *French* nations."[2]

"The *English, French*, and *Venetians* have at *Cilicia*, or *Scanderoon*, their vice-consuls to protect their merchants, goods and ships."[3]

"There is a *consul* resident at *Smyrna* for the *English*, as also for the *French* and *Venetians*, to protect their merchants and trade."[4]

"The *French* and *Venetians* maintain *consuls* here (at *Sidon*); by their means all western christians find a reasonable favorable protection for their trade."[5]

"The *Venetians* are the only western christian merchants that here (*Damascus*) reside, and have here a consul for the protection of them and their trade and goods."[6]

[1] Page 99.
[2] pag. 110.
[3] Page 116.
[4] Page 117.
[5] Page 128.
[6] Page 133.

"They (the English) have here (*Aleppo*) to this end a consul, who is instituted of *Syria* and *Cyprus*, who hath here the pre-eminence over all other *Christian consuls resident*." [1]

" The Pope doth for trade sake allow a gentleman at *Civita-Vecchia* the title of consul for the English nation, to see that the mariners, who are apt enough to give offense, be not wronged nor abused." [2]

" The English, by the authority of the Grand Seignior, have here (*Petrus*) a protecting consul resident, who hath the title of the *consul* of the Morea." [3]

" This company (that of the Levant) settled a consul in *Aleppo*, and a vice-consul in *Tripoly*, the then principal seat of *Syria*, with the titles of *Syria* and *Cyprus*: they also placed another consul in *Chios*, intitled of *Scio*, *Smyrna*, and the *Arches*; as another consul since in *Algier*, and another in *Tunis*; and the last in *Petrus* in *Morea*, strengthened with command from

[1] Page 139.

[2] Page 63, part 2.

[3] Page 138, *idem*.

the *Port* and *Durano* of the Grand Seignior, not only for their peaceable living, but also for the quiet enjoying of these privileges granted unto them as above is said."[1]

"The Levant company maintain at present and pay salary to six consuls in six several places of this empire, and to wait upon these and their factors, they give pay to forty *janisaries* and twenty *druggomen* or interpreters."[2]

"The *Venetians* have ten consuls in sundry parts of the Grand Seignior's dominions, together with sixty *janisaries* and thirty *druggomen*, paid out of the office of *Cottinia*."[3]

"The French maintain here (in the Seignior's dominions) twelve consuls, dispersed into sundry parts of this empire; together with eighty *janisaries* and thirty-four *druggomen*, paid out of the coffers of the French king."[4]

"The *Dutch*, besides their ambassador, whom they call their orator, have only

[1] Page 193.

[2] Page 197.

[3] *Idem.*

[4] Page 198.

three consulships, 12 *janisaries* and 10 *drug-gomen,* whose charge is borne by *the State of the merchants of that nation.*"[1]

A commercial treaty was concluded at Adrianople, between Sir John Finch the ambassador of Charles the second, and the Sultan Mahomet IV, by which English subjects were to have consuls of their own appointing in the sea-ports of Turkey.

A. D. 1657.

By the treaty of commerce, navigation, and marine, concluded at *Nimeguen,* between France and the States-general, merchants of either party had a right to establish consuls in each other's country.

A. D. 1678.

From this period, foreign consuls were established in all the commercial countries of Europe. The treaties and conventions by which their powers and duties were regulated, shall be noticed in our narrative of the consular systems adopted by particular governments.

[1] Page 199.

CHAPTER V.

Of Consuls for the regulation of internal commerce, and the municipal administration of districts.

THE ancient laws and ordonnances of different countries furnish many instances of the regulation of commercial affairs, and the administration of justice, by counts, viscounts, and lords; who, on account of their magisterial authority, had also the title of consul, which was sometimes connected with that of senator and judge.

The first magistrates of Athens were named *Archontes*, who had the same rank and power as a mayor[1] of the present times: at Naples they were called *Demarchi*;[2] at Alexandria *Juridicus*; *prœtor* at Capua and

[1] This word is a corruption of *major* or chief magistrate.

[2] *Populi principes*, or princes of the people.—Saint Augustin's City of God, b. XVIII, chap. 20.

Constantinople, and in the Latin countries, *Dictatores.*

Commercial establishments for the direction of internal commerce seem to have been created, from their obvious utility, at different periods, in different countries, and even in some where civilisation had scarcely dawned.

In the kingdom of Macaçar, situated in the most southern part of the island of *Celibes*, there existed a provost of merchants in each town and port of the kingdom, by whom were decided all disputes connected with commerce. [1]

The English historian Malmsbury calls the count Robert of Glocester, consul of Glocester. In the laws of Edward the Confessor, the municipal officer of a district is named consul; a term synonimous with *Comes*, or count, as proconsul with viscount. [2]

[1] Histoire du royaume du *Macaçar*, par Gervaise. Edition de Ratisbonne.

[2] Bract, lib. I, cap. 8. See also Marca, Histoire de Bearn, p. 198, where he observes, that these terms were employed, in this sense, by the writers of the middle age.

Before the discovery of the West-Indies, there was established in different towns of Spain, a consular court called prior and consuls, for the regulation of internal commerce. The judges were elected annually by the merchants trading to the West-Indies, and had authority to try all civil and commercial causes relating to merchandise imported or exported from these countries, and full power to execute their decisions.[1]

The consulate of Barcelona was established by don Juan I; A. D. 1347.
and that of Perpignan by his successor. A. D. 1388.

René, king of Sicily, established another at Marseilles. A. D. 1572.

The consular jurisdiction of Burgos was established in the reign of Ferdinand and Isabella. A. D. 1492. All the Spanish factories in Flanders, France, England, in the duchy of Brittany, and other parts of Europe, were under its direction; and their agents rendered a yearly account to this commercial court at the great fair of Me-

[1] Spanish rule of trade to the West-Indies, by De Vestia Linage. Translated by captain Stevens, p. 73. London, 1702.

A. D. 1514. dina del Campo. The consulate of Bilboa was established by
A. D. 1543. queen Jeanne; that of Seville, by the emperor Don Carlos.

In the reign of Henry II, under the direction of the enlightened *Hôpital*, similar establishments were created at Toulouse, Caen, Lyons and Bordeaux. They were multiplied and improved by a singular circumstance. Charles IX was one day induced from curiosity to go and hear the debates of the great chamber of the parliament of Paris, and seated in a *lanterne*, or private box, he heard the judge dismiss, without decision, the case of two merchants, which had been pleaded, in all possible forms, during ten or twelve years. Struck with this abuse, he immediately determined to have all commercial disputes decided in a prompt manner, by judges for that purpose, to whom he gave the title of consuls of merchants; these officers were selected from the corps of merchants of wood, fish, gravel and dye stuffs, who assembled for this purpose in the great judiciary hall. The election was annual, performed by ballot, and executed in a most solemn and religious manner. On the day preceding the fête of the Purification of the Virgin, the assembly marched in procession to the church of *Saint-Medicis*, where a solemn mass was performed for the repose of the souls of the deceased consuls and judges. The next day, they attended the mass of the Holy-Ghost, from which they repaired to the hall to decide the election. There, they bound themselves by oath to select men of probity and knowledge; the persons elected bound themselves in the same sacred manner, to conduct themselves well and loyally, and to distribute impartial justice to the poor as well as to the rich, *sola facti veritate attenta*:[1] The form of civil procedure is contained in the ordonnance of 1667.

An author who wrote at the time when those institutions were thus organized, bestows upon them the title of holy and praise worthy.[2]

Lyons was long governed by princes and counts, who took the title of consuls. It is recorded of Amadic III, that he preferred

[1] Loubeau, Institutes du droit consulaire.

[2] Belleforest.

the honors of the cross and a voyage to the Holy Land, to the cares and business of the consulate : *pro defensione crucis et contempto consulatûs.* [1] In the history of Dauphiny [2] it is stated, that in the 1299th year of the Christian era, there was a very serious dispute between the bishop and counts of Gap, concerning the consular jurisdiction of this district, which extended to almost all objects of civil policy and commerce. The nobles assembled and decided the controversy, by ceding the jurisdiction to the dauphine Beatrix, who was considered as the rightful heir.

It is recorded in the history of Brittany, that so early as the year 1088, Alanus, king of the Brittains, signed all his grants in the quality of consul.

In the year 1593, Philip II organized
A. D. 1593. consular courts in the towns of Mexico and Lima, resembling those of Seville and of Burgos, to take cognizance of all commercial and maritime cases, and the viceroy was judge of appeals. These

[3] Guichen, Hist. de Bresse et de Bujey.

[4] By Loubineau, a Benedictine, vol. II, col. 125.

courts were improved by Philip III and IV. This last king granted a yearly salary of five hundred dollars to each of the judges, consuls and priors of the consulate of Lima.[1]

The consulate of Madrid was established by Philip IV,[2] and consisted of a member of the king's council, a prior and four consuls, one of whom represented the crown of Arragon; the second, the estates and kingdom of Italy; the third; Portugal, and the fourth, Flanders and the provinces of the North.

A. D. 1632.

We find the same species of jurisdiction in Corsica, under the name of *Podestats*, established at a very early period, and renewed, in 1777, with certain limitations, which decided all affairs concerning the life, liberty or honor of individuals. To be *Pôdesta,* it was necessary to be able to read and write, and to have a blameless reputation.[3]

A. D. 1771.

[1] Recapitulacion de leges de los Reynes de las Indias. Madrid. De los consulades de Lima y Mexico, libro IX, art. 46.

[2] De la Juridicion del Prior y Consules. Madrid, 1765, libro III, tit. 3.

[3] Code Corse, vol. II, p. 270. Paris, 1678.

Several towns of Italy were long governed by consuls. The consulate of Turin was composed of a president, two legal judges, and two consuls, who were bankers or merchants, one of whom was annually changed.

The consulate of Nice consisted of a president, two legal judges, and two consuls selected from among the merchants, one of whom was also changed yearly. These consulates decided all maritime and commercial questions.[1]

[1] Leggi e Costitutioni di sua maestà, tom. I, p. 216. In Torino, 1770.

CHAPTER VI.

The Nature and Extent of Consular Jurisdiction.

It is surprising to find, that writers on the laws of nations have differed so widely in opinion, concerning the extent of that protection which is due to a consul from the government near which he resides. This dispute, like so many others, originated, and has been continued, for want of a proper definition of terms. In ancient, as in modern times, there existed two species of consuls; the first commercial, and in some respects diplomatic; delegated by his sovereign or government to exercise a particular jurisdiction over his countrymen and their commercial concerns, without being permitted to exercise any other profession than that of a magistrate, counsellor and public agent. The second, a mere merchant, commissioner or broker, whose chief employment is to find in the line of this profession, the means of existence, independence or wealth. The latter subjects himself to the municipal laws of the place of his residence, which are obligatory on the merchant; and unless protected by an express convention, he is liable to a prosecution for debt, and responsable for all infractions of mercantile regulations. In commercial engagements, the quality of the person who contracts them is of no importance. The French and other governments foresaw that the public employment of the consul must necessarily be injured by his private speculations, and very wisely interdicted all interest in commercial concerns. The situation of a trading consul may be embarrassed by adverse circumstances, as well as by imprudence. His public commission gives no claim to privilege against arrest for debt; and if unfortunately he be imprisoned, the consulate loses that consideration and respect which are due from the authorities of the place of its jurisdiction. Those who seek protection from it find none, and the country, government and individuals suffer.

One of the latest writers [1] on the law of

[1] Brown, in his Elements of Civil Law, p. 91.

nations and the admiralty, falls into the error of other civilians, in considering consuls as mere merchants, persons employed in trade, liable to the *lex loci*, both civil and criminal, and not even exempt from arrest in civil suits.

The privileges and immunities of a consul, who is not a merchant, though they may not be secured by a particular contract, yet are generally confirmed by usage,[1] which time has sanctioned as law. The commission he bears, his various duties, and free permission to exercise them, imply a certain consideration and protection from the government near which he resides. The very circumstance of his corresponding with his own government, on commercial and political subjects, and acting as a magistrate and notary in his office, evinces the sacredness of his employment.

Another modern writer[1] has observed, that a consul does not represent his prince; therefore he is not a public minister, and consequently he is not *inviolable*. We

[1] Boucher, in his edition of the *Consulat de la Mer*.

know not what meaning he attaches to this word, which admits of a very extensive signification. A consul may be a merchant; his conduct may be capricious, unjust or dishonorable; his *office,* nevertheless, ought to be sacred and inviolable; and the documents in the chancery are not to be touched nor inspected, without his authorisation or that of his government. Nothing is more true than the position of this writer, that a consul is not a minister. With as much propriety might it be observed, that he is not a king. The consul is inferior in rank and in office; but he is nevertheless entitled to a certain consideration and respect; for he also, in the line of his humble duties, represents his prince or government. He bears a public commission or patent, which authorises him to facilitate and support the interests and commerce of his country, in virtue of treaties, usages, or of the laws of nations and reciprocity.

The importance of this subject has induced us to examine the opinions which several authors have delivered concerning it in their discussions of the rights, privileges and duties of ambassadors.

Wiquefort, whom Bynkershoeck styles *acerrimus vindex legatorum,* the great champion of ambassadors, observes, "that the princes who employ consuls protect them as every good master protects his servant and domestic, but not as a public minister. The Dutch consul was affronted and arrested by the governor of *Cadix*. The States-general of the United Provinces complained to the court of Madrid of this violence committed against the rights of nations, instead of urging the non-execution of treaties, in which they ought to have found the security of their pretended minister, and not elsewhere. They wished to have their consul at Genoa considered as a minister: the senate refused to acknowledge him as such, and observed, that they could grant him only the peaceful enjoyments of those rights and privileges which custom attributes to this sort of employment. Consuls are no more than merchants charged to judge of disputes which may exist between persons of their own nation; and they are subject to the justice of the place of their residence, civil as well as commercial. In 1634, the republic of Venice was on the point of breaking out with pope

Urbain VIII, on account of the violence shown to its consul by the governor of Ancona. He repaired to Venice to inform the senate of this persecution against him; and during his absence, the governor sent a garrison to his house, seized his effects, papers, and even such documents as related to the functions of his employment. The senate complained, and demanded reparation; and with so much warmth, that the French ambassador, dreading a rupture, endeavored to adjust the difference. In the mean time, the consul was condemned to banishment under the pretext of his having unloaded merchandise in time of contagion, though he had done nothing without the permission of the magistrate. The senate was enraged; the ambassador of France renewed his mediation. *Oberti,* the consul, was to be reestablished, then to be recalled, and another, chosen by the senate, to be put in his place. *Oberti* died, and was succeeded in his office by his brother, who was also imprisoned by the governor. The Venetians, to show their indignation, refused audience to the *Nuncio,* and instructed their ambassador not to see the pope, until satisfaction should be received, which the governor was obliged to give."

It is surprising, that a grave diplomatic writer could be so unreasonable as to deduce from premises such consequences as the premises flatly contradict. The facts, which are cited, prove that the governor of *Ancona* was compelled by the pope to give satisfaction to this sage republic; but if this had not been the case, if the doubly outrageous conduct of the governor had been even sanctioned by his master, the circumstance would have afforded no proof that consuls do not enjoy the protection of the rights of nations.

The Turkish bashaw arrested the consul of England, and shut him up in a miserable prison, because the governor of Gibraltar detained a vessel of ten guns sent thither for reparation.[1] If this consul had been an envoy, or minister plenipotentiary, or ambassador, neither of these titles would have prevented his arrest, when the bashaw

[1] Journal du Voyage pour la rédemption des captifs aux royaumes de Maroc et d'Alger, pendant les années 1773, 1774 et 1775, par les Pères, etc.

believed that, by this means, his vessel would be restored; for, at that period, consuls, in Turkey enjoyed all the prerogatives of ambassadors.[1]

When the Christians were to appear before the bashaw, on days of ceremony, they previously assembled at the house of the English consul, who was supposed to exercise over them complete jurisdiction.[2] We know not why the governor detained the vessel of the bashaw; but the conduct of the Turkish potentate would have furnished, to this legislator of ambassadors, as good an argument as that of the governor of Ancona. We suspect that he had been guilty of injustice to some unfortunate consul, seeing that he grants him no better protection than what belongs to "a servant or domestic."[3]

[1] Consulat de la Mer, par Boucher.

[2] *Ibid.*

[3] Wicquefort was Dutch secretary and translator of English intelligence, which trust he betrayed in 1675, by delivering to the English minister *Williamson*, original letters of lord Howard, who had held a secret correspondence with the prince of Orange. During his imprisonment for this great offence, Wicquefort wrote his " longwinded treaties on ambassadors."

The reasoning of Vattel[1] on this subject, evinces a more çorrect judgment. This popular author observes, "That of modern institutions, the most useful to commerce is that of consuls, who are authorised, by their commission, to watch over and preserve the rights and privileges of their nation, and to terminate difficulties which may arise among merchants. The consul, charged with the affairs of his sovereign, and receiving his orders, remains accountable to him for his actions. The consul is not a public minister, and he cannot pretend to his prerogatives; nevertheless, as he is charged with a commission from his sovereign, and received in this quality by the chief where he resides, he ought to enjoy, to a certain degree, the protection of the rights of nations. The sovereign who receives him, tacitly engages to grant him all the freedom and protection necessary to execute his functions with propriety; without which the admission of the consul would be vain and illusory. His functions require, that he be not a subject of the state where he resides, for in this case

[1] Le Droit des gens, par De Vattel; p. 262, édition de Neufchâtel, 1773.

he would be obliged to follow its orders in every respect; nor could he freely execute the functions of his office. These seem to require, that the consul be independent of the ordinary criminal justice of the place of his residence; that he may not be molested nor imprisoned, unless he himself violate the rights of nations by some enormous offence. As he is under the particular direction of his sovereign, and charged to watch over his interests, the respect due to his master requires, that he be sent to him for punishment. He who receives a consul without express conditions, is understood to receive him on the footing established by usage."

The opinion of writers of acknowledged authority, coincides nearly with that of Vattel. In the "*Ambassador of Hottmann*"[*] we find the following observations.

"It appears that we might place in the rank of agents and ambassadors, consuls who settle the disputes of merchants, towns, and provinces, in *Algiers*, *Tunis*, *Tripoli*, and other places of Barbary and Turkey; inasmuch as the prince nominates, authorises

[*] Published in 1663, at Amsterdam, p. 16.

and recommends them by letters, and that, instead of ambassadors, they give advice and sometimes execute their duties with success. The Venetians have consuls in Cairo, in Aleppo, Rosetta, Alexandria, and other celebrated towns, which is of great importance; for besides the knowledge of commerce thence obtained, they receive news from all parts of the world; in which respects they surpass all other states and republics.

"Almost all the consuls sent out of Europe have a jurisdiction sufficiently extensive over subjects of their sovereign. There are places in Europe, where the consuls enjoy a civil jurisdiction more or less limited over the subjects of their master: in others, they can only exercise a *voluntary* jurisdiction; and besides, their general function is to watch over the interests of the commerce of their state, and particularly the observance of commercial treaties; and to assist, by interference and counsels, those of their nation whom commerce has brought to the place for which they are named. They are sometimes acknowledged by *letters of credence,* but oftener by a *patent* and letters of recommendation; and although they are under the particular protection of the rights of nations, they do not enjoy all the advantages which usage attributes to ministers, neither concerning honors, religion, nor the immunities relating to jurisdiction; so that it is only in a very extensive sense that they can be placed in the number of public ministers. Most consuls, out of Europe, approach the condition of ministers; some are at the same time consuls and ministers.

"Sometimes there are consuls general who preside over many places at the same time, or who exercise authority over several consuls."[1]

Another writer[2] observes, that consuls are subjects employed in almost all maritime towns of importance, for the protection of commerce. There are many in the great mercantile towns of Europe, situated on the borders of the sea, or the mouths of rivers. There are many in Africa, in Asia, and in the ports of the Levant. If consuls

[1] Précis du Droit des Gens moderne de l'Europe, fondé sur les traités et l'usage; par Martens, professeur de droit à Gottingue. Vol. I, p. 181.

[2] Le Ministre public dans les cours étrangères, etc.; par du Franquenay. Amsterdam, 1733, chap. XI.

have letters of credence in due form, which authorise them to treat of affairs concerning their sovereign, they may, for this reason, perform the functions of a minister, without having the title; and therefore, as soon as they are acknowledged, they have a right to present memoirs, to have conferences, and to treat with towns and powers, of every thing which regards the commerce of the masters by whom they were sent. They have consequently the right of protection for their countrymen, which they may claim, in case of need, for themselves, their families and public chapels. In some respects their jurisdiction extends farther than that of ministers of any order, as they are sovereign arbiters in commercial disputes. It is for this reason, as well as on account of the emoluments of consulates, that the employment is so much sought, especially in France. It results from what has been said, that consuls, by means of their attributions, may be placed in the rank of ministers.

The consul, although not a minister, enjoys various privileges, and that public safety which is granted to ministers by the laws of nations. Consuls are even considered as ministers; that is to say, in ports of the Levant, in the principal commercial towns of Asia and Africa, at Aleppo, Smyrna, Cairo, Alexandria, Tunis and Algiers.[1]

According to the opinion of Bynkershoeck,[2] consuls " are protectors, sometimes judges, of matters of their nation; usually themselves merchants, they do not represent their prince near a foreign sovereign, but protect the subjects of the prince in every thing respecting commerce. They also often examine and decide disputes which arise among them concerning this sort of affairs."[3]

" Consuls are a species of *residents*, public ministers of the third order, which commercial nations, great and small, send to the principal seaports of Europe, of the Levant,

[1] De la manière de négocier avec les souverains, par M. de Callière, conseiller du roi, etc., chap. I. Paris, 1716.

[2] De foro competente Legatorum, ch. X.

[3] *Pestel*, in his *Commentarii de Republica Batava* (vol. I, p. 268, *Lugduni Batavorum*, 1755), has adopted a similar opinion: " At cives tamen nostri manent cives, qui e. e. *agentium* aut *consulum* munere a populis exteris mandato funguntur, horumque negotia pecuniaria potius, quam ea procurant, quæ ad rempublicam spectant."

of Africa and other places, to facilitate commerce and to protect the navigation and merchants of their nation. For this purpose, they are furnished with letters of credence, and enjoy, on this account, the protection of the rights of nations, without however pretending to other distinctions."[1]

"In some states of Europe, it has been proposed to separate the diplomatic from the consular career. These two form but one; the consul collects facts, the *diplomat* combines them for the formation of a treaty. If the *consulate* be not a ladder to mount to the *embassade*, the *diplomat* apprentice ought to travel with a mission of the court. A perspective ought to be offered to consuls; a pension of retreat to those who have merited it by their services, and an embassy to such as have displayed wisdom in their conduct, and economical views in their correspondence, for such men must be singularly fitted to conduct a negociation. They are intimately acquainted with the business of a tariff, and

[1] *Institutions politiques*, par le baron de Bielfield, tom. II, p. 333. A work which formerly served as a manual for diplomacy.

to make it well, is the result of all the art of the negociator. I know that ambassadors have usually higher pretensions; but they seem to forget, that the strength of nations is founded on agriculture and manufactures. [1]

A late writer [2] observes, that although there be different opinions concerning the character of consuls, the only reasonable one is that which makes them participate in the rights of nations. The object of their mission is to favor commerce, to administer justice to their countrymen, merchants and navigators; to keep them within the bounds of order and decorum, and under the regulations of the ordonnances of their sovereign; to watch over the preservation of their privileges, and the observance of commercial treaties. While they exercise these functions, supported by a commission and *exequatur*, it would be a mere verbal dispute not to grant them the protection of the rights of nations, as ministers of the third order. If the prerogatives of consuls have not been distinctly

[1] Beaujour, Tableau du Commerce de la Grèce, near the end of the second volume.

[2] Borel, de l'Origine et des Fonctions des Consuls, p. 39 and 40.

specified in modern treaties between the sovereigns of Europe, it is because they are too well known to require explanation. These same princes have taken care to describe them in their conventions with powers less enlightened, with Barbary and the Porte."

Numerous historical facts might be adduced to show, that different governments have defended, in the most decisive manner, the rights of consuls. We shall cite a few.

The consul of Lewis XIV was murdered at Algiers; to avenge his death, the town was bombarded and almost reduced to ashes.

The English consul, ill-treated by certain Mahometans, fled to the port of *La Calle;* England, for this insult, demanded and obtained complete satisfaction.

In the eleventh year of the French Republic, *Augé*, a captain of marine, was ill-treated in the road of Tunis, by *Reis Ali-Tatar*. General Hullin was sent to Algiers by the first consul of France, to demand reparation for this outrage committed against the French nation, in the person of one of its officers; and, if refused, the general was instructed to bring back to France M. *Dubois-Thainville*, consul general at that port. The

Reis was summoned before the *Divan*, to answer for his conduct. There, in the presence of the consuls and merchants of different nations, the *Kasnadgi*, who judges causes of great importance, in the name and absence of the dey, pronounced the following sentence: " Seeing that such is the will of Bonaparte, the *Reis Ali-Tatar* shall be strangled and his body thrown into the sea." The sentence was about to be executed in presence of the assembly, when his life was claimed by the consul, and by general Hullin in the name of their government; and the offender's punishment was commuted into that of destitution and the confiscation of his property.

A few weeks after the departure of the envoy, the Dey ordered the consul to depart, or to pay a tribute of 200,000 dollars. The latter boldly replied, that Bonaparte was too great to be his tributary; and this argument acquired such force from the appearance of a French squadron, that the Dey offered any sacrifice rather than lose the friendship of the first consul of France.

In the year 1768, an English merchant ship was driven by stress of weather into the port of Ostend. She had anchored at Spithead, where the sailors had concerted a mutiny, and actually signed the *round Robin.*[1] When the captain came ashore, the British vice-consul [2] was absent. Before the magistrates, he accused three of his men of mutiny; they were arrested, imprisoned, put in irons, and ordered for trial. In the mean time, the consul returned, and demanded their release, for the purpose of sending them to England, to be judged by the Admiralty Court. The magistrates insisted on their right of trial. The case was communicated, first to sir William Gordon, his majesty's minister at Brussels, and afterwards to the Board of Admiralty at London, by whom it was submitted to their solicitor, who decided in favor of the consul. The affair was then laid before the king, by the secretary of state for the Northern department; in consequence of which, the imperial ambassador wrote to Vienna, to order the

[1] Each sailor writes his name in a circle, to show that there was no chief, or ringleader.

[2] M. Mortimer.

government of Brussels to release the sailors, which was accordingly done. [1]

The English Admiralty Court refuses to acknowledge a trading merchant as consul, although he officiate in this quality.

The cargo of the ship *Indian Chief* was claimed by M. Millar, acting as American consul at Calcutta. Destined for Hamburg, she had touched at Cowes, where she was arrested and detained. Sir William Scott observed, in this decision, that the office of consul does not distinguish the national character of the person who bears it, from that of the country where he resides. That persons are conceived to take their national character from that association under which they live and carry on their commerce. M. Millar must take his situation with all its duties; and amidst these duties, that of not trading with the enemies of his country. [2]

We shall here present a statement of two important decisions concerning consular powers; the one by the Imperial Court of

[1] Lex mercatoria rediviva, by Mortimer. Art. *Consul.*

[2] Robinson's Admiralty Report, vol. III, pag. 12. London edition.

Cassation, and the other by the Imperial Prize Court, at Paris.

Can foreign consuls be prosecuted before our Tribunals, for acts made in France by order of their government, and with the authorisation of the French government?

The Imperial attorney-general [1] has declared, after a thorough examination of the subject, that the negative is incontestible; and that this opinion has been consecrated by a decision of the Court of Cassation, of the third vendemiaire, ninth year. The circumstances which gave rise to this question were as follow:—"A Ligurian was summoned before the Tribunal of Correctional Police at Marseilles, concerning certain effects in the hands of the vice-consul of the Ligurian Republic, seized by him, to serve as a proof of a crime committed within that territory. The Ligurian was acquitted, and the vice-consul condemned to restore the objects, and to pay the expenses of the suit; and was summoned, by the former, before a justice of the peace for the purpose of obliging him to restore the said effects.

[1] Count Merlin, member of the National Institute.

The vice-consul declared, that he acted conformably to the orders of his government, and that he ought not to be cited before a French Tribunal, for having executed, against a Ligurian, orders and acts emanating from the Executive Directory and tribunals of Liguria, with the approbation and concurrence of the French authorities; that he had written to Genoa for orders concerning the demand of the Ligurian, which was not within the competency of the Peace Tribunal.

The Ligurian opposed this declaration by insisting that the effects claimed by him were his property; that they ought to have been delivered, with the documents, to the director of the jury, and restored to him by the judgment of the Tribunal of Correctional Police. The Civil Tribunals, regardless of the *Laws of Nations,* thought that the plaintiff had a right to objects which were his property, and therefore condemned the vice-consul to restore them.

The commissary of the government, near the Tribunal of Cassation, was instructed by the Minister of Justice to denounce the Marsellese judge, as acting contrary to the laws of nations and the inviolability of foreign powers; and he observed, in his report, that in all countries it has been a principle, that foreign ministers are not subject to positive laws, nor consequently to the tribunals of the country where they reside in this quality. The Ligurian vice-consul was not amenable to the tribunals in France, even for a personal demand; and much less for an affair directed by the Ligurian executive authority. The laws of nations, and the independence of the two nations, do not permit that a foreign power should be condemned, in the person of its agent, to restitution and expenses in virtue of French laws; or that this agent should personally become responsible for what he had done in the name of his government. The judgment of this tribunal is even contrary to the laws and principles of the French nation. The vice-consul is both a civil and military administrator: with these functions, a Frenchman could not be prosecuted immediately, and without previous authorisation, before tribunals, as responsible for acts relative to his functions. The judgment was therefore an excess of power, a violation of treaties, an opposition to authority, and an attack upon the mutual independence of nations.[1]

A suit was proposed by an American against the French agent of commercial relations at Genoa, which gave rise to the discussion of an important question before the Council of Prizes at Paris; *viz. Whether a consul can be prosecuted without the previous authorisation of his government?*

The judges of the Council addressed to the Minister of Justice, a memoir containing the arguments for their negative decision, of which we shall present a summary review.

Impeachment is well known to signify the means of redress, which may be exercised against a judge, to oblige him to answer, in his private name, for injuries done to individuals by his judicial proceedings.

To impeach a judge in France, it was formerly necessary to obtain the permission of the parliament. According to the existing laws, it cannot be executed without the authorisation of the Court of Cassation.

[1] Répertoire universel et raisonné de Jurisprudence; par Merlin. Art. *Consuls étrangers.*

The measures to be pursued in the prosecution of an agent of the government do not resemble those which must be observed in the case of a judge. It was impossible to submit, to the same rules, two things of an order so distinct; and, in the present question, there are other reasons which make this difference still greater.

Consuls have existed since the introduction of a regular commerce. The object of their mission, especially in maritime ports, is to watch over the preservation of the rights and privileges of their nation, and to terminate contestations which arise among their mercantile compatriots.

It is evident, from the attributions given to them by the ancient and new laws, that consuls, to the character of political agent, may unite that of judge.

But the administrative and judiciary functions, although cumulated on the same head, do not for that reason change their nature. Each continues to be respectively directed by principles inherent in the order of things to which it belongs.

Thus the acts of the political agent are under the immediate and exclusive inspection of the government, and cannot be separated from it by arbitrary actions of prosecution unauthorised by government.

If it were otherwise, an agent, useful and often necessary to the republic in our foreign relations, might suddenly and personally have his character exposed, without the knowledge of his government; and, every instant, operations of great importance to the general welfare might be troubled or suspended by the shock of particular passions.

Infractions against the laws in the administration of justice, as, in every other administration, ought to be punished; but when the safety of persons, accused of these infractions, is under the guarantee and protection of the government itself, the sanction of the government is necessary in legal suits against their persons. This also results from the seventy-fifth article of the constitution, in which it is expressly said, "That the agents of government cannot be prosecuted except in virtue of a decision of the Council of State."

This measure ought, for a still stronger reason, to be observed, when he who proposes the prosecution is a stranger; for, in this case, the affair and quality of persons equally belong to the rights of nations, and, consequently, ought to be regulated by this species of right. For this reason, consuls, without enjoying the plenitude of prerogatives attached to ambassadors and other public ministers, ought to enjoy, in a rank less elevated and for functions less shining, that inviolability and independence which ambassadors and other public ministers enjoy among themselves. Every political agent is the organ of his government, and the government ought neither to speak nor act through an agent who has something to fear. It is therefore necessary, with respect to agents of the government, to follow reasons drawn from their representative character, and not those derived from the ordinary relations of things.

If agents abuse their public character, it is taken from them; but for this purpose, the stranger, sovereign or individual ought to apply to the government itself, which disapproves or supports its mandatory; and no other can deprive him of that inviolability of character with which he is invested.

From all these considerations, the Council

concluded, 1.° That a consul is both a judge and a political agent, from the nature and species of the functions which he exercises:

2.° That as a judge, he might be prosecuted according to the terms of the civil law; but as his character of political agent is the principal and predominant, he cannot be prosecuted without the special and positive authorisation of his government:

3.° That this measure is necessary, whoever be the person that commences the suit, and, with much greater reason, when he is a stranger; for then both persons and things are under the jurisdiction of the law of nations, the discussion of which belongs to government. In no case, therefore, can a consul be prosecuted without the previous permission of his government.

In the year 1800, the consul general of Denmark presented a memoir to the Council of Prizes, for the purpose of obtaining a guarantee for the proceeds of the sale of a Danish prize. This intervention of the consul, opposed by interested corsairs, gave rise to the decision of an important question: "*Whether a consul, acknowledged by the French government, can interfere in particular contestations between French merchants and those of his own nation?"* The commissary of the Prize-Tribunal, M. Portalis, presented the following report to the Council.

The consul of the Danish government is a political agent. When acknowledged by the French government, he may incontestibly fulfil the functions attached to his *mandate;* but can he, by actions or demands, intervene in particular contestations between French and Danish merchants?

The thirteenth article of the *arrété* of the sixth of germinal, admits only the parties, *or their defenders,* who must previously justify *their rights and powers.*

The Danish consul does not act for his own interest, but as charged with the interest of another: he is not a party; he pretends only to exercise the ministry of the defender. Does he justify his *right* and *power?*

It is probable, that he only acts in virtue of his consular title. It is possible that, by this title, he may be authorised to pay particular attention to contestations concerning the interest of Danish merchants. But no title derived from his government can render him the true representative of the parties. To the government belongs the protection, and to the parties the property. A proprietor can dispose of his effects and exercise his rights by himself or by another; but as every one is the arbiter and regulator of his own fortune, it is not permitted to intervene concerning the affairs of another, if he has not received a *power* to this effect. The general mission given to a Danish consul by his sovereign, instructing him to watch over the interests of the merchants of his nation, and especially over those relating to prize-causes, will not suffice to establish this consul the proxy of each of the merchants. According to the principles of political law, the mission of the Danish consul is essentially limited to the good offices of a protector, who recommends; and does not extend to the acts of an attorney, who rules and disposes.

I agree, that a right more ancient and more sacred than political right, I mean the social right, authorises any person to pursue the affairs of one who is absent and ignorant of his personal situation, and who has need of the spontaneous aid of this natural benevolence, of which the germ cannot be entirely extinguished by our vices; a sentiment of which civil rights ought to sanction the effects.

It has been acknowledged in all ages, and among the most polished people, that one man, without the knowledge of another, may do him good; and that if he does no injury to others, he may, without authority, contribute to his advantage.

The Danish consul, without a particular or special *mandate,* might perhaps avail himself of these principles, to justify the steps he has taken near the Council of Prizes, in the cause or affair of his absent compatriots. Who shall defend them, if he does not; when by their remoteness, or other circumstances, it is impossible for them to defend themselves?

Nevertheless, as in our present state of society it is of importance to public order and tranquillity, as well as to the safety of individuals, that measures relating to justice be not popular; it is a constant and universal maxim, that interest alone is the principle of action, and that a person must be a party, or furnished with the powers of the party, to be able to intervene in any litigation. It was thought necessary to prevent the dangerous interference of speculators in affairs in which they have no concern. It was, moreover, believed, that to arrest the indiscretion of a false zeal, it was useful to prescribe limits to this same beneficence.

But there has been established near all the administrations and tribunals, a public ministry, now known in France under the name of commissary of the government, the natural defender of all those who have none; the principal party in important affairs, and the joint party in all. This admirable institution, unknown to the ancients, serves as a barrier against fraud, injustice, violence and abuse. The public party acts, and all rights are preserved; it watches, and every citizen is tranquil; it represents the absent; and, amongst us, one of its principal functions, according to the testimony of *D'Aguessau*, is to facilitate for strangers the approach to justice; to propose their defence; to offer them support, and to be for them the guarantee of national loyalty.

The Danish consul ought not, therefore, to be alarmed, if I support laws which do not permit any person, except the parties or their attornies, to act and to form demands.

The protection which he owes to his countrymen is sufficient to authorise him to enlighten the members of the Council, by furnishing notes, memoirs, or other communications. Never ought we to reject the means of ascertaining truth; from whatever quarter it may come, it has rights over the mind and heart of man.

The Danish consul may therefore recommend and instruct; he may, by the duties of his place, protect indiscriminately the merchants of his nation. But to act more particularly in contestations pending between French merchants and those of his nation, he must have the special power of the party or parties in whose name he is to act.

The attorney of several parties ought to act separately in each cause, for the interest of each client, and not to cumulate, by demands *in globo*, different interests, that often have no resemblance to one another, and which require a separate examination and distinct enunciation.

I conclude then, that the consul's demand, to intervene in particular contestations, is not to be granted; but he may furnish the commissary of the government near the

Council with such notes and memoirs as he may judge useful to the interests of the merchants of his nation.

The Council has adopted the conclusions, and decided, as a general principle, that a consul, a foreigner, acknowledged by the French government, cannot, with this title, and in virtue of his *mandate* alone, as political agent, intervene in particular contestations between French merchants and foreigners, create demands, and act for them and in their name.

It does not require much sagacity to perceive, that the commissary, in his examination of this important question, struggled with difficulties which he knew not how to surmount, with objections supported by reason, wisdom and equity. His premises authorise a decision very different from that adopted by the Council.

What is the Prize Tribunal? Is it not a political institution, under the immediate direction of the government, established for the purpose of judging, in an administrative manner, the legality or illegality of maritime prizes?

What is the object of a consul's mission?

Is it not to protect and promote the commerce of his country, according to existing treaties, usage, or the principle of reciprocity? He is instructed by his sovereign or government, and is engaged by solemn oath, to protect the interests of the merchants of his country. If he be a political agent, as defined in this report, he certainly has a right, when duly received and acknowledged by the government near which he resides, to defend the cause of his countrymen before a political tribunal, regulated by administrative forms, very different from those which belong to civil jurisdiction. This right is implied in the very nature of his functions, and is an essential condition of his reception. The Danish consul was not a merchant; he had not selfish interest to gratify; he acted solely from motives of duty. If, as M. *Portalis* acknowledges, every person, from a natural principle of beneficence, is authorised to support the interests of an absent acquaintance or friend, which require an immediate attention, how much stronger is the right of the consul to interfere in the support of the claims of his fellow-citizens, when to this natural right of *political society* is added that derived from his commission, from the nature of his functions, and his solemn engagements. If truth always commands authority over the *heart and mind*; if under every situation, her light is vivifying, why shut out those rays which the consul proposed to throw, by a reflecting medium, into the interior of the Prize Tribunal? If already sufficiently illuminated, they would have been lost in the midst of its refulgence, but no harm could possibly ensue. To drop the metaphor: it will not be said, that his statement was irrelevant or unnecessary; and to enlightened minds, occupied, not with adventitious circumstances, but with the real merits of the case, it can be of no importance, through what channel the defence was presented, whether through that of the commissary, the attorney-general, or clerk of the court; nor is it of great moment, whether it be entitled a note, defence, instruction or communication.

The commissary represents himself as the natural defender of those who have no protector; as a barrier against all fraud and injustice. We do not question his willingness to plead the cause of him who has no helper; but if the Danish government prefers to his, the mediation and report of its consul, occupied with the interests, laws, orders, and regulations of his country, we see no good reason why he should not be permitted to examine the grounds of decision against Danish property; or to take cognizance of a Danish case, though not furnished with a regular procuration; and particularly when the property, concerning which he is interested, may be endangered by delay and the artful misrepresentation of interested corsairs.

It is probable that the consul did not interfere in the present case without the request of the party. But we will suppose a still stronger case, and such as has occurred, and may still occur.

A prize is conducted to some distant port: the captain, without money, friends or acquaintance, remains there without knowing what to do. His voyage was legal; his papers regular; he trusts to the justice of his cause, and waits for a favorable decision, though he knows not from what authority it may be expected. Certificates of property, or other essential documents, have, without his knowledge, been suppressed by the corsairs, and this circumstance, even in fortunate times, may involve the confiscation of the property. The consul, permitted to examine the register of the Prize-Court, finds that the case is libelled, the time for defence elapsed, and trial ordered. The corsairs urge their claim, and pant and struggle for the confiscation of the property. The consul interferes, arrests the decision; and, in the mean time, obtains from the captain a detailed statement of his capture, in the form of a protest. The fact of the suppression of the papers is proved, on which the plea of confiscation was grounded, and a valuable property restored, which, without his protection, must have been necessarily lost.

In such a case, the consul is neither party nor agent; yet who will deny the propriety of his mediation. He here stands in the same relation to his countrymen as a parent to his child, whose protection is freely exercised without title, *mandate* or procuration. In this situation of affairs, the consul is their natural, their legal representative; there is none else. He is opposed by no authority but that of the court, which, by this opposition, rejects the powers of the Danish sovereign, while it respects the procuration of the most obscure notary. How can the consul detect frauds, abuses and violation of the flag of his nation, if he be not permitted to consult the documents on which this knowledge depends? It is true that prizes are made by private corsairs; but corsairs act by the authority and particular regulations of the government, which is the principal, and therefore accountable for spoliations. The property captured becomes the property of individuals, but it is public with regard to the consul's protection; and, if not opposed by a treaty, he has an indisputable right to take cognizance of the case, and to assist, examine, or support its defence. "A consul is a kind of ambassador which one nation sends into the maritime ports of another, to reside there for the purpose of favoring the commerce of his fellow-citizens."[1]

An association or contract formed between *Skipwith* and *Mountflorence*, concerning cer-

[1] Della Giurisprudenza maritima, by Piantanida.—Milan, 1806.

tain fees and emoluments connected with the American consulate at Paris, gave rise to a dispute so intimately connected with our subject, that we think it useful to present the outlines of its origin, legal discussion and decision.

Mr. Mountflorence had, for some time, acted as consul, and had charge of all the consular documents, when Mr. Skipwith was reappointed to that office by the president of the United-States. The payment of certain claims had not been effected, and Mr. Mountflorence required from Mr. Skipwith, an acknowledgment, or guarantee for his share of commissions, which was to be deducted from the proceeds by the consent of their proprietors. This was refused. The former threatened to retain the consular papers until the latter accepted his proposition; but he afterwards delivered them up to him, with an offer to submit the dispute to the decision of arbiters. This proposition was rejected by Mr. Skipwith. He was then cited before the Commercial Tribunal at Paris, but declined its jurisdiction. A judgment was pronounced against him, grounded on the circumstance of his supposed commercial partnership, which was annulled by the Court of Appeal. The plaintiff had recourse to the Court of Cassation. This tribunal found it sufficient to decide the case, by their answer to a simple question; namely: "*Whether two foreigners, residing, but not domiciliated in France, can, by virtue of a mutual contract there executed, prosecute each other before the French tribunals?*"

The parties were citizens of the United-States, and not domiciliated. The consular convention did not expire till the first of January, 1802. The contract in question was made in 1799, during its existence; but by a misunderstanding between the two governments, it was then paralysed and without effect.

The plaintiff invoked the thirteenth article of the convention, to prove, that disputes between Americans are under the jurisdiction of the French commercial tribunals. This was shown not to be the true sense, by the decision in the following case. *Sands*, an American merchant, seizes, at Havre, goods belonging to *Vance*, another American, who owed him the amount of bills of exchange on Hamburgh, which had been protested.

The arrestation of the goods was authorised by the Tribunal of Commerce. This decision was opposed by Vance, who grounded his appeal on the twelfth article of the consular convention, and referred the case to the consul of the United-States. Sands insisted, that this article related only to maritime commerce; and this opinion was supported by the court, whose judgment was confirmed by the Civil Tribunal. The decision was annulled by the Court of Cassation, on the grounds, that all disputes between Americans in France, or between Frenchmen in the United-States, are submitted, without distinction, to the respective consuls of the nation; and that no territorial officer, civil or military, can interfere therein.

Mountflorence argued, that *Skipwith* could not be his own judge in an affair in which he was personally interested. The Court observed, that he was in a situation not anticipated by the convention, and that the solution of the problem was not to be sought therein; that the question was simply, "*Whether a stranger not domiciliated in France, can be prosecuted before the French tribunals for the execution of a contract made in France with another non-domiciliated stranger?"*

In the farther discussion of this subject, the Court observed, that a stranger of this description can certainly be prosecuted when the contract has for its object, the construction, equipment, or sale of a vessel.[1]

It is also certain, that strangers are responsible to the French tribunals, or local judge, for bargains made between themselves, in French fairs and markets; a maxim universally acknowledged, and consigned in the *procès-verbal* of the discussion of the Code Napoleon.[2] This principle, which was probably derived from usage, has been consecrated by an express law.[3] But the contract in question does not belong to the class here specified.

According to the Roman law,[4] every contract belongs to the jurisdiction of the judge of the place where it was formed. But all the French authors who treat of this subject,

[1] Ordon. of Marine of 1681, B. I, t. ii, art. 1.

[2] Sixth thermidor, ninth year.

[3] Ordon. of Marine, 1673, tit xii, art. 17, and art. 420 of the Code of Civil Procedure.

[4] Law 19, §. 1 and 2, D. *de Judiciis.*

assert that it has no force nor vigor. A contract, passed between strangers not domiciliated, resembles a contract made in their own country, at or before their departure for France; with this difference, that the one is signed in the former and the other in the latter country; but as to the question, this difference is nothing; for, with the exception of two cases, foreseen by the fourteenth and hundred and eleventh articles of the Code Napoleon, the place, where the contract was signed, has no influence with regard to the competency of the judges to whom it belongs.

The French tribunals cannot take cognizance of a contract made out of France between two strangers, not domiciliated in France, of which one declines the jurisdiction.—A principle which may be expressed in few words: *Actor sequitur forum rei.*

It results, however, from the fourteenth article of the Code Napoleon, that strangers, for ordinary debts, of which the payment is exacted by other strangers, may voluntarily acknowledge the French tribunals, which then assume, with regard to them, the character of arbiters. But if one of the two foreigners, who have formed a contract in or out of France, decline the authority of the French tribunals, the case belongs to the domiciliary judge. This rule admits of one exception, agreements made in fairs.

The contract in question related to "*Indemnities and sums due by the government of the French Republic to Americans and other citizens, for the detention of vessels in French ports, by embargo or otherwise; and for supplies furnished for the use of the French colonies.*"

In all this, the parties cannot be considered as agents, factors, or commissioners of merchants for mercantile contracts. The provisions furnished for the French colonies were for their consumption, and not for sale. There was no commercial act, and therefore, those who solicited the payment of the amount of the articles, did not solicit the payment of a commercial debt.

The detention of vessels was an administrative, not a commercial act. The indemnity demanded did not constitute a commercial claim; and as there was nothing really commercial in the contract between the parties, the plaintiff cannot *subpœna* the defendant, except before the judges of the place of his residence.

M. *Mountflorence* then presented a letter written by M. Livingston, late minister plenipotentiary of the United-States at Paris, and formerly chancellor of the Court of Justice of the state of New-York, dated in April, 1805, which certified, "That a Frenchman or other foreigner, may prosecute another foreigner before the tribunals of the United-States, for any matter originating within the jurisdiction of the United States." He also produced another certificate to the same effect, from a former magistrate of Massachusets, and from these documents claimed the right of reciprocity, which requires, said he, that the French tribunals take cognizance of contestations between Americans, on account of contracts made in France.

This reason was considered as a mere sophism. If the Roman law be observed (said the Court) in the United-States, this is no proof that it ought to be observed in France, with regard to Americans. The French legislation does not choose to exercise this authority.

The eleventh article of the *Code civil*

states, that a oreigner shall enjoy in France, the same civil rights as those which are or shall be granted to Frenchmen, by the *treaties* of the nations to which the foreigner belongs.

To justify the pretension of M. *Mountflorence*, it is not sufficient, that a Frenchman, by American laws, may prosecute another Frenchman before the American tribunals for the execution of contracts made in the United-States; this right must also be established by a treaty between the two governments; and it is well known that no such treaty has ever existed.

No conclusion, therefore, can be drawn from the usage in the United-States. America has her laws, and we have ours.

The plaintiff then produced a *non-official* copy of a circular letter of the Department of State of the United States, of July, 1805, addressed to all the consuls in France, to certify, "That no judiciary power was invested in the consul, except that expressly granted by the laws of the United-States, and tolerated by the government under whose jurisdiction he resides; and that every case which cannot be arranged by his friendly intervention, ought to be submitted to the local authorities."

It was observed, that if the decision of this pretended letter were real, it was posterior to that of the Court of Appeal. The Court could not divine, that in sending two Americans to plead their cause in their common country, it acted contrary to the intentions of their government; and of what importance is it for us, that the government of the United-States consents that Americans may prosecute each other before our tribunals. This consent, were it real, is not, neither can it be a law for us; it cannot remove the boundaries in which our laws have circumscribed the jurisdiction of our judges, nor force them to mingle in affairs not embraced by our laws. The government of the United-States may delegate to the French government the administration of justice for her citizens in France; but the former cannot oblige the latter to accept this delegation against her consent.

Considering, therefore, that the parties are both foreigners, not domiciliated in France; that the action is personal, and not commercial; that the contractors are in no wise subject to the French tribunals; that no arbitration has taken place, and that the principle of reciprocity invoked is not applicable, the treaties between the two states having decided nothing to this effect; the appeal of the plaintiff is rejected, and he is condemned to pay a fine.

January 22, 1806.

We shall cite another important case now pending before the Supreme Court of France.

A mercantile association was formed at Paris, in 1793, by Messrs. *Lecouteulx* and *Cheriot;* the chief object of which was to export to the United States the productions of Europe, and to import into France those of the former country. One of the company, Lecouteulx, died, and it was stipulated that, in this event, he was to be replaced by his brother. This partner, from different motives, refused to fulfil his obligations, and *Cheriot* suspended payment. By a clause of the act of society, all contestations which might take place between the associates, were to be submitted to arbitration

To this the parties had recourse for the termination of their dispute. The arbitral decision, which was drawn up in a very able manner, supported the interests of *Cheriot.* This decision was homologated by the French consul at Newyork, and a legal copy forwarded to M. Lecouteulx, who protested against this ordonnance, alledging that an arbitral decision, passed in a foreign country, by foreign arbiters, against a Frenchman, for the profit of a foreigner, was not susceptible of execution in France; and this doctrine was supported by the Civil Code. (Articles 2123 and 2128.)

In behalf of *Cheriot* it was argued, that these articles relate to contracts, or obligations received by foreign officers, and judgments rendered by a foreign judge, and not to arbitral decisions; that the act of the consul was legal and valid. This principle, after a long discussion before different tribunals, has been submitted to the decision of the Court of Cassation, and the report of the Attorney-General has not yet appeared.

CHAPTER VI.

Of the Consular system of the United-States of America.

THE consul of the United-States is nominated by the president, by and with the advice and consent of the Senate. Age is not a qualification. Before he receives his commission from the president, he takes an oath of office, and gives a renewable bond, to the amount of two thousand dollars, in which he is joined by two respectable merchants, for the faithful discharge of his duties according to law. This instrument of writing is deposited at the department of State.

When he arrives at the place of his residence, he presents this commission, in person, or through his minister, to the minister of Foreign Relations, who obtains from the sovereign authority, permission to exercise his functions, which is confirmed by a letter of *exequatur*.

By the constitution of the United-States it is ordained, that, in all cases affecting consuls, the Supreme Court of the said states shall have original and exclusive jurisdiction.[1]

The American consul has no authority except what may be expressly granted by a law of congress and acknowledged by the government in whose jurisdiction he resides. His duties are described in different acts of Congress,[2] and in the consular instructions of the Department of State, of which he is fournished with a copy.

1.° The consul is authorised to receive the protest or declaration of a citizen of the United-States, whether captain, master, merchant, passenger or sailor; and also of a foreigner relative to the personal interest of an American citizen; and this document, duly authenticated, is as legal and binding as the original would be in the courts of the United-States.

[1] Constitution of the United States, act III, sect. 2.

[2] April 14, 1792, of which the seventh and eighth sections are repealed (vol. VI, p. 28); of February and March, 1799, contained in the fourth volume.

2.° In countries where the laws permit, it is the duty of the consul to take possession of the intestate property of his fellow-citizens, of which he is to make an inventory, in the presence of two American merchants, or two other respectable persons selected for this purpose. He is to announce his death to the secretary of state, and also to the public, through the medium of a newspaper, published within the limits of the consulate; he is to examine and settle the accounts of the deceased, and to transmit the balance to the Treasury Department of the United-States, to be there held in trust, for the benefit of the true claimant. If a legal representative appear, before the balance is thus transmitted, the effects are delivered to him, on his payment of certain fees hereafter specified.

3.° In cases of stranded vessels not represented by a master, owner or consignee, the consul saves as much of the property as he can, for the benefit of the proprietors.

4.° At the expense of the United-States, the consul furnishes reasonable sums for the relief of sick, captive, or shipwrecked seamen, within his district; and he finds means to transport them home, on board of American vessels, where, if not diseased or disabled, they are obliged to perform a sailor's duty. For every hundred tons burthen of the vessel, the master is compelled to receive two such seamen, for whose passage he cannot demand more than ten dollars each; and if, in this respect, he refuse to obey the orders of the consul, he forfeits and pays the sum of one hundred dollars, which is recovered for the use of the United-States, in any court of competent jurisdiction. The certificate of the consul is acknowledged as *primá facie* evidence of this refusal.

5.° When by their own consent, seamen and mariners are discharged in a foreign country, the master or captain is obliged to present to the consul the *rôle d'équipage*, or list of the crew, and to pay for each sailor therein designated, three months wages more than are then due, two thirds of which sum he is to receive upon his engagement on board of any vessel, to return to the United-States; and the other third is to be retained to create a fund for the support and homeward passage of destitute seamen. The consul is to transmit to the Treasury

Department, half-yearly accounts of all sums thus received.

It has been decided, by the attorney-general of the United-States, that this provision of *extra* pay does not extend to stranded vessels, nor to those condemned as unfit for service; but if the vessel be sold, or if her original voyage be changed, the consul is to demand three months *extra* pay, though a passage may be offered to seamen on as good terms as those on which they were shipped.[1]

6.° All legal and reasonable sums, advanced by consuls for the relief of seamen, are reimbursed by the secretary of state.

Accounts for the relief of seamen in Great Britain were to be settled by the consuls, with the agent for seamen; in Europe, north of the Pyrenees, Italy excepted, with the minister at Paris; in Europe, south of the Pyrenees or in Italy, with the minister at Madrid.[2]

7.° On his arrival at a foreign port, the master or commander of an American vessel is obliged to deposit with the consul, his

[1] See the annexed letter addressed to the American consul at Genoa.

[2] Circular of the Department of State, Aug, 1, 1801.

register, sea letter, and Mediterranean passport; and in case of refusal, he is to forfeit and pay the sum of five hundred dollars, which is recovered, for the benefit of the United-States, in any court of competent jurisdiction. When the captain produces a regular clearance, it is the duty of the consul to deliver to him the said papers.

8.° If a consul shall falsely and knowingly certify, that the property of foreigners belongs to citizens of the United-States, he is to forfeit and pay a sum not exceeding ten thousand dollars, and to be imprisoned for a term not longer than three years; which circumstances are to be decided by the court to whose jurisdiction the case appertains.

9.° If the consul grant a passport or other papers certifying that an alien, whom he knows to be such, whether male or female, is a citizen of the United-States, he shall forfeit and pay a fine not exceeding one thousand dollars.

10.° If an American vessel be condemned as not sea-worthy, or if she be lost or sold to foreigners, it is the duty of the consul, with the consent of the captain or agent, to cancel the register, and return it to the Treasury Department. If not delivered to him, he is to communicate this circumstance to the secretary thereof, that recourse may be had to the bond.

11.° The consul is also instructed to detain marine papers, which bear clear marks of fraud and forgery; for which offence the penalty is to be applied in the United-States.

If the offender be a foreigner, he is to be brought, if possible, to punishment before a competent court, or authority, in the country where the offence was committed.

12.° Consuls were formerly authorised to grant certificates to American prize vessels, purchased for citizens of the United-States. This privilege was greatly abused, and was therefore annulled by the government.

13.° When seamen are impressed on the high seas, or in port, it is the duty of the master of the vessel to which they belonged, to make a protest of the fact before the consul, of which a copy is to be transmitted to to the Department of State.

14.° With regard to American prizes conducted into French ports, American consuls "may exercise the same jurisdiction as the

French consuls exercise in the countries where they are most favored."[1]

"When vessels, having letters of marque and reprisal, put into a foreign port, where there is an American consul, or other public agent of the United States, the commander is obliged to produce his journal, commission, and certificate to such consul or agent, who may go on board and number the officers and men, and examine the guns; and if the same shall not correspond with the commission and certificate, such consul or agent shall forthwith communicate the same to the secretary of the navy."[2]

"The consul or public agent of the United States is also authorised to claim and receive two *per cent* on the net amount of the prize money arising from captured vessels and cargoes, and on the net amount of the salvage of vessels and cargoes recaptured by the private armed vessels of the United States;

[1] Letter of March 3, 1813, addressed to David Bailie Warden, consul general of the United States, by his Excellency the Duke of Bassano, minister of Foreign Relations.

[2] Act concerning letters of marque, prizes and prize goods, June 26, 1812, § 11.

which sum is destined for the support and maintenance of such persons as may be wounded and disabled on board of the private armed vessels of the United States in an engagement with the enemy."[1]

15.° The consul at London, Paris, and on the Barbary coast, is charged with the business of prize cases, concerning which, his duties are defined in a general, though not in a special manner.

The law[2] on this subject, announces that the president of the United-States was authorised by the Senate, to appoint agents, with fixed salaries, in foreign countries, for the purpose of taking special cognizance of prize cases, and of the detention and imprisonment of seamen; and to correspond, on these subjects, with the executive of the United-States.

The president was also authorised[3] to allow an annual salary, not exceeding two thousand dollars, to the consul charged with this business, except for the consulate

[1] Act of Congress concerning letters of marque, etc. June 26, 1812, § 17.

[2] Vol. III, p. 322.

[3] Law of April 14, 1792.

at Algier, to which double this sum was accorded.

The consulship of Paris was created, in 1794, by Mr. Monroe, the present secretary of state, who appointed to that office Fulwar Skipwith, esquire, the former secretary of legation, whose appointment was afterwards approved by the president, and confirmed by the senate of the United States. On this subject, Mr. Monroe observed, "that a short experience had already demonstrated the interest which his country had in the appointment of some person here, known to and respected by the French government, and responsible to that of the United-States, to take charge of the commercial affairs of their citizens. [1]

"The duties of the consul here, will be those of consul general, and in strictness the commission should be correspondent. They may, however, be performed under that of consul *only*, for I presume those in the ports will respect him in either character. [2]

"Your ordinary commercial concerns, in

[1] Letter to the commissary of Exterior Relations.

[2] Letter to the secretary of state, December, 1794,

which my support may be deemed necessary, I will thank you to communicate with me as heretofore, through Mr. Skipwith, the consul in this city; for as he is charged with those concerns, and obtains redress, if possible, without my intervention, he is thereby enabled officially to report to me correctly those cases in which he cannot succeed, and, of course, in which my interference may be useful, which report forms generally the basis of my application.[1]"

Instructions to consuls were communicated by Mr. Monroe, through the channel of the Consular Office at Paris.[2]

The duties of the consul at Paris, in relation to prize cases, are pointed out in the following circular letter, dated the first of August, 1812.

contained in Mr. Monroe's work, *On the Conduct of the Executive in the foreign affairs of the United States.*—Philadelphia, 1797.

[1] Circular to the consuls of the United States in France, June, 1795.

[2] Letter from Mr. Monroe to Fulwar Skipwith, Esq. consul general.—Paris, April, 1796.

A statement of consular fees, specified in acts of Congress, and established by law.

	Doll.	Cents.
1.° For the authorisation of any act, under the seal of the consulate............	2	»
2.° For a certificate of the discharge of a seaman or mariner in a foreign port.....	»	50
3.° For the verification of the delivery or landing of merchandise at a port.....	1	»
For administering an oath concerning the same............................		25
4.° For a certificate of drawback..........	1	75

As the consul in the execution of this instrument signs his name and administers an oath, two dollars are usually paid.

5.° For the verification of letters of attorney, concerning the transfer of any stock of the United States, or for the receipt of interest thereon...............	»	50

6.° A commission of two and a half *per cent* is allowed for the receipt and payment of the amount of wages due on the discharge of seamen in foreign ports.

7.° For the preservation and management of the property of intestates, *five per cent* is paid on the gross amount, except when delivered over to the legal heir or representative, before a final settlement; in which case *two and a half per cent* is paid for whatever portion of it does not consist of money; and *five per cent* on the gross amount of the residue.

8.° Ten dollars *per annum* are granted for useful printed documents on the subject of quarantines and epidemical diseases, which must be transmitted to the Department of State.

EXTRACTS

FROM

TREATIES AND CONVENTIONS,

Between the Government of the United States and that of other nations, concerning the rights, privileges, and duties of Consuls.

THE Consular Convention,[1] between the United-States and France, was concluded in 1788, in virtue of the 19th article of the treaty of commerce of the 6th of February, 1778. The object of this Convention was to determine and fix the functions and prerogatives of the consuls and vice-consuls of the two respective powers.

The consuls and vice-consuls of each

[1] It was framed and signed by Thomas Jefferson, minister plenipotentiary of the United States, and Montmorin Saint Herem, minister and secretary of state of Lewis XVI.

country were to present their commissions, according to the form of their respective governments. The *exequatur*, necessary for the exercise of their functions, was to be delivered without expense. On the exhibition of this instrument, the governors, commandant, justices of the peace and other officers, having authority in the place of the consulate, were obliged, without exacting any fee or tribute, to grant the consuls that preeminence, authority and privileges, which were reciprocally stipulated.

Full and perfect immunity was granted to the consuls, vice-consuls, chancellors and secretaries, concerning the chancery and its papers. They were also exempt from personal services and taxes of every kind, with the exception of their possessions moveable and immoveable, which were subject to the duties fixed by the laws of the country. Consuls or vice-consuls concerned in commerce were subject to all the taxes, charges and impositions of merchants; and though they placed the arms of their sovereign or nation above the outer door of their house, it did not render it an asylum, neither for persons nor effects.

The consuls and vice-consuls had the right of establishing agents in ports or places of their department, who might be of their own or of a foreign nation. They could have no particular rights, privileges, nor immunities.

The consuls and vice-consuls had the exclusive right of receiving in their chancery, or on board of vessels, the declarations and all other acts of captains, seamen, passengers and merchants of their nation, even their testament or other act of their last will; and copies of these acts, duly legalized by the consuls, and bearing the seal of the Office, were to have the same force in justice as the originals would have before the tribunals of either country. In cases in which there was no testamentary executor or lawful heir, they had also the exclusive right of managing the succession of persons of their nation, who died within their consular department.

They had also exclusive authority in cases of shipwreck and of average, when no persons were interested therein, except those of their own country.

They were also authorised to exercise a

police or jurisdiction over the vessels of their respective nations, and to arrest and transport from the country, all deserters from vessels, whether captains, officers or sailors.

Crimes or infractions of the public tranquillity, were under the jurisdiction of the judges of the country.

This convention was to be in force during twelve years.

By the convention of 1800, between the French Republic and the United States of America, which was to operate for eight years, it was agreed, "That the parties shall have a mutual right to appoint agents for the protection of trade; who are to reside in any place not excepted by either government." "Before he exercises his functions, he must be accepted and furnished with an *exequatur* in the usual form, by the government in whose jurisdiction he is to reside; and to enjoy the rights and prerogatives of the most favored nations."

During the French revolution,[1] the Committee of public Safety, having examined the letter of the minister plenipotentiary and of the consul general of the United-States, at Paris, concerning the seizure of American vessels, decreed: that the Commission of Marine and Colonies shall immediately deliver to the consul of the United-States, at Paris, a copy of each decree which shall hereafter be rendered by the Committee of public Safety, relating to vessels, which, in cases permitted by decrees of the National Convention, may be seized by cruizers or war vessels of the Republic.

In the treaty of commerce, of the 19th of November, 1794, between the United-States and England, it was stipulated, in the sixteenth article, that the contracting parties may respectively appoint consuls for the protection of commerce, who shall enjoy the rights and privileges which belong to them in virtue of these functions. But before the consul can act in this quality,

[1] Brumaire 3, third year.

he must be acknowledged according to the usual forms, by the party to whom he is sent; and it is formally declared, that in case of unlawful or improper conduct, with respect to the laws of the government, it is right and fit to punish a consul conformably to the laws, if they apply to his case; and to remove him from his place, or from the country of his residence, provided that the offended government give, to the other, reasons to determine it thus to act."

In the treaty of commerce between the United-States and Holland, of the 8th of October, 1782, it was agreed by the contracting parties, that each shall have the liberty of establishing, in the ports of the other, consuls, vice-consuls, agents or commissaries, whose functions shall be regulated by a particular convention, when one of the two parties shall think fit to form such establishments.

In a treaty of commerce with Sweden, concluded the 3d of April, 1783, the United-

States stipulated, that each of the contracting parties should have the right of mutually establishing in their respective ports, consuls, vice-consuls, agents or commissaries, whose functions were to be regulated by a particular convention.

In the treaty[1] of friendship, limits and navigation of 1795, between the United-States and the king of Spain, it was stipulated: "that consuls shall be reciprocally established, with the privileges and powers which those of the most favored nations enjoy in the ports where these consuls reside or are permitted to be.[2]

In the treaty of amity and commerce of 1799, between Prussia and the United-States, it was mutually agreed: "that the two contracting parties shall grant to each other the liberty of having each in the ports of the other, consuls, vice-consuls or agents, and

[1] Executed by Thomas Pinckney, envoy extraordinary.

[2] Art. 19.

commissaries of their own appointment, who shall enjoy the same privileges and powers as those of the most favored nations. But if such consuls shall exercise commerce, they shall be submitted to the same laws and usages to which the private individuals of the nation are submitted in the same place.[1]

An article of the treaty of commerce of 1788, between the said powers, contains a similar regulation.

In 1787, the United-States concluded a treaty with the emperor of Morocco, in which it was agreed, "that disputes between citizens of the United-States shall be decided by their consuls, whose decisions, if necessary, are to be enforced by the aid or assistance of the government. If a Moor wound or kill an American citizen, or that the latter kill or wound the former, the case shall be decided by the laws of the country, and the consul shall assist at the trial, and shall not

[1] Art. 25.

be answerable for the escape of the delinquent.

"When no testament or will appears, the consul shall take possession of the effects of an American citizen. He shall not be answerable for the debts of his countrymen, and shall enjoy all the privileges which the consuls of other nations enjoy."[1]

The United States, in 1795, made a treaty with the dey of Algiers, in which it was stipulated, "that the property of American citizens dying intestate, was to be under the immediate direction of the consul. That he shall decide the disputes of Americans, except with a subject of the regency, in which case its laws are to apply. Every personal security shall be given to the consul and to his household; permission to exercise his religion in his own house; to travel where he pleases within the limits of the regency; to appoint his own drogman, and to visit any vessel in the roads. In the event of a war, to embark with his countrymen, with his

[1] Executed by Thomas Barckly, Esq. appointed for that purpose by the ministers plenipotentiary, John Adams and Thomas Jefferson.

and their effects; and to import, from any foreign country, free of duty, whatever article he pleases for his house and family."[1]

In 1791, a treaty was made with the bey and regency of Tunis, which gave powers to the American consul similar to those secured afterwards by that of 1797.

If the consul did not act in conformity with the usages of his country, his conduct was represented to the government, by that of the country of his residence. His family and *suite* were protected. His provisions and furniture paid no duty. Unless bound by writing, he was not responsible for the debts of his countrymen. The effects of persons dying intestate were under his management. He was constituted judge of disputes between his fellow-citizens, and of persons under his protection. He presided at the trial of commercial, civil, or criminal mat-

[1] Art. 13, 16, 17, 18 and 21. This treaty was executed by Joseph Donaldson, Esq. appointed for this purpose by David Humphreys, commissioner plenipotentiary at the court of Lisbon.

ters, between Tunisians and those under his protection.[1]

In the treaty of 1797, with the bey and subjects of Tripoli, it was agreed, that the privileges, immunities and jurisdiction of consuls were to be on the same footing as those of the most favored nations respectively.[2]

Form of the commission of the American Consul.

The President of the United States of America, to all who shall see these presents, greeting.

Know ye, that reposing special trust and confidence in the abilities and integrity of A. B. of   I have nominated, and by and with the advice and consent of the *Senate,* do appoint him consul of the United States of America, for the city of   and

[1] This treaty was negociated by Messrs. Eaton and Cathcart.

[2] Made by Joel Barlow, Esq. consul general of the United States.

such other parts as shall be nearer thereto than to the residence of any other consul or vice-consul of the United-States within the same allegiance, and so authorise and empower him to have and to hold the said office: and to exercise and enjoy all the rights, preeminences, privileges and authorities to the same of right appertaining, during the pleasure of the president of the United-States for the time being: he demanding and receiving no fees or perquisites of office whatever, which shall not be expressly established by some law of the United-States; and I do hereby inform all captains, masters and commanders of ships and other vessels, armed or unarmed, sailing under the flag of the said States, as well as other of their citizens, to acknowledge and consider him the said accordingly; and I do hereby pray and request His Majesty, etc. governors and officers, to permit the said fully and peaceably to enjoy and exercise the said office, without giving, or suffering to be given unto him any molestation or trouble; but, on the contrary, to afford him all proper countenance and assistance, I offering to do the same for all those who shall, in like manner, be recommended to me by his said Majesty.

In testimony whereof I have caused these letters to be made patent, and the seal of the United-States to be hereunto affixed.

Given under my hand, at the city of Washington, etc. etc.

By the PRESIDENT.

Secretary of State.

Form of the Consular Bond.

Know all men by these presents, that we are held, and firmly bound to the United-States of America, in the sum of two thousand dollars, money of the said United-States, to the payment whereof we bind ourselves jointly, and severally, our joint, and several heirs, executors and administrators.

Witness our hand and seals this

The condition of the above obligation is such, that if the above bounden consul of the United States in certain foreign ports, shall truly and faithfully discharge the duties of the said office according to law; and also, shall truly account for all monies, goods, and effects, which may come into his possession, by virtue of the laws of the United-States, or of his said office; then the above obligation to be void, otherwise to remain in full force.

Signed, etc.

To the consuls and vice-consuls of the United-States of America, residing in ports of France, or in those over which her Imperial Prize Court has jurisdiction.

Gentlemen,

Be it known, that the president of the United-States, by and with the advice and consent of the senate, has been pleased to superadd to my consular duties, those of "*Agent of American Prize Causes at Paris,*" and has authorised and directed me to aid and protect American citizens in the prosecution of said causes, in *bureaux* where they may be produced and discussed; and particularly before the Imperial Prize Court, and his Majesty's Council of State. I am also instructed to detect and expose every species of fraud, or violation of the laws of nations and of the American flag; all voluntary neglect, or sacrifice of the property, rights and interests of American shippers, merchants and insurers; and to render an account, to the Executive of the United-States, of every circumstance, which I may consider worthy of its notice, concerning the arrestation, detention, or release of American seamen, and of vessels and cargoes in France, or in countries to which the regulations and decisions of her maritime courts and authorities do or shall hereafter extend.

In order to execute more effectually the general and special instructions of the president, and of the secretary of Foreign Relations of the United-States, on this head, you are hereby requested to inform the captain, supercargo, or agent of every American vessel captured and conducted to, or arrested in the port or ports of your consular department, that it is my public duty, and consequently my great desire, to give to claimants every useful aid and advice; to seek for them, as much as in my power, prompt and impartial justice; and vigilantly to watch over and protect their interests. It is also proper to apprise them, that nothing more is necessary than the *procuration* of the captain, or consignee, or attorney in fact, to enable me to perform all that can be required in the prosecution of a claim; and that this document will be cancelled when the case is finally adjudged.

Moreover, it may be useful to observe, that my services are offered without commission, or pecuniary or other compensation.

You are intreated, gentlemen, to report to me every case of capture and of sequestration; to acknowledge the receipt of this *circular,* and to communicate its contents to the commercial and banking houses within your district, which have relations with those of the United-States. On my part, I tender you my goodwill, friendly aid, and correspondence whenever you may think them useful in relation to your public duties.

DAVID BAILIE WARDEN.

February 25, 1813.

Mr. Schee having this day communicated to me your refusal to act, without my advice, concerning the discharge of the crews of the American schooners the *Erect* and *General Green*, of which he is the owner, it is my duty to submit to you the following observations on this subject.

It appears that these vessels sailed from the port of Philadelphia for that of Genoa, prior to the declaration of war by the United-States against England; that the crews were shipped for the voyage; that the voyage was broken by an unforeseen casualty, which obliged Mr. Schee to lay up the vessels in your port, where they still remain. The seamen, unwilling to continue on board, solicit and obtain their discharge without the intervention of the consul. Their refusal would have given rise to a curious question concerning the duration of their lien or contract with the vessel, which it is not our business here to examine. The points which require discussion in relation to your consular duties, are those concerning the manner and conditions of discharge. With respect to the first, the laws are clear and positive. Though seamen, with their own consent, be discharged in a foreign country, it is, nevertheless, the duty of the master or commander, to pay, to the consul, three months wages more than are due, of which he is to give two-thirds to each seaman, upon his engagement on board of a vessel to return to the United-States; and to retain the other third for the maintenance and passage home of destitute seamen. If the master refuse to comply with the conditions of the law, the consul ought to have means to enforce its execution, by the arrestation of his ship, goods, or person; but on this head the act is silent, and the consul is left to decide as his judgment may direct.

The question for information is, whether under the peculiar circumstances of this case, you have a right to demand three months extra wages. Mr. Schee argues, that the rupture between the United-States and England was an unforeseen circumstance, over which he had no control; that the risk of capture rendered it impossible for the vessel to return immediately, and perhaps, not before a considerable lapse of time, to the port to which she belongs; and therefore that the contract between the captain and the seamen ceases to exist. In other words, he seems to consider her in the same situation, with regard to her crew, as if captured, stranded, or condemned. To this it may be objected, that there is still some chance of avoiding the enemy and completing the voyage; and yet the dread of capture by the English, and merciless corsairs of Barbary, which cover the Mediterranean, would have probably frightened the seamen from their engagement in the homeward voyage, if it had been possible for the captain to have proposed to put to sea. This case is singular, and has not been anticipated, neither in our marine laws nor consular instructions.

In a circular letter of July, 1805, addressed to consuls by the Department of State, it is observed, that according to the opinion of the attorney-general of the United-States, consuls have no claim for extra pay, in cases of vessels stranded or adjudged as not seaworthy; that this provision is restricted "to voluntary sales of vessels and discharges of their crews in the ordinary course of trade," or to "an alteration of the original voyage." In the present case, the voyage was not changed; the vessel remains unsold; she is neither stranded nor condemned: but the Mediterranean being covered with the corsairs of two enemies, is for her unnavigable; a circumstance, which, by parity of reason, may form another exception to the provision of the act concerning the extra pay of seamen.

Mr. Schee, in his letter to me on this subject, states, that the crew, by contract, were not entitled to receive any portion of their wages before their return to the United-States; that they agreed not to demand the additional advance allowed them by the laws; that they have received the whole amount of their pay, of which, to several of them, twelve months were due; that, if authorised by me, he is willing to deposit, at your consulate, one month's extra wages for each seaman. In conversation, he has, moreover, observed, that all of them, except two, are provided with funds, (which remain in the hands of his agent) to carry them to a port of embarkation for the United-States.

Their detention since the date of their discharge, is attributed to the difficulties of the case which prevented your official decision; to the want of passports, or the intervention of the authorities of Genoa; and, therefore, Mr. Schee may not be considered as responsible for the expenses incurred since the date of the receipt in full of which you have transmitted copies.

Under all these circumstances, it seems to me to be your duty to prevent these seamen from being lost to their country; and, for this purpose, to accept the deposit of one month's wages for each, destined for the relief of others; to procure passports and a *feuille de route,* to enable them to proceed to Bordeaux, and to advance reasonable sums for the travelling expenses of those who have not funds sufficient for this purpose, which may be done without any charge to the United-States, by instructing the consul at Bordeaux, or other port, to deduct the amount from the wages advanced, by the captain of the ship with whom they have embarked. There are, at present, more than twenty American vessels in the port of Bordeaux, several of which, as I am informed, require additional seamen, who will receive wages to the amount of twenty-five dollars per month. If those in question should not arrive in season to find employment there, by proceeding to the port of Nantes, Mr. Breuil, supercargo of the *Bellona,* which has not her complement of men, will engage them on liberal terms on board that schooner. They may be transported, in a very economical manner, by the *feluccas* or coasting boats, to Marseilles, (where they may be placed under the direction of our consul) and thence, by the canal of Languedoc, to Bordeaux, the port of embarcation.

Ed. Caffarena, Esq.
American consul general.

EXTRACTS

RELATING TO CONSULS,

FROM A WORK ENTITLED,

A View of the conduct of the Executive of the United-States, etc. By James Monroe, late Minister Plenipotentiary to France. —*Philadelphia*, 1797.

It is important that no public character of the United States should be in France, which is not acceptable. You will inquire into the consuls; and inform, how they are approved, and whether they be deserving. *Although the president will avoid, as much as possible, to appoint any obnoxious person consul, it may happen otherwise, and must be considered as accidental.* Mr. Alexander Duvernat goes for Paris in the quality of vice-consul, and Mr. Fauchet said that he had nothing to object to him.

Consulates are established in every port

of France, where they are conceived useful. But perhaps you may find it adviseable to mark out some other places for such offices.[1]

I HAVE received the letter by which you inform me, that you have nominated Mr. Skipwith, provisionally, to the office of consul for the department of Paris, and I have written, in consequence, to the Committee of Public Safety, to request that the *exequatur* of his commission may be granted. The numerous affairs which your countrymen have to discuss at Paris, have proved, for a long time past, the necessity of confiding their interests to a commercial agent, who should be especially charged with this detail.[2]

THE inclosed letter from one Binard, of Brest, speaks of his having been appointed

[1] Instructions, page 6.—From the Secretary of State to Mr. Monroe.

[2] Letter of the commissary of Foreign Affairs to the minister of the United-States, p. 51.

vice-consul of the United-States there, by Mr. Burrat Carnes, our late consul at Nantes. In this he is mistaken, as Mr. Carnes had no right to appoint a vice-consul under himself, and probably went no farther than to appoint him an agent, as consuls may lawfully do. Mr. Dobree, having succeeded Mr. Carnes, will probably take similar measures with respect to an agent, but it is desirable that you should immediately examine this matter well, and cause to be done what shall appear beneficial to our trade.

If a vice-consul should appear to be really necessary, you will inform me by the first opportunity.[1]

I SHALL immediately state the affair of the consul in the Isle of France; upon which, however, permit me respectfully to add, that the appointment of a person, not an American, perhaps an Englishman, to the office of consul, has not only been the cause of the disrespect shown to our authority, but

[1] Letter from the Secretary of State to Mr. Monroe, p. 54.

even of the embarrassments to which our countrymen were exposed there."[1]

"I UNDERSTAND by a letter from colonel Burr, that Mr. John B. Prevost takes an immediate passage for France, to enter into your family; his expectation being founded on the new office of consul general, which, at your instance has been created and given to Mr. Skipwith, I inclose his commission."[2]

I HAVE just received a letter from colonel Humphreys, our minister at Lisbon, advising that, as our treaty with Algiers is not yet concluded, it will be improper for our merchants and others to adventure into the Mediterranean, until further advised on the subject. I therefore notify this to you, that you may communicate the same to all our consuls within the French republic."[3]

[1] From Mr. Monroe, to the secretary of State, p. 60.

[2] From the secretary of State, to Mr. Monroe, p. 256.

[3] From Mr. Monroe, to Fulwar Skipwith, consul general of the United-States at Paris, p. 337.

" BUT the United-States could not expect that a man of such extended correspondence in trade, would confine his agency to the affairs of the United-States alone. It must certainly have been understood, as in all like cases where foreign merchants are appointed consuls, that while as our consul he protected our commerce, he would continue free to carry on his usual mercantile business. If an idea had been entertained that he must have relinquished this as a condition of holding the American consulate, assuredly he would have refused the latter."[1]

[1] From the secretary of State, to the French minister in the United States; on the subject of Mr. Parish, American consul at Hamburgh, p. 368.

CHAPTER VII.

The French Consular System.

THE code, which explains the rights, privileges and duties of French consuls, was chiefly borrowed from ancient capitulations, treaties and ordonnances, between the French kings and the Porte. Under the minister *Colbert,*[1] it was reduced to a regular system, to serve as a constitution for French subjects residing in the states of the *Grand Seignior*, in the echelles,[2] or ports of the Levant, or

[1] In 1688, the Department of Marine was united to that of Finance, and the direction of both given to *Colbert.*

[2] In the *ceratinus portus,* or great port of Constantinople, each commercial nation that traded there, had a particular place for its vessels, named *scala,* in French *échelles,* which originally signified the apparatus employed to go on board of, or descend from a vessel. The author of the *Voyage dans la Troade,* observed to me, that the word *escale,* employed by the *Provençaux,* was borrowed from the Turks, who, to this day, give the name *iskelé,* or *eskelé* to little ports of

of the Mediterranean. At the distance of eight hundred leagues from the seat of government, it was impossible to communicate timely instructions to the consul, concerning various circumstances not clearly defined by ordonnances, regulations, or local usage; and this officer was invested with absolute authority over the conduct and concerns of his countrymen, who had not renounced their citizenship, and who resided in, or merely visited the consular district. He acted at the same time, as parent, counsellor and judge, and as sovereign arbiter within his jurisdiction; being accountable only to the government by whom he was appointed. The execution of so important a trust, as that of judging men and their affairs, required a large portion of moral and intellectual knowledge, which was not to be attained, without precocity of talents, at a very early age. For this reason, no person could

their capital, and that this term is of Hebrew origin. In the Dictionary of Buxtorf, a passage of the Talmud is cited, which shows that איסכלרת *aiskaleth, scala,* signified the ladder of a vessel.—*Moukar at iskele emoukar at esphiné—vendidit scalam navis cum vendidit navim.* p. 165.

receive a commission before he entered his thirtieth year. The office of consul general was reserved for him, who, in the long exercise of his functions as consul, had, by his abilities, probity, and useful services, done honor to himself and to his country.

Before his departure for the place of his residence, the consul took the oath required by the laws; and on his arrival, presented his patent to the ruling sovereign, by whom he was, by *pareatis*, accredited. For ports of the *Levant*, the *exequatur* of the Ottoman Porte was demanded by the French ambassador, at Constantinople. As soon as the consul was formally acknowledged, his predecessor in office, or *chargé des affaires* of the consulate, convoked a general assembly of the nation, to whom was exhibited the commission of the new consul, and the *barats* or *exequatur* of the authority by whom he was acknowledged. These documents were enregistered in the chancery of the consulate. This ceremony being finished, the consul was installed in his functions. His first employment was to seek particular information concerning the commerce of the place, the character and conduct of his countrymen, the credit of his nation, and the ceremonies and customs necessary to be observed.

For each consulate, there was a chancellor who was nominated by the king, and who performed the duties of clerk, notary and summoner. There were also *vice-consuls, élève vice-consuls*, *drogmans*, *agents*, and *deputies*.

In places where there was no resident French minister, the consul general, in virtue of a diploma, or *barat* of the Grand Seignior, was qualified with the title of *Baliosbey*, or ambassador, and enjoyed all its corresponding prerogatives and privileges. His person and family were inviolable and sacred. His mansion, on which waved the flag of his nation, served as an asylum, not only for his countrymen, but also for foreign christians, and even for Musselmen and Moors, who there sought refuge. A detachment of janissaries was always at his command, to protect him against the fanaticism and barbarity of Musselmen and Moors. In visits of ceremony, at religious or other *fêtes*, at births or rejoicings of the reigning family, he wore his uniform and sword, and was accompanied with a *cortège,* composed of the drogmans, deputies, merchants, captains, clerks and private individuals of the nation, who reconducted him to the consular house. A fine of thirty livres, applied to the redemption of captives, was exacted from him, who, without a valid motive, refused to assist at these public processions. At solemn *fêtes,* the consul received the holy water, the incense and torch, and kiss of the Sacred Book, from the hands of the minister of the altar. His spouse, though considered as unworthy of these honors, on account of her sex, was allowed to place herself at the side of her husband, even on the bench reserved for the devoutest aspirations.

All war vessels, in sight of the flag of the consular house, were obliged to honor it with a royal salutation. In the event of death, the funeral of the consul was distinguished by a public procession; and the sympathy of his colleagues was expressed, by raising the flag of mourning on the summit of their respective mansions.

Great as these honors were in time of peace, in that of secret or open war, they were entirely withdrawn by the Barbary powers. All respect and homage for the officer, and fellow feeling for the man, were lost and forgotten. Laws, usages, treaties and humanity were then equally disregarded. The papers of the consulate were seized as lawful prey; his house was pillaged, and himself immured in a dungeon, perhaps decapitated, or given in barter as a vile christian slave.

Senator Volney [1] informs us, that Monsieur de *Sanci*, the French ambassador, suspected of having connived at the escape of a prisoner, was himself confined during four months: that the son of the ambassador of Lewis XIV, Monsieur *de la Haye*, received a stroke by order of the vizir, which broke two of his teeth; and was afterwards immured, during two months, in a dungeon, where the candle was sometimes extinguished by noxious vapors: that M. Bouis, the French consul at Alexandria,

[1] *Considérations sur la guerre actuelle des Turcs.* Other instances of their barbarity to consuls are cited in a work by *Paruta*, entitled, *Historia della Guerra di Cipro*, 1645, p. 36.

in 1777, was killed by the shot of a pistol, and a French interpreter secretly strangled at Constantinople.

Of Vice-Consuls.

THE vice-consuls, of the department of the consul, were subordinate to his instructions, though they were authorised to correspond with the secretary of State of the Department of Marine. To be appointed consul, it was necessary to have been employed three years in the quality of vice-consul. In case of absence, or of death, he was replaced by an *élève* of integrity and talents, who, like the provisional vice-consul, enjoyed half the salary of the office, as long as he acted as a suppliant. If, from incapacity or other motive, there was no *élève* fitted for this post, the consul was authorised to commit the affairs of the vice-consulate to a person of confidence, until the government decided the choice. In Barbary, there were no vice-consulates; and, as this office required much local knowledge, it was thought wise and prudent to fill it by *élèves* of approved conduct and capacity, who had resided, at least six years, near the consuls of Barbary.

Of Élève Vice-Consuls.

THE élève vice-consuls were chosen, by preference, from among the sons and nephews of the consuls of the Levant and of Barbary, from the age of twenty to twenty-five. They lived in the family of the consul, and rigidly obeyed his instructions. They studied the laws, ordonnances and regulations, and the oriental languages, particularly that of the Turks. At the close of the year, they were examined by the drogmans in the presence of their preceptors, and of the consul, who transmitted a certificate of their progress to the secretary of State of the Marine Department. This officer, to form a still more correct judgment of their application and capacity, exacted from them every year a memoir on a subject proposed by himself. To give them a general knowledge of consular administration, they were sent successively from one department to another. Those who constantly showed most application and intelligence, and whose conduct was regular, were advanced without consideration of length of service. To each of the two *élèves*, most distinguished for their behaviour, by the performance of their duty and their progress in the different prescribed objects of instruction, his majesty granted a yearly gratification of three hundred livres. A service of two or more years was required of the *élève*, before he obtained the *brevet* of vice-consul, which was granted only to merit; to those who, with zeal, patriotism and exemplary conduct, united a knowledge of the government, manners and local customs, and a thorough comprehension of the duties of the office, growing out of edicts, ordonnances, treaties and private instructions. The *élèves* were not permitted to borrow money upon any pretext. They could not form a marriage engagement without his majesty's consent, which was difficult to obtain, unless it were connected with important considerations, and sanctioned by the mutual approbation of the parents.

Of Drogmans.

THE drogmans of the Levant were selected from among the *élèves*, by the French ambassador near the *Ottoman Porte*, who rendered an account to the secretary of State of the Marine Department, of their merit, talents, capacity and conduct, in order to have the nomination confirmed by his majesty. To give a certain consideration to the first drogman, he had a brevet of secretary interpreter to the king. An annual pension of fifteen hundred livres, taken from the funds of the Chamber of Commerce of Marseilles, was granted to the two drogmans of the greatest merit; and this commission and pension were continued as long as they remained in active service. Intimately acquainted with the secrets of diplomacy, and having great influence in the management of affairs and treaties, negligence or dishonesty was dangerous and unpardonable. To prevent involuntary errors, they were enjoined to execute promptly, and punctually, under pain of revocation, or other punishment, all orders and instructions of the ambassador, the consul, or vice-consul. In diplomatic and commercial arrangements, and in visits of every kind, they were the intermediate agents of their own officers, and those of their residence. Their functions were, therefore, exceedingly delicate and important. An incorrect translation, or the suppression of a document, an unfaithful report, the want of intelligence, of honesty, and even of courage to communicate, in a proper manner, the expressions of others, on subjects of national dispute, might be attended with the most unfortunate consequences. To prevent abuses and intrigues, which the mysteries of the seraglios might for ever conceal, the drogmans, without permission, could not visit the authorities of the country. Leave of absence was not granted except in cases of absolute necessity; and then they were deprived, till their return, of one half of their salary. The drogmans could not trade, nor borrow money, nor marry without the king's consent. Educated and supported, from their earliest years, at the king's expense, it was thought reasonable to continue them in service as long as their faculties permitted. When attacked by infirmities, they received a pension proportioned to their age. The drogmans employed in Barbary were chosen from among those of the Levant, by the secretary of State of the Marine Department; and a preference was given to those who, with the necessary acquirements, were most intimately acquainted with the Arabian language.

The education of élèves destined for the place of drogmans, commenced in France, and was completed in the Levant. The king, by whom they were appointed, recommended to their parents and preceptors, a regular education, and the study of oriental languages.

Of the Chancellor.

The functions of the chancellor were usually performed by the drogmans; if necessary, he was aided by a clerk, at the expense of the chancery. His duty was to receive all acts and protestations of which he was to transmit copies to the secretary of State of the Marine Department; and disobedience or neglect was punished by a fine of three hundred livres, which was applied to the redemption of captives; and in case of refusal, the curate of the nation was charged by the consul to perform his duty.

The chancellor was obliged to keep five registers. The first, for acts, obligations, and contracts; the second, for the *procès-verbaux* of the Assembly, and deliberations of the nation; the third, for the ordonnances of the king, the orders and instructions of his majesty, and of the ambassador, consul or vice-consul, and the decisions of the secretaries of the Marine; the fourth, for deposits, and the fifth, for manifests of entry.

The pecuniary concerns of the consulate were all managed and recorded by the chancellor.

Of Agents.

WHEN it was considered as necessary or useful, the consuls were authorised to appoint agents in places of their department, to whom commissions were granted by the government. These agents were chosen from among French merchants residing in places where there existed French commercial establishments. Their province was to be useful to their countrymen; to watch over the execution of the laws; and to communicate to the consul, whose orders they obeyed, whatever occurred of importance in the place of their residence. They had no salary, no claim for fees or retribution. His majesty reserved to himself the recompense due for useful and essential services.

Of National Assemblies.

As often as the commerce, interest, or safety of the nation required, National Assemblies, consisting of French subjects, were convoked by the officers of the king. On extraordinary occasions, captains and other persons were invited to attend, to listen to or take a part in the instructions, and absence was punished by a fine. To prevent more than one interest from influencing the deliberations, admittance was refused to more than one associate of a commercial house or establishment. Bankrupts were formally excluded. The consuls and vice-consuls, guided by a spirit of justice and impartiality, had no deliberative voice in the Assembly; though they had power to dissolve it, when they perceived that, notwithstanding their observations, decisions contrary to the orders of the king were to be carried into effect. The *procès-verbaux* of the Assembly were inscribed on the register by the chancellor.

His majesty himself decided concerning the abuse of authority, or any injustice committed by consuls. He permitted any subject to complain to the National Assembly, of vexations or oppressions; but as consuls are often requested, from interested motives, to pursue measures contrary to their duties, by which their authority is compromitted and exposed to contempt, calumnious complaints were punished with rigor; and all were of this description of which the facts were not completely verified.

Of Deputies.

The Deputies were charged with national and commercial affairs: they were chosen annually by the Assembly of the Nation. The exercise of their functions required age and experience; and no merchant could be elected before he attained his twenty-fifth year, and had resided, two years at least, in the department. Bankruptcy was then, as it is still supposed in France, to leave an impression never to be effaced from the civil life of the merchant, in consequence of which he became incapable of all public employment. A bankrupt, therefore, could not be a deputy, nor could he assist at his election. No preference in the choice was manifested by the officers of the king. Representatives were always necessary to the nation, and the Deputation was never vacant. To avoid the abuses which result from the perpetuity of administration in the same hands, and also to prevent the same person from being continually charged with public affairs, a merchant could not be elected twice in succession, unless there were no other eligible candidate for office.

If a merchant compromitted the character of an honest man, by employing illicit means to obtain election, he was, on that account, rendered unworthy of the public confidence, and was for ever excluded, not only from the Deputation, but also from the National Assembly.

The deputies, when they thought it necessary, convoked the assemblies; they conferred with the consuls and vice-consuls, and co-operated with them to render their administration useful. Three times a year they communicated, to the Chamber of Commerce at Marseilles, a report on the state of commerce and navigation.

The consular jurisdiction extended to all affairs of commerce, police, and justice, civil as well as criminal. The prominent duty of consuls was to render justice to merchants; to give them protection; to support the credit of commerce against the spirit of cupidity and bad faith; and he who refused to submit to the authority of the consul, was considered as guilty of disobedience to his king.

Consuls could not trade, either directly or indirectly; because personal interest blinds men with regard to their public duties.

It was considered that a man who borrows money, is, in some measure, dependent on his creditors; and if an officer, that he, by this means, enervates authority and lessens his character. For these reasons, the French consul was not allowed to borrow money, under pain of revocation.

It was supposed, that the interests of the state required from the consuls a life of celibacy, unless marriage was suitable to their condition; and the king reserved to himself the right of judging of its propriety.

Without the king's permission, the consul could not quit his post, or abandon the affairs committed to his care; and his absence, without powerful motives, was always refused.

When leave of absence was obtained, the vice-consul of greatest merit, talents and experience, was called by the consul to exercise his functions.

In case of the consul's death, the *élève* informed the most ancient vice-consul of this accident, and he filled the place *per interim;* until his arrival, the *élève* dispatched those affairs which did not admit of delay, and afterwards exchanged places with the vice-consul. If there were no officer of this grade, the *élève* remained *chargé d'affaires* until the government disposed of the place.

The priests could not celebrate a marriage without the consul's permission; and disobedience to this regulation was punished by transporting them to France.

All captains, masters and patrons of merchant vessels were obliged to present to the consul their commission, clearance and manifest, to give a faithful report of the voyage, and they could not put to sea without his permission and certificate. As long as they remained in the roads, or ports, they were under consular police. All French subjects were obliged to apply to the consul for protection, advice, or justice, and could not have recourse to another authority.

No instrument of writing, made where a consul resided, was legal, unless authenticated by his seal and signature. Bills and testaments, marriages, and acts of separation of husband and wife, policies of insurance, bottomry, bonds, and all species of maritime contracts were made legal at the consulate.

The goods and effects of intestate Frenchmen, for which there was no attorney; and shipwrecked property, for which there was no factor, were committed to the consul's care.

With the approbation of the deputies, he had the power of transporting to France, those of his countrymen whose life and conduct were proved to be scandalous and immoral. This power extended to persons of an unfortunate temper (*humeur fâcheuse*), who annoyed society with their quarrels and disputes.

In civil offences, which admitted of bail, the decisions of the consul were provisional; and definitive, in criminal matters, for which corporal punishment was not assigned. Persons convicted of crimes were transported in irons to France, with a *procès-verbal* of their delinquency, to be judged by the competent tribunal.[1]

In cases of assassination, or wounds, the

[1] Edict of May, 1779, Art 35.

consul was aided by a surgeon, whose duty it was to make a formal report of the case.

Throughout the kingdom of France, the decisions of consuls were executed, by virtue of *pareatis*, like the sentences of other judges. The highest Court of Judicature acknowledged their authority in every kind of disputes.[1]

In 1742, a dispute, concerning the settlement of an account, was carried before the Parliament of *Aix*, by which Court it was returned to the consul of Spain, to whom its decision belonged.

The settlement of another account, in 1750, was referred, by the Court of Admiralty of Marseilles, to the French consul at Constantinople.

Private contestations between consuls and French merchants, charges against the former of speculation, extortion, or contravention to the laws, were formerly referred to the Court of Admiralty at Marseilles. This

[1] Senator Volney has severely inveighed against this authority of consuls, and the magnitude of their salaries; some of which he states to be from sixteen to eighteen thousand livres. *Considérations sur la guerre actuelle des Turcs*, p. 88.—Londres, 1788.

Court was suppressed in 1790. Trials of this kind, according to the present Civil Code, are under the jurisdiction of the Imperial Courts, and must be authorised by the Council of State. Appeal may be made to the Court of Cassation.

If the consul contract debts, or commercial engagements towards the inhabitants of the place of his residence, he is responsible to the tribunals of that place.

The statement which we have given of the French consular system, has been drawn from different edicts concerning the residence, commerce and navigation of the French under the direction of the consulates in the *echelles* of the Levant and of Barbary. Two of the most important of these edicts or regulations, with the capitulations renewed in the time of Lewis XV, have been lately printed at the imperial press, in a quarto form, of two hundred and thirty-four pages, by the order of government.

The first of these edicts was published at Versailles, in June, 1778, the object of which was to define the judiciary functions and police, which the consuls of France were to exercise in foreign countries, concerning French residence, commerce and navigation.

The second edict, or ordonnance, was issued in March, 1781, and was intended not only to modify and add to the former, as experience dictated, but to give it more strength and solidity, establishing an uniform administration throughout the consular jurisdiction, supported by the same principles, and directed and protected by the same authority.

In the year 1660, the following instructions were drawn up by the minister Colbert, in the name of the king, to serve as a guide to French consuls in foreign countries, concerning their correspondence on subjects connected with diplomacy.

As commerce is their principal occupation, it is their duty to acquire accurate information concerning the productions and manufactures of the country, the merchandise imported by sea and by land; if by caravans, as in the Levant; the quality and yearly quantity of merchandise; to inquire whether the subjects of the prince have any commerce by sea, of exportation or importation, and to what extent; how the commerce of foreign nations is carried on, and what are the mutual advantages resulting therefrom; the number of vessels trading with Spain and with Portugal; the value, weight and standard of the coin of each country; the nature of the exchange, condition and extent of manufactures, and names of the different nations whose products are transported to the Levant; and as a great number of five-sous pieces pass from France and Italy to that country, it is the king's will that the consuls shall carefully examine the matter, and communicate to him their advice concerning the best means of preventing the continuation of this disorder, which draws yearly considerable sums out of the kingdom, and injures its manufactures, by substituting in their place those of England and of Holland.

The capitulations between the court of France, and the Ottoman Porte, were treaties, or, according to the oriental expression, *sacred imperial diplomas.* The first was obtained, in 1535, by Francis the first, from Soliman the second, sirnamed the Canonist, in favor of commerce and the Roman catholic religion. In 1604, they were renewed, with additions, by Henry IV.

At the request of Lewis XIV, all nations who had no ambassador near the Porte, were obliged to traffick under the banner of France, and under the protection of the French consuls, residing in ports of the Levant, to whom they were obliged to pay certain fees or duties.

The consuls were made sole judges of all disputes or contestations between French merchants and other persons; and were to enjoy all the privileges of the laws of nations, with complete jurisdiction over the persons and property of the subjects of their nation.

The capitulations were again renewed, with considerable additions, in 1740, under the reign of the sultan *Mahmoûd;* and served as a ground-work for a treaty, containing eighty-five articles, concluded between that sultan and Lewis XV; the leading principle of which is, that ambassadors and consuls shall enjoy all the privileges of the laws of nations; and that interpreters, merchants, and other subjects of France, shall be entitled to protection and safety.

The ancient ordonnances and regulations have been readopted as the best guide for

French consuls; though the powers they give are modified and limited by the laws of the country in which they reside. In ports of the Levant, the authority of the French consul has been gradually forced to yield, in several respects, to that of the *Cadis*, who judge disputes between Turks and strangers according to the usages of commercial nations.[1]

During the consular government in France, which existed from the nineteenth brumaire, eighth year, to the *Senatus Consulte* of the twenty-eighth floreal, twelfth year, consuls were named "*Commissaires des Relations Commerciales*," Commissaries of Commercial Relations. The ancient title was readopted, when that form of government ceased.[2] In the year 1803, consuls were placed under the direction of the minister

[1] *Origine et progrès du droit et de la législation maritime, etc.* par Azuni.—Paris, 1810.

[2] The author, or the editor of the *Gentleman's Annual Pocket Remembrancer for 1803*, published, at Philadelphia, has inserted therein a list of American and French consuls; the former, residing in France, are styled *Commercial agents*; the latter, *Commissaries of Commercial Relations*. This error ought to be corrected.

of Exterior Relations; though on maritime subjects they necessarily correspond with the minister of Marine, and on those which are commercial, with the minister of Commerce and Manufactures.

The consuls of France, since the almost total extinction of foreign commerce, are diplomatic, as well as commercial agents. Charged with the economical and political administration of the nation, they communicate all kinds of information, which they consider as useful to be known by their government, concerning the customs, politics, navigation and commerce of the country. The consul is upheld by his government, as the natural counsellor and defender of his countrymen; and those who refuse his mediation and interference, are considered as aliens, unworthy of national protection.

Ministers and consuls are instructed to prosecute, before the local authorities, and according to the legislation of the country, those who falsify the French stamp on cloth destined for the commerce of the Levant: which shows that Frenchmen remain subject to the consular jurisdiction, according to laws and established conventions.[1]

The French consul is also agent of maritime prizes. He visits the vessels, seals the hatches and cabins, makes an inventory of articles that cannot be sealed, places guardians, and draws up *procès-verbal* of all particulars relating to the prize, according to the declaration of the officer by whom it was made; which is afterwards verified by the testimony of two of the persons composing the crew. The captain and sailors of the prize are afterwards examined; the papers translated, and transmitted, with the *procès-verbal*, to the department of the Marine. It is the duty of the consul to receive, and communicate the complaint of the captured, and to oppose his authority to all species of bribery and concealment.[2]

If the merchandize of a prise, clearly legal, be in a state of perishing, the consul, without waiting the decision on the case, is permitted to have it estimated by four domi-

[1] Imperial decree of Sept. 21, 1807, art. 25.

[2] Reg. of November, 1779.

ciliated merchants of the place; and to order a provisional sale; the amount of the proceeds of which is established by their certificate. In the mean time, the goods are deposited in a magazine, shut with two keys; one kept by the consul, and the other by the merchants.

The consuls, as administrators, are charged with the comptability of the Marine. Their duties concerning this important trust are too extensive for our notice. They are laid down in the Ordonnances of the Marine, and in different circular letters.[1] The victualling and repair of vessels; the subsistence and passage to ruined colonists, and civil and military officers, are under their direction. They have authority over sailors in port, with the faculty of deciding their contestations, and of arresting and disposing of deserters.

All acts of births, marriages, divorces and deaths, which are to have civil effect in

[1] Ministerial circular of Messidor 13, ninth year. Ministerial marine circular of Prairial 28, tenth year. Arrêté of the Council of State, Nivôse 1, ninth year. Circulars of Frimaire 30, and Thermidor 24 and 26; likewise Fructidor 2, eleventh year.

France, are executed in the Chancery of the Consulate.[1] The consuls are charged with the property of shipwrecks, and that of Frenchmen dying intestate.

If a vessel touch at a foreign port, where a French consul resides, having a will or testament on board, the person in whose possession it is, must deposit at his office one of the double originals, closed or sealed, which the consul transmits to the Minister of the Marine.

The consul is charged with the delivery of passports, except those destined for the ministers' messengers or couriers.

In the United-States, the duties of French consuls are much circumscribed by the forms of judicature, and the spirit of republican laws; and complaint is made, that the powers given to them, by the treaty of 1778, and Consular Convention of 1780, of judging their countrymen in civil and commercial matters, have been annulled by the conditions of the treaty of 1801. Though charged with the successions of intestate Frenchmen, they cannot execute the trust without the

[1] Code Civil, Art. 991.

permission of the local authorities. The right of entry, and of departure for prizes, was secured by the twenty-fourth article of the treaty of 1801; but the right of sale not being actually defined, it was granted rather by reciprocity than by express convention. The consuls also complain, that they are not aided by the civil authorities in their arrestation of sailors who have deserted from their vessels.

The French consul cannot leave his post, without the permission of his government.[1] He is answerable for his private, as well as public conduct. The instructions of an enlightened consul general[2] to his colleagues, contain this excellent observation: "In a foreign country, Frenchmen are generally judged by their consuls, and the latter by their conduct. When you reflect that it

[1] By an imperial decree of March 16, 1813, M. Theremin, French consul at Leipsick, was deposed, "for having abandoned his post without necessity, at a moment when his presence was most necessary to the army, and for not having manifested that courage and zeal which we have a right to expect from a public "functionary."

[2] M. De Beaujour.

depends on you to cause the French name to be cherished and respected, you will feel all the dignity of your mission."

To an officer, with powers so extensive, may, without much impropriety, be applied the following lines: "*In civem patremque geras: tu consule cunctis. Non tibi, nec tua te moveant, sed publica vota.*"

Pensions of Consuls before the revolution.

The pensions or salaries of retreat were founded on the duration and nature of the service, as follows:

To consuls general, after 15 years service in the Levant and in Barbary		2500 livres.
	after 20 years	3500
	after 25 years	4500
	after 30 years	5000
To consuls,	after 15 years service	1500
	after 20 years	2000
	after 25 years	3500
	after 30 years	5000
To vice-consuls,	after 15 years service	900
	after 20 years	1500
	after 25 years	2000
	after 30 years	3000

The drogmans had pensions of retreat proportionate to their age,

To those of 60 years	3000 livres.
of 65 years	3600
of 70 years	4000

The salaries of consuls were regulated by an *arrêt* of the council of November 27, 1779: they were paid quarterly.

Of the Dress or Uniform of the Consuls.

The uniform of the consuls general, consuls, vice-consuls and *élève* vice-consuls, consisted of an embroidered royal blue colored coat, lined with scarlet serge, and vest and small clothes of the latter color; with copper gilt buttons bearing the king's arms. Those who had a commission in the military service, were permitted to wear the epaulettes of their rank. No other subject of his majesty could wear a blue embroidered coat, or a blue coat with a red vest. The drogmans had the choice of the oriental or the French dress. The latter was composed of a coat of a sky-blue. Its lining, and the vest and small clothes, were of the color of chamois leather.

The agents of the consul were not permitted to wear a uniform.

Of Consular Dues or Fees.

In the origin of consular establishments, the duties on the entry and departure of vessels were paid, by the consul, to the privileged company of merchants, from whom he received a regular salary.

The consulates of the ports of the Levant and of Barbary, formerly belonged to two merchants of Marseilles, who enjoyed their emoluments. This excited the jealousy of the *African Company*, and the envy of the government; the Marsellese merchants lost all their privileges, except those derived from the consulate of Smyrna, which, in time of peace, gave two millions of francs per annum, though it was subject to considerable expenses. The salary of the consul or factor, was three thousand livres per annum.

The impolicy of this system was too obvious to be of long duration. The government reserved the proceeds of consular fees for the expenses of ambassadors and consuls.[1] In 1767, the salaries of consuls were increased by a decree, which forbids them to trade, either directly or indirectly, under pain of revocation.

The French consular fees, in Spain, were

[1] *Manuel des Commissaires, etc.* p. 32.

originally one half per cent on all merchandise exported to, or imported from France. By an *arrêt* of the Council, in 1660, they were regulated as follows. In the ports and havres of Biscay and Gallicia, twenty-four reals of plata were paid for every vessel and bark. For the ports of Seville, Cadix, San Lucar, etc. seventy reals for every vessel and bark. For the ports in the Straits of Gibraltar and in Catalonia, thirty-six reals of plata for every ship, and twenty-four for a bark or polacre. By a decree of the twenty-fourth of May, 1728, the consul at Cadix was authorised to exact *anchorage* duty on vessels loading or discharging, at that port, at the rate of twelve and a half dollars for a large vessel, and five and a quarter for a small one. Of the first sum, the vice-consul retained two, and of the second one dollar. Fine merchandise in bales, consigned to Frenchmen, paid an additional duty of one real per ton, of which the consul retained one half; the other was for the use of the poor.

By an ordonnance of the twenty-first of July, 1731, every master, captain or patron of a vessel, which loads in any port merchandise for the account, or to the consignment of French merchants and strangers, was ordered to pay to the French consul residing in the place of unloading, the consular and national duties fixed by regulations, tarifs and usage.

By an *arrêt* of the Council of the ninth of December, 1776, the consular duties were fixed at three per cent. on the value of merchandise imported or exported by French vessels. The delinquent was subject to bodily arrest, and to a fine of one thousand franks, which was not to be considered as comminatory. The merchants, captains and patrons of vessels, on their return to a port in France, are obliged to exhibit a receipt of the consul for the payment of these duties, who is responsible, in his private capacity, for those which have not been paid.

On the proceeds of prizes, the consul has no claim; but he has a right to a retribution of five livres for every two hours occupation on board the prize vessel. For the employment of his chancellor, during the same space of time, one half of this sum is allowed. For the inventory, unloading and attendance on the sale, the consul has thirty sous per hour, and the chancellor one half of this sum.

The maximum of subsistence for officers is a dollar per day, and eighty dollars for a passage home. Soldiers and seamen may receive one half of a dollar per day, and sixty-five dollars for their passage; besides medicine for the sick, and clothes for the naked. On all payments, three per cent is deducted for the Chest of Invalids.

Consular fees were regulated by an *arrêt* of the Council of State, the third of March, 1781; and this regulation, which was originally intended for the consulates in the Levant, was afterwards applied to those in other countries.

A statement of Consular Fees.

	fr.	cent.
A policy of insurance....................	4	»
Contracts of marriage, testaments, donations and codicils...........................	12	»
Copy of said acts.......................	4	»
Said acts for captains and artisans.........	6	»
Copy..................................	2	»
For sailors, *gratis*.		

	fr.	cent.
For the execution and registry of a solemn testament, for merchants and traders....	12	»
Copy..:............................	2	»
Said acts and copies for sailors, *gratis*.		
For putting seals on the house or magazine of a merchant, the copy included.........	6	»
For inventories and sales, *per* hour........	1	»
Acts made during that time.............	»	50
For acts of deposit for the sum of 50 francs or less.........................	1	50
Idem above 50 francs..................	3	»
For duties on deposits, 2 *per cent.* For discharges on sums deposited of 50 francs and under............................	1	50
Idem, above 50 francs..................	3	»
Copy of said acts on discharges of deposit...	1	50
For transactions, emancipations, or sale of real estate.........................	6	»
Copy of said acts......................	2	»
Acts of discharge, attestation, procurations, obligation, or registry of a document....	1	50
Copy................................		50
Certificate of health for a vessel..........	3	»
Idem for a passenger...................	2	»
The said acts for sailors, *gratis*.		
For the bill of lading and manifest of a cargo, two copies.........................	10	»
For a petition or simple demand..........	1	50
For a petition, and execution upon a judgment made in consequence, with signification to the party.....................	3	»

	fr.	cent.
For information or inquest, each deposition.	»	60
For copy of said deposition..............	»	20
For an act of protest of a bill of exchange, with signification and answer, the whole supposed to form but one act............	1	50
For a copy.............................	1	35
For the verification of documents, the registry included..........................	3	»
Copy.................................	1	»
For the minutes of a writing of contestation between the parties, not exceeding one page.................................	1	»
For the opening of a *procès-verbal,* called the consulate..........................	1	50
For the deposition of each witness, copy included.............................	»	80
For acts of partnership, and dissolution of societies..........................	6	»
For the freighting and *nolissement* of a vessel.	3	»
The patents are certified gratis.		
For inquest or information, copy included, for each witness.....................	»	80
For the *consulate,* made by a captain on his arrival.............................	3	»
For the travelling expenses of a chancellor two leagues from his residence..........	6	»
From two to four leagues................	9	»
For a day or more, *per* day............... besides the expense of acts.	12	»
For assignations, significations, and other similar documents....................	1	50

	fr.	cent.
For the authentication of accounts produced by a captain for the salary of his crew.....	1	»
For the registry of a certificate of a merchant for the purpose of establishing himself in another port..........................	18	»
For the registry of the certificate of a clerk..	6	»
For writing, 50 centimes *per* page, each page to contain twenty or twenty-two lines, and each line twelve syllables.............	»	50

The French consuls are authorised to receive the civil acts of citizens of their nation.[1]

In time of peace there were French consular establishments in the following towns and ports.

In Spain.

At Madrid, a consul general, who was *chargé d'affaires,* with a chancellor.

At Cadix, a consul general.

At Andalusia, a vice-consul and a chancellor.

At Seville and San Lucar, a vice-consul.

[1] Decision of the Council of State, Brumaire 4.

At Malaga, a vice-consul.

At Carthagena, a consul.

At Alicant, a consul and vice-consul.

At Valentia, a vice-consul.

At Gijon and ports of the Asturias, a consul.

At Corogna and ports of Gallicia, a consul.

At St. Andero, a consul.

At Majorca, a consul.

At Barcelona, a consul and vice-consul.

At Teneriff and ports of the Canaries, a consul.

At Oran, a consul.

In Portugal.

At Lisbon, a consul general and vice-consul.

At Oporto, a consul.

At the island of Madeira, a consul.

At the islands of Fayolle and Azores, a vice-consul.

In Italy.

At Leghorn, a consul.

At Charles-Fort, a vice-consul.

At Rome, a consul and commercial agent.

States of the church, a commercial agent.

At Civita-Vecchia, a consul.

At Naples and ports of the kingdom, a consul general.

At Messina, a vice-consul.

At Palermo, a consul.

At Cagliari and ports of Sardinia, a consul.

At Ancona, a consul.

At Porto-Ferrajo, a vice-consul.

At Pesaro, vice-consul.

At Venice, a consul.

At Ragusa, a consul general and *chargé d'affaires.*

At the Venetian islands, a consul general, *chargé d'affaires,* and vice-consul.

At Trieste, under the emperor's domination, a consul general.

In Great Britain and Ireland.

At London, a consul, who is marine agent.

At Bristol, a consul.

At Hull, a vice-consul.

At Edinburgh, a consul.

At Dublin, a consul.

At Cork, a vice-consul.

In the Echelles of the Levant and in Barbary.

At Morocco, a consul general and *chargé d'affaires*, near the emperor of Morocco; a chancellor and drogman.

At Magador, a vice-consul.

At Algiers, a consul general, *charge d'affaires,* vice-consul and drogman.

At Alexandria, a consul general, vice-consul, chancellor and drogman.

At Rosetta, a vice-consul, chancellor and drogman.

At Seyde, a vice-consul, chancellor and drogman.

At Aleppo, a vice-consul, chancellor and drogman.

At Tripoli, in Syria, a consul and drogman.

In Turkey, a vice-consul, chancellor and drogman.

At Smyrna, a vice-consul, chancellor and drogman.

At Constantinople, an ambassador, who acts as consul general.

At Rhodes, a vice-consul and drogman.

At Leio, a vice-consul and drogman.

At Cyprus, a consul and drogman.

At Salonica, a consul and drogman.

At Cance, a consul, chancellor and drogman.

At Morea, a consul general, vice-consul and two drogmans.

At the Dardanelles, a vice-consul.

At Bassora, a consul and chancellor.

At Bagdad, a vice-consul.

At Tunis, a consul general and *chargé d'affaires* near the bey, vice-consul, chancellor and drogman.

At Tripoli in Barbary, a consul general and *chargé d'affaires* near the pacha bey, vice-consul, chancellor and drogman.

At Athens, a vice-consul.

At St. Jean d'Acre, a consul, chancellor and drogman.

In the North.

At St. Petersburgh, a consul general and vice-consul.

At Cronstadt, a vice-consul.

At Gottenburg, a consul.

At Warsaw, a consul or agent.

At Elsenor, in Denmark, a consul.

At Drentheim, in Norway, a consul.

At Berghen, in Norway, a consul.

At Christianstadt, a vice-consul.

At Amsterdam, marine and consul general, and chancellor.

At Rotterdam, a marine agent.

At Hamburgh, a consul general.

At Nastock, a vice-consul.

At Dantzick, a consul general.

The United-States of America.

At Philadelphia, a consul general.

At Boston, a consul.

At Rhode-Island, a vice-consul.

At Portsmouth, a vice-consul.

At Baltimore, a consul.

At Richmond, a vice-consul.

At Newyork, a consul.

At Wilmington, a vice-consul.

At Charleston, a vice-consul.

At Savannah, a vice-consul.

East Indies.

At Moka, an agent.

At Sumatra, an agent.

At Canton, in China, a consul, chancellor and two interpreters.

At the Cape of Good-Hope, an agent.

At Batavia, an agent.

Of treaties between France and other Powers, in relation to Consuls.

In the year 1604, the sultan Mahomet concluded a treaty at the request of Henry IV, in which it was agreed, that all the commercial nations of Europe, including the English, may freely traffick under the banner and protection of France, and in obedience to the French consuls. (Art. 3.) Venetians, English, Spaniards, Portuguese, Catalans, Ragusans, Genevese, Anconitans, Florentines, and generally all other nations of every description, may freely come and traffick in our countries, under the sanction and protection of the banner of France, obeying the French consuls who reside in our havres and ports. The subjects of France, and those of friends, allies and confederates, may, with our permission and protection, freely visit the holy places of Jerusalem; and the religionists who remain at that city, and serve the church of *Kamama*, (the Holy Sepulchre of Jesus Christ), may there remain, go, come or return with safety. (Art. 4.) The French consuls, established for the welfare and protection of merchants, shall not be made prisoners, neither shall their houses be sealed or burned. They shall pay no duties on victuals or provisions for their house, and claims against them must be referred to the Porte. (Art. 19.)

In the treaty of 1612, between the Grand-Seignior and the States-General, it was stipulated, that, in disputes with consuls, established for our commerce, the consul is not to be arrested, nor shall his house or goods be sealed, but he may be cited before the Imperial Court of the Grand-Seignior. (Art. 12.)

In the treaty of 1740, between Lewis XV and the sultan Mahmoûd, it was agreed, that if any murder or tumult take place among Frenchmen, their ambassadors and consuls shall decide concerning it, according to customs and usages; without being disquieted by any of our officers. (Art. 15.) If any person enter an action against consuls, established for mercantile affairs, they shall not be imprisoned, nor shall their house be sealed; and their cause shall be heard at our Port of Felicity. (Art. 16.) The consuls of France, in commercial towns, shall have precedency over the consuls of Spain, and those of other kings, as is the custom at our Port of Felicity. (Art. 18.) The consuls of France, and those who depend upon them in the quality of religious persons (*religieux*), merchants, and interpreters, are permitted to make wine in their houses, and to import it, or grapes, free of duty, for their ordinary use. (Art. 40.)

Besides the precedency mentioned in the foregoing articles, in favor of the ambassadors and consuls of the most magnificent emperor of France, as the title of emperor has been attributed *ab antiquo,* by my Sublime Porte to his said majesty, his ambassadors and consuls shall also be treated and considered, by my Port of Felicity, in a manner suitable to the honors of this title. (Art. 44).

By a treaty of peace, made on the twenty-sixth of Frimaire, tenth year of the French republic, between France and the Regency of Algiers, it was agreed, that the asylum of the French consul shall be sacred; that no public force can be there introduced, if not required by the consul from the chiefs of the Algerian republic. (Art. 16).

The French republic concluded another treaty, the same year, with the Sublime Porte, in which it was stipulated: "That the French republic shall enjoy, in Ottoman countries bordering on the Black-Sea, the same rights, privileges and prerogatives, for her consuls and agents, as France formerly enjoyed in the other parts of the states of the Sublime Porte, in virtue of ancient capitulations."

A convention was signed at Prado, in 1769, between the courts of France and Spain, by which the contracting parties agreed, "That consuls are acknowledged reciprocally, after having presented the diploma of their sovereign; they are to enjoy certain immunities: they shall not be arrested or imprisoned, even in the quality of merchants, except for atrocions crimes; they are exempt from the charge of lodging soldiers, except in cases of necessity, when all the houses of the town or city are occupied: they are free from all tribute and personal service. They may wear a sword and cane, and place an inscription over the door of their house. Their papers are not to be seized under any pretext, unless concerned in commerce; and in this case, they are to be treated as temporary foreign merchants. In case of need, the magistrate may demand a juridical declaration for the purpose of justice. The consul is never to be wanting in those attentions due to governors and other persons who represent the king and magistracy. The consul, when authorised by his sovereign, may nominate vice-consuls; but they shall not be natives of the country where they reside. They may visit the vessels of their nation, demand all useful informations, accompany their officers to the custom-house, to ministers and to authorities; and without their permission, no magistrate nor custom-house officer can go on board. Sailors who desert are put at their disposition, until an opportunity presents of sending them home. Captains, sailors, or passengers, if injured or oppressed by the consul, may have recourse to the justice of the country. Vessels and merchandise, saved from shipwreck, are to be put at the disposition of the captain. The heritage of Frenchmen, temporally residing in Spain, and of Spaniards in France, who die with, or without a testament, is to be liquidated by the consul, conformably to the thirty-third and thirty-fourth articles of the treaty of Utrecht; and the entire proceeds are to be delivered to the present or absent heirs."

In the sixth article of a convention between the said powers, concluded on the twentieth of January, 1768, it was stipulated, that the consuls, vice-consuls and deputies, being the interpreters of the nation which they represent, must accompany, whenever necessary, masters, captains and patrons; and also the officers of customs when they go on board of vessels to perform the visit of *fondeo;* and no magistrate shall receive the declaration of the captain, patron, or sailor, but in presence of the consul; for this is the only means of avoiding frauds and mistakes, and of securing the free administration of justice; besides, it has been prescribed by former ordonnances, that all navigators shall obey the consuls, and respect them as their immediate superiors, conformably to the sixth article of the treaty of 1725; it being well understood, that the consul must be informed of the hour; and if he does not appear, nor send a person to represent him, at the time appointed, the obligation of this article shall be considered as forfeited.

In the year 1774, another convention was concluded between France and Spain, by which it was agreed, "That the captains of French and Spanish vessels, on their return to the port of their departure, shall present certificates from the consuls, vice-consuls, or other officers of the nation, to testify that they sold or unshipped their cargo at the port of their destination."

" They shall also exhibit certificates from the consuls, expressing the quantity, quality and destination of the new cargo."

" The consuls of both nations established at Dunkirk and Ostend, shall be obliged to present to each other, a statement of the vessels of the two nations, which shallhave carried from these ports salt and tobacco; and this statement must comprehend the name and tonnage of the vessel; the name of the captain, and the number of the crew; the quantity of salt and tobacco, and the place of destination. The same formalities shall be observed by the consuls, or vice-consuls, established in the Mediterranean. The consul shall have power to examine cases of prohibited merchandise, and to institute such proceedings against the captain and crew, as may be authorised by his court. Contraband articles shall be subject to confiscation."

"Cases of shipwreck shall be under the protection of the nation to which they belong."

France, in her treaty of commerce with England, concluded in 1786, stipulated, "That it shall be permitted to their majesties respectively, to establish in the kingdoms and countries of each other, for the advantage of their subjects who trade there, national consuls, who shall enjoy those rights, immunities and freedom, which belong to them in virtue of their duties and functions; and they shall afterwards agree concerning the places where the said consuls may be established, and also concerning the nature and extent of their functions. The convention relative to this subject shall be executed immediately after the signing of the treaty, of which it is to constitute a part."

This convention was executed on the seventh of January, 1787, of which the sixth article is as follows:

"Their majesties having stipulated, by the forty-third article of the said treaty, to determine the nature and extent of the functions of consuls, it is agreed, that the convention, relative to this subject, shall be framed in the space of two months; and that, in the mean time, the consuls general, consuls and vice-consuls, shall act conformably to established usages concerning consulates, in the respective states of the two sovereigns; and that they shall have all the privileges, rights and immunities, which their quality supposes; and which are given to the consuls general, to the consuls and vice-consuls of the most favored nations."

In the treaty of commerce and navigation

concluded at Saint-Petersburgh, in 1787, between France and Russia, and maintained by the treaty of peace of the tenth year, it was agreed, "That the consul general, consul, and vice-consul of the contracting powers, shall not, without express permission, be subjects of the government near which they reside. They shall respectively have exclusive authority over the crews of their nations in the ports of their residence; as well for the general police of seamen, as for the examination and decision of their contestations." Cases of average, in which Frenchmen only suffered, were regulated by the French consul; and the same power, in a similar case, was given to the Russian consul, art. 5, 6 and 7.

In the settlement of disputes, the parties might have recourse to the authority of the vice-consul, whose decisions were acknowledged by the consul, as valid and legal.

By the seventh article of the treaty of commerce of the second of April, 1776, between France and Ragusa, sovereign power was given to the French consul over the vessels of his nation, in criminal as well as in civil matters.

THE French republic, in her treaty of peace with his majesty the king of the Two Sicilies, concluded the nineteenth of Vendemiaire, fourth year, stipulated, "That every French citizen, and those composing the house of the ambassador or minister, consuls and other agents accredited, and acknowledged by the French republic, shall enjoy, in the states of his majesty, the king of the Two Sicilies, the same freedom of worship as the inhabitants of the most favored non-catholic countries." (Art. 10.)

On the twenty-second of Messidor, seventh year of the French republic, the Executive Directory decreed as follows:

" The consul general and consuls of foreign nations, in the French republic, may communicate directly with the authorities, judiciary or administrative, of their respective *arrondissements*. They may apply to a minister, through their ambassador, as intermediary, who must communicate with the minister of Foreign Affairs. (Art. 2.) When there is no minister, nor ambassador, the consul general may be the intermediary of the consular agents of his nation." (Art. 3)

On the fourth of Messidor, eleventh year of the republic, the French government decreed, that no commercial house could be established in the Levant, in Barbary, or in the ports of the Black Sea, without permission of the government; that applications for this purpose were to be made to the minister of the Interior, through the Chamber of Commerce of Marseilles. The ninth article authorised the French consul to send back to France every individual who went there without permission, and whose residence might do injury to the nation.

The French republic, on the first of Messidor, eleventh year of its reign, decreed, that its laws, statutes and regulations expressly forbid the consul from carrying on any species of trade, directly or indirectly, or forming a commercial association on their own account. And we say with justice, that our consuls, since the regeneration of our republic, have every where shown themselves faithful to its principles. No where do they mingle in the interests of commerce, except to protect, extend, and render it more and more favorable to their fellow-citizens, and never for their own benefit. The commercial agents of nations allied to France, even those of Russia, the Teutonic Hans, and Austrian states, have disinterestedly hastened to imitate this fine example.

It is quite otherwise with the English consul, who every where trades on his own account, or that of the government, to the injury of his fellow-citizens; every where drenching them even to loathing. One while a public agent, another, a simple individual, he employs every method to accumulate a fortune, and increase the fisc of his isle. Monopoly, brokerage, stock-jobbing, arbitrary taxes, all is agreeable, because all concurs to his interest. He is a trader in Smyrna, a commissioner in Holland, and a pirate in Barbary.

Of the Salaries of French Consuls.

The salaries of French consuls are as follow:

The consul general, 30,000 franks, besides his travelling expenses, (at the rate of 16 franks *per post*) and those of his passage, and of his first establishment. The latter is estimated at about one-third of the salary.

	franks.
The salary of the consulship of Newyork is	18,000
of Charleston...........	18,000
of New Orleans.........	18,000
of Boston..............	12,000
of Philadelphia..........	12,000
of Baltimore............	12,000
The vice-consul of Newyork.............	10,000
Other vice-consuls....................	6,000

The travelling expenses, passage, and bureau expenses of every consul, are fixed by the government.

Before the revolution, the French consuls general at Cadix and at Madrid, had each a yearly salary of 40,000 franks; that of the consul of Barcelona was 10,000 franks, which was the salary of the second class of consuls. The first, besides the fees of office, had 20,000 franks for yearly expenses.

CHAPTER VIII.

The English Consular System.

The English consul was originally elected by merchants from among the members of their own association; and was recommended by them to the secretary of State, as the candidate of their choice. This officer presented the nomination to the king, who, under his sign manual, issued a commission, which explained the nature and object of the appointment. This mode of election was observed but for a short period of time. Ministers of State, from different motives, claimed and obtained the privilege of appointing consuls. Interest, private friendship, and national policy, all concurred to invest them with this authority. The consul was a merchant, united in close commercial ties with the association to which he owed his appointment and continuance in office. With the mercantile concerns of the port of his residence, he had a minute and practical acquaintance; but his mental extended no farther than his visual sight. He felt no interest in the rich productions of his country, when wafted to another port. His views and interests were very different from those of his government, which required an agent not only acquainted with the local and commercial concerns of the place of his residence, but also with those of the whole country; a person who had talents to furnish naval, statistical, or political information, and whose opinions were not to be warped by selfish or pecuniary considerations : in short, an officer qualified to represent his government where there was no minister, and who would not, by a dishonorable or mean action, degrade his office or the commission of his majesty. Though the emperor *Pertinax* was a merchant, as were also some of the wisest and best men of antiquity, still it was believed, that this employment, and that of a consul, were, in most situations, incompatible; that in spite of the stubbornness of virtue, the latter might, if he traded on his own account, act partially, and thereby injure the interests of his country.

The appointment of consuls was, therefore

confided to the secretaries of State, for the *southern* and *northern provinces.* The consulates of the southern kingdoms of Europe are under the direction of the former; and those of the northern under that of the latter, with the exception of a few, over which certain commercial corporate companies have an unlimited controul. The English government, struck with the political and commercial advantages of consular establishments, selected, for their direction, men of talents and respectability, naval or military officers, with a salary suitable to their situation; whose particular duties are to support the dignity and privileges of the nation; to exercise a certain jurisdiction over English commerce and navigation; and to furnish the government with prompt information on every subject connected with its interests.

The admission of an English consul, though the right be not stipulated by treaty, is seldom or never refused. In every commercial and civilized country, the institution is extremely important; and the authority which, in time of peace, refuses to receive a consul, does real injury to itself. The advantages are so obvious, that generally neither the person nor commission is rejected. Nevertheless, there is a curious distinction on this head. Though the right of sending a consul, by one government to another, be secured by treaty, his admission may be refused, if proper reasons be assigned; but the commission itself, without a violation of peace and amity, cannot be rejected. This is certainly a nice distinction. The person, the choice of the king, is turned away, mocked and insulted, and majesty itself thereby offended; whilst the scrap of parchment remains at its post, in all the dignity and plenitude of office.

A government, free and independent, ought never, without reasonable motives, to tolerate the rejection of an officer of its appointment; for, by this tame submission, the ignorant flatterer may occupy the place destined for the enlightened patriot.

The most savage tribes of America pay honor and respect to an agent or ambassador, though they may reject the presents and offers which he brings. Corinth, the luminary of Greece, owed her destruction to the circumstance of having wantonly illtreated a simple individual sent from Rome, for the object of commerce.[1]

The British government has two kinds of consular commissions; one founded on an existing commercial or other treaty; the second, on sufferance, permission, or reciprocity. They were formerly written in Latin, the language of diplomacy among European nations, but now in English. We have subjoined, with a translation, a copy of the ancient commission.

Without permission from the secretary of State, the English consul cannot return home, nor absent himself from the place of his residence. When permitted to leave his post, he appoints a deputy to exercise the functions of his office; who, when approved by the secretary, is an officer of the crown, in virtue of the commission signed by the consul; and, without permission, the consul cannot regain his delegated authority. The vice-consul corresponds with the public officers, as if he were consul; and, if necessary, appoints, within his jurisdiction, subordinate agents or deputies.

[1] Cicero.

The English consul has power to call a general meeting of the British merchants and factors for the discussion of commercial affairs; and for the purpose of levying sums on trading ships, for the relief of shipwrecked mariners and charitable purposes. All matters are decided by the majority at such meetings.[1]

The succession or effects of Englishmen, dying intestate within the consul's jurisdiction, are entrusted to his care.

All British or Irish captains, within ten days after their arrival in the ports of Portugal, are obliged to deliver upon oath, to the consul or deputy consul, a manifest of the cargo, to communicate the name of the consignee, and do not receive the clearance outward from the consul until the duties are paid, which are destined for the use of distressed seamen, shipwrecked mariners, and other charitable purposes.[2]

The duties, at Lisbon, are recovered by the British consul general, according to the weight or tonnage, which is valued, by two

[1] Statute 10, George II, 2 ch. 14, and statute 9, George II, ch. 25.

[2] Statute 9, George II, ch. 25.

British merchants, on the place; one chosen by the consul general, the other by the master of the ship, within ten days after the goods are unladen. In case of disagreement, a third person is chosen, after the expiration of five days, who is obliged to decide the valuation in the course of three days.[1]

The general duties of the consul are as follow:

1.° To acquire an accurate knowledge of the language employed by the court and authorities where he resides; so that he may be enabled to converse with ease upon subjects relating to his duties.

2.° To make himself acquainted, if he be not already, with the laws of moral nature and of nations; with commercial regulations, with the tarif, or specification of duties on articles imported or exported, and with all the municipal ordonnances and laws.

3.° It is his duty to support the dignity of his office, and thereby secure esteem and consideration.

4.° To protect from insult or imposition, British subjects of every description within

[1] Statute 8, George I, chap. 17, §. 1.

his jurisdiction. If redress for injury suffered is not obtained, he is to carry his complaint, by memorial, to the British minister residing at the court on which the consulship depends. If there be none, he is to address himself directly to the court; and if, in an important case, his complaint is not answered, he is to transmit the memorial to his majesty's secretary of State.

5.° When insult or outrage is offered by a British subject to a native of the place, the magistrate thereof complains to the consul, who orders the offender to give immediate satisfaction; and, if he refuses, he resigns him to the civil jurisdiction of the magistrate, or to the military law of the garrison, always acting as counsellor or advocate at his trial, when there is question of life or property.

6.° It is the duty of the consul to take exclusive cognizance of cases of offences committed at sea, within the territorial limits of the sovereign near whom he resides, and to transport the parties to Great Britain for trial.

7.° To relieve all distressed British mariners; to give, for their support, six sous per day; to transport them home on board the first British vessel sailing for England, and to transmit, to the Navy Office, as often as required, an account of his disbursements.

8.° To give free passes to all British subjects who wish to return home, instructing the captains of the king's packet-boats or ships of war, to receive them on board.

9.° He is not to permit a merchant vessel to leave the port without his passport, which he is not to grant until the master and crew thereof have paid all just demands.

10.° It is his duty to claim and recover all wrecks, cables and anchors belonging to British ships, found at sea by fishermen or other persons; to pay the usual salvage, and to communicate a report thereof to the Naval Board.

11.° To attend, if requested, all arbitrations, where property is concerned, between freighters and the masters of British ships; to imprison disorderly seamen, at the request of the captain; and even the captain himself, if guilty of unjust or improper conduct[1]

[1] It may be observed, that though an action can be afterwards brought, before the Court of England, for false imprisonment, in the case of a sailor whose mas-

12.° To complain against all oppressive regulations, arbitrary proceedings or imprisonment, or infraction of treaties in relation to the commerce of his country.

13.° To prepare, and transmit to his government, annual or periodical reports, concerning the quantity and value of articles shipped to every port.[1]

14.° Finally, it is his duty, in a catholic country, not to hold assemblies for protestant worship, unless the privilege be granted by the authorities of the place or stipulated by treaty. To defend protestants in the free exercise of their faith; not to insult or ridicule the established religion; nor to suffer a bible, common prayer, or religious book to be seized, as heretical, in the house of a protestant; and, if carried off, as has sometimes happened, by a priest or friar, he is to be prosecuted by the consul at common law.[2]

ter is absent on a voyage, yet the consul may unjustly suffer by the want of evidence.

[1] In the third volume of *Macpherson's Annals of of Commerce*, pages 425, 432, 467, 474, 480, 493 and 560, several of such reports are noticed.

[2] *Lex Mercatoria Rediviva*, enlarged and improved by Mortimer, vol. I, art. Consul. Dublin, 1795.

The British consul, residing on the coast of Barbary, has been usually charged with the execution of treaties.

That of 1751, between the king of Great Britain and the emperor of Morocco, was made by William Pettigrew, esquire, his Britannic majesty's consul general.

Another was concluded the same year, at Tripoli, between the dey and Robert White, esquire, the British consul general, and a third, at Tunis, by Charles Gordon, esquire.

The consul is distinguished from the merchants or inhabitants of the place where he resides, by various privileges, derived from treaties, from usage or reciprocity. He is respected in a particular manner. On his arrival, a free entry is given to his furniture and baggage; he is exempt from certain internal duties; he sits with the magistrates on the bench, when he acts as consul for his countrymen, in their disputes with the natives; he is freed from the general duty of lodging the military; to maintain his authority over seamen, he is furnished with a guard; masters of vessels show him respect and obedience; he is charged, by his government, with the distribution of presents; he corresponds with the secretary of State, and with the minister residing at the court on which the consulate depends.

In some places, English consuls have salaries from the crown; in others, they have nothing but the pecuniary dues or fees of office. Where English factories are established, those fees are regulated by a stipend on the burthen of the ship, or length of the voyage, and it is worthy of remark, that unless there exists a commercial treaty, the claim for fees cannot be supported. If a master refuse to pay them, the consul cannot detain his ship, for the owners and freighters would bring an action for damages; but he may seize and appropriate, for his fee, any valuable article of furniture belonging to the cabin.[1]

In a late publication,[2] the pecuniary advantages of consular establishments are urged as sufficient motives for their multiplication and support. " The duties of customs

[1] Opinion of the chancellor Hardwicke.

[2] Reflections on the Commerce of the Mediterranean, etc. etc. by John Jackson, Esq. F. S. A.—New-york edition.

alone, upon a very few cargoes of merchandise, will more than pay the salaries of all our consuls in the Mediterranean; and had England three times the number there, it would always be of increased advantage to this country."—"When a man of war goes into any port of the Mediterranean for supplies, the vice-consul, usually a Greek or Italian, will not furnish them unless he has a prospect of gaining thirty-five per cent, exclusive of the usual commission." "No British accredited consul would suffer this within his jurisdiction. In France, the subject of consuls has always been a principal object, both in the time of the monarchy and of the republic; the late conduct of the French in sending an immense number of consuls and commercial agents to all ports and cities of any consequence in the *Morea, Levant,* Egypt, etc. etc. ought to have been sufficient to open the eyes of the English." "They were treated by the French government, in the most handsome manner, which would always operate in their favor, and make them appear in the eyes of the people, where they were established, as men of real consequence. They had men of war to attend, and every respect outwardly shown them, equal to so many ambassadors."

In all its commercial treaties, the English government has granted but little judicial authority to its consuls, except to those in the Barbary states.

In the year 1645, *Richard Anthony*, consul of the English nation in *Andalusia*, in the name of the "*Vassals* of Great-Britain," obtained from Don Philip, a *cedula* of privileges, of which one was that of appointing a *judge-conservator*, who had special and exclusive cognizance of all causes, civil or criminal, between Englishmen, whether as plaintiff or defendant; and also of suits of the latter with Spaniards, or persons of other nations.

In a treaty with Spain, made in 1667, it was stipulated, that the goods and estates of Englishmen, dying without will in that kingdom, were to be put into inventory, with their papers, writings, and books of accounts, by the consul, or other public minister of the king of Great-Britain, and placed in the hands of two or three merchants, named by the said consul, or public minister, to be kept for the proprietors or creditors; and that neither the *Cruzada,* nor any other judicatory whatsoever, should intermeddle therein; which, also, in the like case was to be observed in England, towards the subjects of the king of Spain.

In 1670, the queen governess of Spain, at the request of the English consul,[1] renewed the privilege of a *judge conservator* of English causes. I ask justice, said this consul, when he demanded the removal of vexations experienced by the English merchants, at Seville, and the observance of certain articles of peace, which had been shamefully infringed.

By an article of the treaty of commerce and navigation, concluded, in 1713, at Utrecht, between queen Anne of Great-Britain, and Philip the fifth of Spain, it was agreed: "That the consul who shall reside within the dominions of the king of Spain, for the help and protection of British subjects, shall be named by the king of Great-Britain, and when named, shall exercise the same power and authority, in the execution of his charge, as any other consul formerly had

[1] Art. 27.

within the said dominions." "In like manner, the authority of the Spanish consul, residing in England, shall be as extensive as that of any consul who had been there established."

In a treaty of amity and commerce, between Charles II, king of Great-Britain, and prince Charles Emanuel II, duke of Savoy, concluded at Florence, in the year 1699, the following form of judicial procedure was adopted by the contracting parties.

"All differences and disputes between the subjects of his British majesty, or with those who are not subjects, shall be pleaded before and decided by a judge, called the *delegate* for the English nation. This delegate shall be one of the ministers of his royal highness, established as consuls of the sea; and shall be chosen by his majesty's subjects residing at *Nice*, *Villa-Franco* or *Saint-Hospice*. He shall be continued as long as the national electors shall think proper; though not longer than the time limited by his royal highness, for the office of consuls of the sea. This delegate shall determine briefly, and expeditiously, all the said differences without the formality of law-suits, according to reason, only regarding the truth of the fact, and without any other expense than that of the writing. From this sentence appeals shall only be made to the Court of Consuls for the sea, established at Nice, in which the said delegate is also to have a sitting, as one of the judges; and from this court there shall be no appeal. But if his majesty's subjects, in the said ports, should grow too numerous to decide their differences in the manner prescribed, the following regulation shall be established.

"The subjects of his majesty shall choose out of the English nation three men, who, for their lives and morals, bear the reputation of the greatest integrity; one of whom shall be nominated as the national delegate, who, with four arbitrators, chosen by the plaintiff and defendant, shall decide all disputes; he shall have the casting voice, when the votes of the arbitrators are equal on both sides, and shall be continued in office during three years."

In a treaty of navigation and commerce between Anne, queen of Great Britain, and Lewis XIV, concluded at Utrecht, in 1713, it was agreed: "That it shall be free for their royal majesties, for the advantage of their subjects trading to the kingdoms and dominions of the other, to constitute national consuls[1] of their own subjects, who shall enjoy that right and liberty which belongs to them, by reason of the exercise of their functions; but as to the places where such consuls are to be appointed, both sides shall afterwards agree between themselves."—(*Supp. art.*)

In articles of peace and commerce between Great Britain and Portugal, concluded at London, January 29, 1641, it was agreed: "That the consuls nominated and appointed by the most renowned king of Great Britain, for the aid and protection of his subjects residing in the kingdoms and estates of the most renowned king of Portugal, shall fully and freely exercise the functions and office of consuls in the said kingdoms and estates, though they profess not the Romish religion."

In another treaty of peace and alliance

[1] *Consules nationales ex subjectis suis instituere.*

between Great Britain and Portugal, made at Westminster, in July 10, 1654, it was stipulated, "That the consuls, who shall hereafter reside in any part of the countries of *Portugal*, for the aid and protection of the people of Great Britain, shall be nominated and appointed by the said lord king of Great Britain, and thus nominated, and appointed, shall have and exercise the same authority, as any consul, either of this or of any other nation whatsoever, now does, or ever hereafter shall exercise, on the territories of the said king, although he does not profess the Roman catholic religion; and in all cases, that are to be tried, concerning the people of Great Britain, the judge conservator shall be deputed, and no appeal allowed from his court, but to the *Senate of References*, where the controversies, that are arisen, by putting in the appeals, shall be decided within the space of four months at farthest."

WITH the Barbary powers, in 1675, the English government imitated the example of France, and secured extensive privileges for her consuls.

In the treaty of commerce, made and concluded at Adrianople, in 1675, between Mahomet IV, sultan of the Turks, and Charles II, king of Great Britain, the ancient agreements made in the reign of queen Elizabeth, of James I, and Charles I, were repeated and confirmed. It was agreed, "That all Englishmen, who are slaves, or who shall be demanded by the ambassador or consul of the English nation, shall be delivered up to the English ambassador or consul. That all disputes between subjects of the crown of England, shall be judged by the ambassador or consul of the nation. That in case of any lawsuit, or other quarrel with any persons of the English nation, neither the *cadis*, nor any other of our ministers of public justice, shall hear or decide the cause, unless the ambassador, consul or drogman of the said nation be upon the spot. Our ministers shall not have power to commit English consuls to prison, nor to seal up their houses, nor to send them away, nor to dispose of their offices or functions. But in case of a difference or lawsuit with the consul, a certificate shall be drawn up, and addressed to the Imperial Court, to the end that the ambassador may protest, and be answerable for him. The English consul shall take care of the goods and effects of Englishmen dying intestate. It is expressly stipulated, in the imperial capitulations, that in all disputes and lawsuits with the English nation, our magistrates ought not to hear nor determine a cause, unless the ambassador or consul be present."[1]

Another treaty was concluded in 1716, between *England* and the *dey* of *Tunis*, by which it was stipulated, that the ships of this town were to carry a certificate of the British consul, showing their nationality; that the clearance of vessels expressing the quantity, quality and value of goods, was to be certified and delivered by the said consul. That differences happening between subjects of Great Britain, were to be decided by the British consul only.

The same year it was agreed with the *dey*

[1] Art 12, 16, 23, 26, 35 and 57.

of Tripoli: "That the English consul was to have entire freedom and safety of his person and estate; permission to go on board of any ship in the road; to have the liberty of the country, a place to pray in, and that no man shall do him any injury in deed or word." That merchant ships, though not belonging to *Great Britain*, shall have free liberty to put themselves under the protection of the British consul.

In 1728, articles of peace and commerce were executed between the most high and renowned prince, George II, and the most high and glorious, mighty and right noble prince Muly, king and emperor of Fez and Morocco, of which the second article is as follows:

"The king of Great Britain's subjects, residing in Barbary, shall not be obliged to appear before the *cadi*, or justices of the country; but only the governor of the place and his Britannic majesty's consuls are to take cognizance of, and adjust the differences they may have with the natives of the country."

Another treaty of peace and friendship, between the king of Great Britain and the emperor of Morocco, was executed in 1751. By the third article it was agreed: "That if any dispute shall happen between the English and the emperor's subjects, the same shall not be determined by a judge, but ended and adjusted by an English consul, and the *coyed,* or mayor of the town, where such disputes shall happen."

A copy of the English Consular Patent.

GEORGIUS REX.

Georgius secundus, Dei gratiâ *Magnæ Brittaniæ,* Franciæ et Hiberniæ rex, fidei defensor, etc.

Omnibus et singulis ad quos presentes litteræ pervenerint, salutem; quum expedire compertum sit ut in oppido Alicante in regno *Hispaniæ,* probus aliquis constituatur vir, qui subditorum nostrorum rebus mercatura causa ibi loci commorantium vel appelantium in communi prospiciat, et consulis officio fungatur; sciatis igitur quod nos fide, affectu, prudentia, et in rebus gerendis præsertim mercatoriis experientiâ dilecti nobis et fidelis, subditi nostri *Samuelis Tucker*, generosi, omnino confidentis, eumdem nominavimus et constituimus, et per præsentes, nominamus et constituimus consulem nostrum in dicto oppido *Alicante*, una cum membris et pertinentibus quibuscumque; dantes eidem et concidentes potestatem pariter ac mandatum quoscumque subditos nostros prædictum oppidum ejusquæ ditiones et territoria incolentes et frequentates, vel in illis locis, postibus, et oris mercaturum facientes et facturos de negocia tractantes aut tractaturos, juvandi, et protegendi iisque secundum validos pacis, et fœderum inter coronas *Magnæ Britanniæ* et Hispaniarum earumque regna conclusa, et ad commerciorum celebritatem facientes, tractatus et articulos, consilium auxiliumque præstandi dictos subditos nostros eorumque, onerus, bona et res quascumque, cum opus fuerit, eorum judicibus, et magistratibus quibusvis, defendendi differentias, controversias, litesque quæ inter eos moventur vel accidere possunt, cognoscendi, decernendi, et componendi, eos in omnibus juribus, articulisque mutui commercii, libertatem, et frequentiam spectantibus tuendi, et conservandi ac unum vel plures deputatos, sive proconsules, prout illi visum fuerit, substituendi, qui in prædictis locis vel eorum quolibet ejus vices supplere possint, ceteraque omnia faciendi et præstandi quæ ad subditorum nostrorum commodum, mutuæ inter utraque regna populosque amicitiæ incrementum, mercaturæque utrinque exercendæ frequentiam et securitatem conducere poterunt, tandemque etiam omnibus, et singulis juribus, honoribus, immunitatibus, libertatibus et emolumentis. Quibus aliis quispiam in prædicto oppido consul de jure fructatur, vel frui poterat, utendi, fruendique. Serio autem rogamus serenissimum ac potentissimum regem catholicum fratrem nostrum, et unicè petimus ab omnibus aliis quorum ulto modo interesse poterit (id quod subditis nostris per præsentes firmiter injungimus) ut dictum *Samuelem Tucker*, consulem nostrum in oppido prædicto cognoscunt et habeant acceptum. In quorum omnium fidem has litteras manu sigilloque nostris regiis munitas expedire fecimus.—Dabantur in palatio nostro divi Jacobi, undecimo die mensis decembris, anno domini millesimo septengentesimo vicesimo-octavo, regnique nostri secundo.

Ex mandato serenissimi domini regis.

HOLLES NEWCASTLE.

Translation.

GEORGE REX.

George the second, by the grace of God, of Great-Britain, France and Ireland, king, defender of the faith, etc.

To all and singular to whom these presents shall come greeting: whereas, it hath been found expedient, that some person of known probity be appointed to act as consul in the town of Alicant, in the kingdom of Spain, and to take care of the commerce of our subjects, who reside, or commonly go there to trade. Know ye, therefore, that we entirely confiding in the probity, affection, prudence and experience, especially in mercantile affairs, of our trusty and faithful subject *Samuel Tucker,* gentleman, have nominated and appointed, and by these presents do nominate and appoint him our consul, in the said town of *Alicant*, together with all its members and appurtenances; giving and granting unto him, full power and commission to aid and protect all our subjects, that inhabit or frequent the said town, its territories or jurisdiction; or who do or shall carry on a trade, or transact business in the ports, harbor and coasts; advising and assisting them, agreeably to the articles and treaties of peace and alliance relating to trade, and firmly concluded between the crowns of Great Britain and Spain, and their respective dominions; and to defend our said subjects, in case of need, in their trade, goods and whatever else shall appertain to them, before all judges and magistrates; and to take cognizance of, determine and compose all differences, controversies and litigations, which do or may happen between them; and to defend and preserve them in every thing relating to their right, liberty and freedom of mutual trade and commerce; and farther (as he shall think fit) one or more deputies, or vice-consuls to act for him, in all, and every of the aforesaid places, and to do all and every thing which may promote the good of our subjects, the increase of mutual friendship between the two kingdoms and people, and the freedom and security of commerce: and farther that he use and enjoy all and every the rights, honors and immunities, liberties and emoluments, which any other consul, in the aforesaid town, did or could of right enjoy: and we earnestly intreat the most serene and potent catholic king, our brother; and we desire all others whom it may in any wise concern, in a friendly manner, (what we strictly enjoin all our subjects by these presents) that they acknowledge and admit the said *Samuel Tucker,* as our consul in the aforesaid town. In witness whereof, we have caused these our letters to be made patent, and signed and sealed with our hand. —Given in our palace, at Saint-James, the eleventh day of December, in the year of our Lord 1728, and second of our reign.

By his majesty's command,

HOLLES NEWCASTLE.

The preamble of the commission of the first English consul general in Spain, granted in 1640, and inserted in the *Fœdera*,[1] is as follows:

"Whereas we are given to understand how convenient and necessary it is for the good of our loving subjects trading to *Alicant*, in the kingdom of Valencia, to have some person of judgment and experience, able to govern and direct them, in their just and lawful occasions, to be placed and appointed as consul there, know ye," etc.

The following copies of English consular *commissions*, transcribed from the *Fœdera* of *Rymer*, are alluded to in chapter IV.

Pro consule mercatorum, infra Insulam de Candia. [2]

Rex omnibus, ad quos, etc. salutem!

Sciatis quod nos, de gratiâ nostrâ speciali, ac ex certa scientia et mero motu nostris, necnon certis A. D. 1530.

[1] Vol. XX, p. 430.

[2] Fœdera, tom. XIV, p. 389.

causis et considerationibus nos specialiter moventibus, dedimus et concessimus, ac per presentes damus et concedimus, dilecto subdito nostro *Dionisio Harrys*, de civitate nostra Londoniæ mercatori, officium sive locum *magistri, gubernatoris, protectoris*, sive *consulis* omnium et singulorum mercatorum aliorumque ligiorum et subditorum nostrorum prædictorum, tàm infrà *insulam* sive *civitatem de Candye* quàm infrà omnes et singulas portus villas et crecas eisdem insulæ, sive civitati adjacentes frequentantium, morantium, mercandisantium, sive negotiantium, ipsumque *Dionisium magistrum, gubernatorem, protectorem*, sive *consulem* mercatorum, aliorumque ligiorum et subditorum nostrorum prædictorum constituimus et ordinavimus, ac per præsentes constituimus et ordinamus.

Dantes et concedentes *eidem Dionisio* plenam tenore præsentium potestatem et auctoritatem ad omnia et singula quæ pro ordinaone regimine, gubernatione, et conservatione mercatorum aliorumque ligiorum et subditorum nostrorum prædictorum, bonorumque et mercandisarum suarum, prout sibi melius videbitur, ordinandum, exercendum, et perimplendum.

Habendum, occupandum, et exercendum officium sive locum prædictum ac cætera præmissa præfato *Dionisio* per se, sive per sufficientem deputatum suum, sive sufficientes deputatos suos, durante vitâ suâ, cum omnibus et omnimodis feodis, præeminentiis, juribus proficuis, commoditatibus, avantagiis, et emolumentis quibuscumque, in tàm amplis et consimilibus modo et formâ prout aliquis alius sive aliqui alii hujusmodi sive consimile officium aut locum in insulâ, civitate, portu, sive villis et crecis prædictis, vel alibi ex dono sive concessione nostris, sive aliquorum progenitorum sive prædecessorum nostrorum quondam regum angliæ, habuerunt et gravisi fuerunt, habuit et gravisus fuit:

Eo quod expressa mentio, etc.

In cujus, etc.

Teste rege apud *Chelsehith,* vicesimo-sexto die aprilis.

Pro Laurentio Strozzi.

Rex omnibus, ad quos etc. salutem![1]

Quia nonnulli mercatores et alii subditi hujus regni nostri Angliæ habent intentionem, Deo volente, partes exteras, maximè ipsos Italiæ, cum suis propriis seu conductis navibus bonis et mercibus, frequentare.

Tantò libentiùs quanto liberiùs et commodiùs in eis, cùm illinc applicuerint, poterunt conversari, volentes ipsorum quieti et utilitati quantum possumus providere, ac per experimenta aliorum nationum pro certo scientes oportere inter eos aliquem magistratum peculiarem erigi et creari, cujus judicio et diffinitioni lites et contentiones, quas inter ipsos subditos nostros mercatores seu alios, dùm in illis partibus morum traxerint, suboriri contigerit, submitti debeant.

Cùmque intellexerimus civitatem Pisanam, inter alia loca Italiæ, maximè propitiam futuram aptàmque et convenientem pro residentia mercatorum nostrorum hujusmodi.

[1] Fœdera, tom. XII, p. 270.

De fidelitate igitur probitate ac egregiis virtutibus dilecti nobis *Laurentii Strozzi*, mercatoris Florentini plenissimè confidentes, de gratiâ nostrâ speciali, et ad humilem supplicationem mercatorum regni nostri Angliæ, et aliorum subditorum nostrorum partes Italiæ, et præcipué dictam civitatem Pisanam portumque ibidem, partesque adjacentes frequentantium, frequentare vè in futurum volentium, *ipsum Laurentium* præficimus, constituimus, et ordinamus consulem et præsidentem superfactis omnium et singulorum subditorum nostrorum, ad dictam civitatem, partesque illic ut præmittitur adjacentes confluentium.

Damusque et concedimus *eidem Laurentio*, quantum in nobis est. facultatem et potestatem causas, questiones, controversias atque lites, quas inter ipsos subditos nostros in partibus ipsis moveri contigerit, audiendi, discutiendi, terminandi, et diffiniendi summariè et de plano, sine strepitu et figura judicii, quotiens ad id per alteram partium hujusmodi dissidentium requisitus fuerit, cæteraque omnia et singula faciendi, exercendi, et expediendi, tàm in judicio quàm extra quæ ad officium consulatûs et præsidentiæ hujusmodi de jure seu consuetudine aliarum nationum spectare noscuntur.

Mandantes omnibus et singulis subditis nostris antedictis, cujuscùmque statûs, gradus ordinis, dignitatis vel præeminentiæ existant, tàm mercatoribus quàm aliis, qui in futurum ad dictam civitatem Pisanam portumvè seu loca illic adjacentia accedere, concurrere, habitare, seu residere curaverint, quatinus *eidem Laurentio Strozzi* in exercitio suo officii consulatûs antedicti abedientes sint, assistentes, et obtemperantes in omnibus, prout decet.

Et, quia dignus est operarius mercede, utque ipse *Laurentius* tantò diligentius officium hujusmodi pro pacificandis subditorum nostrorum differentiis exequatur, quantò merita et studia sua ab eis gratiùs intellecta cognoverit, volumus et concedimus, quòd ipse *Laurentius* habeat et percipiat de valore et æstimatione omnium et singulorum mercium et rerum venalium quas in dictis civitate et portu per subditos nostros hujusmodi modo mercatorio emi aut vendi contigerit, quartam partem unius ducati de quolibet centenario ducatorum ; præsentibus, durante vitâ naturali *præfati Laurentii*, in omnibus et per omnia valituris, donec has literas nostras, per intimationem publicam *eidem Laurentio*, faciendam, nos aut aliquis successorum nostrorum regum Angliæ, aliis literis patentibus, duxerimus aut duxerit revocandas.

In cujus, etc.

Teste rege apud Westmonasterium, quarto die junii.

Per ipsum regem.

De consule, infrà Insulam de Syo, constituto.[1]

Rex, omnibus ad quos, etc. salutem.

Sciatis quòd nos, de gratia nostra speciali ac ex certa scientia et mero motu nostris, nec non certis causis et considerationibus nos specialiter moventibus, dedimus et concessimus ac per præsentes damus et concedimus dilecto et fideli nostro *Baptistæ Justiniano*, quondam *Jeronimi* mercatori de Syo, officium sive locum magistri, gubernatoris, protectoris sive con-

A. D. 1513.

[1] Tom. XIII, p. 353.

sulis omnium et singulorum mercatorum aliorumque ligeorum et subditorum nostrorum infrà portum insulam sive terram de Syo frequentantium, morantium, mercandizantium, sive negotiantium.

Ipsumque *Baptistam magistrum*, gubernatorem protectorem, sive consulem mercatorum aliorumque ligeorum et subditorum nostrorum prædictorum constituimus et ordinavimus, ac per præsentes constituimus et ordinamus;

Dantes et concedentes *eidem Baptistæ* plenam, tenore presentium, potestatem et auctoritatem ad omnia et singula, quæ pro ordinatione regimine, gubernatione et conservatione mercatorum aliorumque ligeorum et subditorum nostrorum prædictorum bonorumque; et mercandisarum suarum prout sibi meliùs videbitur, ordinandum, exercendum, et perimplendum;

Habendum, occupandum, et exercendum officium sive locum prædictum ac cætera præmissa *præfato Baptistæ* per se vel per sufficientem deputatum, sive sufficientes deputatos suos, durante vitâ suâ, cum omnibus et omni modis feodis, præeminentiis, juribus, proficuis, commoditatibus, avantagiis, et emolumentis quibus cumque, in tàm amplis et consimilibus modo et formâ, prout aliquis alius, sive aliqui alii, hujus modi sive consimile officium, et locum in portu insula sive terra prædicta, vel alibi, ex dono sive concessione nostris, sive aliquorum progenitorum, sive prædecessorum nostrorum quondam régum Angliæ, habuerunt, et gavisi fuerunt, habuit et gavisus fuit; eo quod expressâ mentio, etc.

In cujus, etc.

Teste rege apud *Westmonasterium*, quarto die aprilis.

Per breve de privato sigillo.

By the treaty of amity, commerce and navigation between his Britannic majesty and his royal highness the prince regent of Portugal, signed at Rio de Janeiro, February 19, 1810, the consuls of the contracting parties are amenable to the laws of the country where they reside.

By the tenth article, Great Britain has secured the ancient privilege of appointing special magistrates, named *judges conser-*

vators, in certain ports and cities of the dominions of the prince regent, to try and decide all causes of British subjects which may be brought before them; and it is curious enough, "*that the benefit of the English laws, the acknowledged equity of British jurisprudence, and the singular excellence of the British constitution,*" is considered as a fair return for this privilege.

"It is, however, to be understood, that in the cases of treason, contraband trade, and other crimes, for the detection of which provision is made by the law of the land, that law shall be enforced; it being mutually declared, that false and malicious accusations are not to be admitted as pretexts or excuses for vexatious visits and searches, or for examinations of commercial books, papers or accounts; which visits or examinations are never to take place, except under the sanction of the competent magistrate, and in the presence of the consul of the nation to which the accused party may belong, or of his deputy or representative." (Art. 7.)

His Britannic majesty and his royal highness the prince regent of Portugal have resolved, that each of the high contracting parties shall have the right to nominate and appoint consuls general, consuls, and vice-consuls in all the ports of the dominions of the other contracting party, wherein they are or may be necessary, for the advancement of commerce, and for the commercial interests of the trading subjects of either crown. But it is expressly stipulated, that consuls, of whatsoever class they may be, shall not be acknowledged nor received, nor permitted to act as such, unless duly qualified by their own sovereign, and approved of by the other sovereign in whose dominions they are to be employed; consuls of all classes within the dominions of each of the high contracting parties, are respectively to be placed upon a footing of perfect reciprocity and equality; and being appointed solely for the purpose of facilitating and assisting in affairs of commerce and navigation, they are only to possess the privileges which belong to their station, and which are recognised and admitted by all governments, as necessary for the due fulfilment of their office and employment. They are in all cases, whether civil or military, to be entirely amenable to the laws of the country in which they may reside, and they are also to enjoy the full and entire protection of those laws, as long as they conduct themselves in obedience thereto." (Art. 9.)

"His royal highness the prince regent of Portugal, desiring to protect and facilitate the commerce of the subjects of Great Britain within his dominions, as well as their relations of intercourse with his own subjects, is pleased to grant to them the privilege of nominating and having special magistrates to act for them as judges conservators, in those ports and cities of his dominions in which the tribunals and courts of justice are or may be hereafter established. These judges shall try and decide all causes brought before them by British subjects, in the same manner as formerly, and their authority and determinations shall be respected; and the laws, decrees, and customs of Portugal, respecting the jurisdiction of the judge conservator, are declared to be recognised and renewed by the present treaty.

"They shall be chosen by the plurality of British subjects residing in, or trading at the port or place where the jurisdiction of the judge conservator is to be established; and the choice so made, shall be transmitted to his Britannic majesty's ambassador or minister resident at the court of Portugal, to be by him laid before his royal highness the prince regent of Portugal, in order to obtain his royal highness's consent and confirmation; in case of not obtaining which, the parties interested are to proceed to a new election, until the royal approbation of the prince regent be obtained. The removal of the judge conservator in case of neglect of duty or delinquency, is also to be effected by an application to his royal highness the prince regent of Portugal, through the channel of the British ambassador or minister resident at his royal highness's court. In return for this concession in favor of British subjects, his Britannic majesty engages to cause the most strict and scrupulous observance and obedience to be paid to those laws, by which the persons and property of Portuguese subjects residing within his dominions are secured and protected, and in which they (in common with all other foreigners) enjoy the benefit, through the acknowledged equity of British jurisprudence, and the singular excellence of the British constitution. And it is further stipulated, that in case any favor or privilege should be granted by his Britannic majesty to the subjects of any other state, which may seem to be analogous to, or to resemble the privilege of having judges conservators, granted by this article to British subjects residing in the Portuguese dominions, the same favor or privilege shall be considered as also granted to the subjects of Portugal residing within the British dominions, in the same manner as if it were expressly stipulated by the present treaty." (Art 10.)

"And it is further agreed, that in cases of apprentices or sailors deserting from vessels belonging to the subjects of either of the high contracting parties, while within the ports of the other party, the magistrates shall be bound to give effectual assistance for their apprehension, on due application to that effect being made by the consul general, or consul, or by his deputy or representative; and that no public body, civil or religious, shall have the power of protecting such deserters." (Art. 14.)

"This tarif or valuation shall be determined or settled by an equal number of British and Portuguese merchants of known integrity and honor, with the assistance, on the part of the British merchants, of his Britannic majesty's consul general or consul; and on the part of the Portuguese merchants, with the assistance of the superintendant, or administrator general of the customs, or of their respective deputies.

"And it shall be revised and altered, if necessary, from time to time, either in the whole, or in part, whenever the subjects of his Britannic majesty, resident within the dominions of his royal highness the prince regent of Portugal, shall make a requisition to that effect, through the medium of his Britannic majesty's consul general or consul, or whenever the trading and commercial subjects of Portugal shall make the same requisition on their part." (Art. 15.)

The Residence of English Consuls.

There is one English consul in Sweden: four in Portugal, *viz.*

At Lisbon, a consul general.

At Oporto, a consul.

At Faro, a consul.

At Madeira, a consul general.

In the Brazils, a consul general and four consuls.

In Russia, a consul general and four consuls.

In Norway, four consuls.

In Spain, a consul general and ten consuls.

In Italy, eleven consuls.

In the United-States, there is a consul general in the eastern states, residing at New-york; and a consul general for the southern states, who resides at Philadelphia. There are also nine consuls established in other ports of the United-States.

In Barbary, there are eleven consuls general and agents, seven of whom are appointed by the Turkey Company.[1]

Of the Salary of English Consuls.

Lorenzo Strozzi, English consul at Pisa, in 1485, received a quarter *per cent* on all

[1] See the Court Calendar for 1813, art. *Consuls.*

the sales and purchases made by the English in this city and port.[1]

In 1640, the consul general for England at Alicant, in Spain, had the ancient allowance of two ducats on every British ship trading to that port; and also a quarter *per cent* for all merchandize of ships trading thither.[2]

Sir John Temple, the first English consul acknowledged by the congress of the United-States, had a yearly salary, from his government, of eighteen hundred guineas. The salary of colonel Barclay, the late consul general, at Newyork, was twelve hundred guineas; that of colonel Hamilton, consul at Norfolk, was nearly the same.

[1] Fœdera, vol. XII, p. 270.

[2] *Ibid.* vol. XX, p. 430.

CHAPTER IX.

The Consular System of Holland.

THE *reglement* of the king of Holland, established by a decree of October 15, 1807, contains all that is valuable of former regulations, on the subject of the Dutch consulate. It was printed in the language of the country, with a French version, and consists of thirty-six articles, of which we shall here present a free translation.

The commercial agents, in commercial towns and foreign ports, shall have the title of consul. As soon as they receive their commission, they solicit the *exequatur* of the government of the country in which they reside. When acknowledged, they shall make themselves known as consuls, in presenting their commission and *exequatur* to the local authorities. In their relations with them, and with other functionaries, prudence and perfect discretion are recommended. On one hand, they are to conduct themselves in such a manner, that the prerogatives and considerations attached to their employment, by treaties and by usage, may be preserved intact; and, on the other, they are not, by exaggerated pretension, to give room for complaint, or discussions between the respective governments.

The captains of vessels, carrying the Dutch flag, are obliged to present the sea-letter, and list of the crew, to the consul, accompanied with a note, describing the date and name of the place of his departure, and also the nature and destination of his cargo.

The consuls of towns, situated on the Mediterranean and the gulf of Venice, as well as those residing at Cadix and Seville, shall oblige the Holland captains to exhibit to them, the quittances for duties of the Commission of the Levant; and they shall observe, in this respect, until it is otherwise determined, the regulation of the States-General of the twenty-eighth of October, 1791.

It is the duty of the consul to render all services which depend on him, to captains and sailors of the Dutch nation; to supply their ignorance of language and of foreign laws, in serving as their interpreter and defender near the colleges, and different functionaries of the country. He shall also protect, on all occasions, the interests of Dutch merchants; support their rights, and observe not only the execution of treaties and customs actually in vigor, but also the introduction of new and higher duties, or other measures, which may be hurtful to commerce.

In disputes between captains and sailors, the consuls shall employ all their influence to examine and terminate them in a prompt manner; and in case of need, they may invoke the aid of the local authorities to execute and support their decisions.

They shall also employ their influence to arrange and terminate, in an amicable manner, all disputes which may arise between Dutch merchants, established in the place of their residence.

They are authorized to legalize all documents and commercial certificates, which are to have legal effect in Holland, such as protests of average, policies of insurance, *procès-verbaux* of valuation, and other similar acts.

They shall seal all acts legalized by them, as well as the passports which they shall deliver to our subjects, with a seal, bearing the royal arms, with these words: *Consulate of Holland at* according to the model, which shall be presented with this regulation. They shall place the royal arms above the entry of their dwelling, for the advantage of Dutch captains and seamen: but this sign shall have no effect in rendering the consular habitation an asylum inaccessibleto the local authorities.

The consul shall endeavour to save the wrecks of vessels and cargoes, for the use of the proprietors; and he may exact for his trouble the indemnity granted to merchants in a like circumstance; but if the proprietor, attorney, or correspondent be on the spot, the consul is entitled to no recompense; nor is he to interfere except at his request.

The consul will grant passports to Dutch seamen, who have been shipwrecked or who have escaped from an enemy's prison; and he shall send them home by sea, on board of vessels of the nation, and denounce to the government, the captains who refuse to receive them. If war, or other circumstances, render their return by water impossible, the consul shall send them home by land; and he may give them, on the king's account, ten Dutch sous for every day they are obliged to stay in any port or town; and two sous for every hour's march, from his residence to the nearest consulate on the road to Holland. The sum advanced shall be expressed on the passport of the sailor; and the consul shall be reimbursed according to his specific statement, addressed annually to the minister of Foreign Affairs.

If a Hollander die within the *arrondissement* of the consul, without leaving a known heir, or testamentary executor, the consul shall make an inventory of the succession, which he shall take care of, and transmit to the person to whom it belongs.

The consul shall render all the services in his power to the vessels of the king, which may touch or sojourn at the place, or in the neighbourhood of his residence, and he shall aid their commanders in rendering their mission successful.

The consuls shall not exact from captains, nor from merchants, greater consular fees than those assigned by regulations already or hereafter to be formed, or established by long usage.

If an inhabitant of Holland sell his vessel in a foreign port, the consul shall receive her papers from the captain, cancelled and cut, which he shall transmit to the regency by whom they were delivered.

The consuls shall not be permitted to nominate vice-consuls, for places within their *arrondissement,* without having shown, to the government, the necessity of this nomination; and the vice-consul shall be no charge to the state.

Without an express authorisation, no consul shall accept the consulate of a foreign nation. He cannot leave his post without the permission of the minister of Foreign Affairs, or of the legation to which he is subordinate; and he must take care that the public service does not suffer in his absence.

The consul shall keep a register of every consular act, or official report, which, in case of death or resignation, shall be committed to a trusty person, who shall deliver it to the successor of the consul.

The consuls, before the end of February, shall make an annual report to the minister of Foreign Affairs, on the commerce of their district, in which they shall point out the means, which, according to their opinion, may be usefully employed to vivify and extend commercial relations with Holland. They shall also transmit to him a copy of their *exequatur*, and inform him of warlike measures and contagious disorders.

They shall, from time to time, inform the legation, to which they are subordinate, of every important occurrence, particularly concerning the commerce of their place of residence; and they shall furnish, every six months, an exact list of Holland vessels which have visited the ports of their districts.

Until new orders are given, these duties to the minister of Commerce, shall be performed by the consuls at Cadix, Seville, and on the Mediterranean sea, in every thing respecting the trade of the Levant. The consuls, in their correspondence with the minister of Foreign Affairs, shall separate subjects which require deliberation or particular determination.

The consuls in the Turkish empire, or Barbary regencies, shall continue to observe the regulations which concern them, until there is substituted a general and definitive instruction.

The costume of the consuls shall consist of a deep blue coat, with a silver galoon, an inch and a half in breadth; a white vest, with a similar galoon; small clothes of black silk; and they shall wear this dress, which is purely civil, on all solemn occasions, and as often as they shall publicly exercise their functions.

The expense of this costume, and of the seal and arms of the nation, shall be borne by the respective consuls. The postage of letters, received from the minister of Foreign Affairs, or from any of our legations, shall be reimbursed.

The form of the consular oath is as follows:

"I swear obedience to the constitution of the kingdom, and fidelity to the king.

"I promise and swear, that I will faithfully execute, in every respect, the commission with which I am entrusted, conformably to the instructions and orders which have been, or which shall hereafter be given me; and that I will contribute, as much as in my power, to every thing which can advance the interests of the commerce and navigation of Holland. *So help me God.*"

The consuls, after their nomination, shall send this form of oath, written and signed by them, to the minister of Foreign Affairs; and they shall renew it, before this minister, the first time they are in the place of his residence.

The ministers of Foreign Affairs, of Commerce, and of the Colonies, are charged with the execution of this decree.

Given at the Royal Palace of *Bois*.

Treaty of peace between Spain and the States-General of the United-Provinces, concluded at Utrecht, 1714.

Art. 22. The consuls established for the aid and protection of their subjects, shall have and enjoy the same power and authority, in the exercise of their charge, and also the same exemptions and immunities as any other consul has had, or shall have in the said States.

The treaty with the regency of Algiers, of 1726, stipulates that the consul was to judge the disputes of his countrymen, and not to be molested in any respect.

The treaty of Munster, between Spain and the republic of the United-Provinces, 1648, (Art. 16.), guaranteed certain rights, freedoms, immunities and privileges of consuls.[1]

[1] The *reglement* concerning Dutch consuls was communicated to me by Sylvanus Bourne, esquire, consul general of the United-States, at Amsterdam.

CHAPTER X.

The Russian Consular System.

At the time when Peter the Great was occupied in forming a plan of commercial communication with the most remote countries, he was struck with the advantages which might be derived from consular establishments, and he determined to appoint agents in the principal towns of Europe, for the direction and management of commercial concerns.

His instructions to his consul[1] at Cadix, dated in November, 1723, are worthy of notice.

After some preliminary observations concerning the means by which European nations enriched themselves in their commerce with Spain, he instructs his consul to set out for that country, accompanied with the prince Scherbatoff, in the quality of

[1] Jacques Jewreinoff.

travellers; and when the former arrived at Madrid, he was to visit the Russian minister, the prince Gallitzin, who was ordered to present him to the court, to have him acknowledged in his public quality, and, at the same time, to procure permission for the Russians to have commerce with that city. Meanwhile, the prince Scherbatoff was to form an acquaintance with the merchants of the country, and to learn from them in what manner its foreign commerce was transacted. He was to communicate, to the consul, the result of this information, and to present him to those persons whose confidence and friendship he had secured.

The Russian consul was to enjoy the honors, privileges and prerogatives bestowed upon the consuls of other nations.

It was his duty to give all possible protection to Russian merchants; and to settle and judge all matters between them, except those of a criminal nature. He was to ascertain the quantity, species and value of the merchandise in demand; and to endeavour to remove all obstacles to the rising commerce of Russia.

If it appeared, that the Spaniards voluntarily demanded the productions of his country, and in a considerable quantity, he was authorised to contract with them for the articles required; but not for more than was necessary for the consumption.

The consul was also instructed to furnish particular information concerning the merchant fleet, of twenty or thirty foreign vessels, which sailed yearly for America, stating the quantity and species of Russian merchandise on board, the time of its departure, and the quantity of cordage which it consumed.

He was to take care, that the Russian vessels enjoyed the rights and privileges granted to other nations.

Alexis Wischianoff was to remain at Madrid, to act in concert with him concerning commercial business.[1]

In the treaty of commerce, of January 17, 1769, between Russia and Sicily, it was agreed, that the contracting parties were each at liberty to establish consuls general, con-

[1] Borel, *de l'Origine, etc. des Consuls,* p. 88.

suls and vice-consuls, for the advantage of the commerce of their subjects, in all the ports of entry and of commerce of their respective states. These officers were to enjoy the privileges, prerogatives and immunities of the most favored nations. They could not be chosen among the born subjects of the sovereign near whom they resided, unless by his express permission. (Art. 27). They were instructed not to occupy themselves with the affairs of the vessels of their nation, except in an amicable manner, and as the arbitrator of disputes between captains and sailors, relative to their service, expense, wages or nourishment. They were not to mingle in the affairs of merchants, or of individuals of their nation, domiciliated in the respective states, except when they voluntarily submitted to their arbitration. Should the parties at issue think themselves injured by the decision, they might reclaim against it, and have recourse to the ordinary tribunals of the country, where they were domiciliated; to which the consuls themselves, in every thing which concerned their own affairs, were to be equally subordinate. (Art. 18.)

Russia, in the year 1781, claimed the right

of establishing consuls in the provinces of Moldavia, Valakia and Bessarabia. The Porte, afraid of their influence with the Greek princes and the inhabitants, gave no direct answer to this demand, founded on a positive article of the treaty of pacification. The Russian court renewed its claim, with a boldness which required an immediate reply; and the Turkish ministers sacrificed their *Reiss Effendi*,[1] and issued a diploma, acknowledging and receiving *Lascharoff*, as consul general of Russia, with a choice of residence in any part of the three provinces.[2]

By an edict of the empress Catherine, of November, 1785, approved by Austria, the consuls of his majesty the emperor of the Romans, residing in Russia, were promised all the protection of the laws; but they were not permitted to exercise any sort of jurisdiction, though merchants, or others of their countrymen, might apply to them as arbitrators of disputes. It was their duty

[1] The minister for Foreign Affairs.

[2] Life of Catherine II, by W. Tooke, F. R. S. vol. II, p. 114; first American edition.

to witness the preservation of the property of absent heirs or minors.

Russia, in virtue of the eleventh article of the treaty of Cainadgé, acquired the right of naming consuls for any place in the Ottoman empire, who were to enjoy the same rights and privileges, as the English or French consuls residing in that country, or those of the most friendly or favored nation.

By the treaty of commerce of the twenty-first of January, 1783, the consul was to be furnished with janissaries, for the protection of himself and family; to have wine for his use, free from duty. His house was not to be sealed under any pretext; he was not to be arrested, nor was he personally to appear before the tribunals. The pachas and commanders were to defend Russian merchants from the insults and rapacity of pirates. Lawsuits, for a sum exceeding four thousand aspres, were to be brought before the Divan, and not before another tribunal. The minister and consuls were judges of all cases, even of murder, between Russian subjects.

In the commercial treaty of the seventh

of June, 1801, between Russia and Sweden, it was stipulated, that the consul's presence was necessary in the execution of the laws relating to the succession of his countrymen, who died without testament, or who left no person to represent the heirs. (Art. 2.)

The consul was to be under the particular protection of the laws, and to enjoy the same rights and immunities as those of the most favored nations. He had no jurisdiction over his countrymen. Though chosen as the arbitrator of their disputes, they might still have recourse, in case of need, to the competent authorities. It was the duty of the consul to assist in a search for deserters on board of merchant vessels; and to aid in quelling any disturbance or riot among his countrymen. To ascertain the character of Swedish merchandise, imported into Russia, a certificate from the Russian consul, in Sweden, was required. If the vessel sailed from a port where there was no consul, this certificate was supplied by one from the Custom House, or magistrate of the place. The same precaution was observed concerning goods, imported from Russia into Sweden. For a certificate of the origin of property, or other consular document, the fee was two *rixdhalers* of the bank. (Art. 19.)

In cases of bankruptcy, the consuls respectively were permitted to intervene for the absent debtors and creditors of their nation.

This treaty is similar to that of December, 1787, between Russia and Portugal, which was renewed in 1798.

In time of war, the Russian consuls are recalled, and those of the enemy obliged to withdraw beyond the frontiers. Catherine, in her famous edict against "the impious and seditious principles of the French revolution," granted the French consuls but three weeks for the settlement of their affairs.

CHAPTER XI.

Consular System of Denmark.

At Algiers and Morocco,[1] the Danish consul exercised an authority similar to that of the French consul, concerning the property of his countrymen, their conduct and litigations. He was not to be molested, neither in his person nor his effects. He named his interpreter and agent; enjoyed the free exercise of his religion, and was at liberty to depart, with his effects, whenever he pleased. All provisions for the use of his family were free of duty.

At Genoa, the Danish consul was authorised to take charge of the effects of his countrymen, dying without leaving a testament or executors.[2] The inventory of the effects was made by a notary in the presence of an ordinary judge, and two merchants of

[1] See the treaty of commerce, of May 16, 1772, with Algiers, and that of July 25, 1747, with Morocco.

[2] See the treaty of July 30, 1789.

the nation; and were kept for the use of the absent heirs, minors or creditors.

At Saint-Petersburg, the Danish consul is the natural arbiter of the disputes of his countrymen; and his decisions, made by the request of the parties, are acknowledged and supported by the government; but, in every thing respecting their own affairs, the consul is subordinate to the laws and tribunals.[1]

[1] See the treaty of commerce, of November, 1782.

CHAPTER XII.

Consular System of Portugal.

THE Portuguese consular system grew out of the Spanish, which it resembles.

The consul is named by the king, from whom he receives a commission, which must be acknowledged, in the usual form, by the government of his place of residence.

The great end of the institution, being the advantage and safety of national commerce, the first duty of the consul is to exert his credit, intelligence and zeal, in support of these two objects; in the establishment and protection of commercial houses; in procuring entry for Portuguese productions; in supporting the freedom of navigation, and watching over the execution of privileges and exemptions accorded by existing treaties or conventions.

The consul corresponds with the Supreme Tribunal of Commerce, at Lisbon, and with the minister of his country in that of his residence, who aids him by his counsel, and supports his representations.

The consul keeps a register of all vessels entering or leaving the port or ports of his department, and also of goods imported or exported. He legalizes the passports and other papers, which the captains of vessels are obliged to present to him, and transmits a copy, by extract, of the manifest of the cargo, to the Tribunal of Commerce, to which he also sends, in the month of January, an annual report of all vessels, which have sailed to or from the ports of his consular department.

The consul is bound to exercise a sort of police over his countrymen; to see that they observe good faith and probity in their affairs, and that they do not violate the laws and usages of the country. He is obliged to denounce those who have disgraced the Portuguese name, to the judges of the Tribunal of Commerce, who take cognizance of the case. He is charged with the settlement of disputes or altercations between his countrymen, who are obliged to acknowledge his jurisdiction, and sentences of arbitration instituted by him, with their consent.

Commercial and maritime contracts are not received as legal, unless executed at the consulate.

For the transmission of important communication, he is permitted to employ an extraordinary courier.

He is authorised to appoint vice-consuls within his jurisdiction; but nominations of this kind, at Dublin, Cork, Hamburgh, Carthagena, Marseilles, etc. must be approved by the Tribunal of Commerce, or confirmed by the sovereign.

The consul general has one half of the emoluments of the vice-consul.

To render the consular office more respectable, the consul is permitted to wear the uniform of the officers of the royal navy.

Of Consular Fees.

For the management of goods, *ab intestat*, the usual mercantile commission is allowed:

	fr.	cent.
A vessel with three masts pays..........	60	»
A vessel with two masts................	30	»
For the legalisation of a signature.......	7	10

For four pages of a translation regularly written.................................. 25 »
For administering an oath............. 10 »

Besides the instructions given to the consul by the Tribunal of Commerce, at Lisbon, there are others, which are private, from the Marine Department, and that of Exterior Relations.[1]

[1] This statement was communicated to me by a Portuguese gentleman, residing at Paris.

CHAPTER XIII.

Consular System of Austria.

AUSTRIA, in different treaties of peace with Algiers, secured certain consular privileges, concerning the property and litigations of her citizens. Her imperial consul was to have the first rank in the line of consuls; to grant passports, to regulate the affairs and settle disputes of his countrymen, and to preserve, for the use of the lawful heir, the effects of those who died within his jurisdiction, without appointing an agent or testamentary executor. Litigations between Austrians and Mussulmen, were to be decided in the presence of the bey and divan; and all controversies between Austrians, by the intervention of their consul, who was to exercise all the functions of his office without impediment; to live in all security and tranquillity; and was not to be molested, neither in his person nor effects.[1]

[1] Treaties of 1727 and 1748.

By an edict of the empress of Russia, the consuls of his majesty, the king of the Romans, were to intervene concerning the property of absent heirs or minors, and might be chosen as the arbiters of disputes.[1]

Austria and Tripoli agreed, that the imperial consul was to have precedence over other consuls, and to enjoy all the usual rights, privileges and freedoms; to grant passports; to regulate the affairs of his countrymen.[2]

The regency of Tunis granted similar privileges.[3]

In the treaty of navigation and commerce, between the emperor of Germany and the crown of Spain, concluded at Vienna, it was agreed, that national consuls might be established in all the ports and principal towns of commerce, who were to enjoy all the rights, authorities, liberties and privileges of the most favored nations; to be arbiters of the disputes of merchants and of seamen; and, in the event of their death, to preserve their effects for the lawful heirs.

[1] November 1, 1785.
[2] Treaties of 1748 and 1749.
[3] Treaty of 1725.

A SHORT ACCOUNT

OF

THE LIVES AND WRITINGS

OF THE MOST DISTINGUISHED

CONSULS OF DIFFERENT COUNTRIES.

BARLOW (Joël), late minister plenipotentiary of the United-States, at Paris, was consul general of the United-States at Tripoli, in 1797.

He is author of the following works:

1.° *The Columbiad.*

2.° *Advice to the Privileged Orders.*

3.° *The Conspiracy of Kings,* and other poetical productions.

4.° *Project for the establishment of a National University.*

5.° *Discourse on the celebration of American Independence.*

Consuls of France.

Beauchamp (Joseph), born in 1752, was a relation of the celebrated Lalande, with whom he studied astronomy, and afterwards became distinguished in that science. He was originally destined for the church; but having abandoned the priesthood, he accepted, in 1795, an appointment to *Mascate*, in Arabia, as consul general of France. In 1798, he was called to Egypt, by general Bonaparte, who, in the year following, sent him on a secret mission for Constantinople. On leaving the port of Alexandria, he was arrested by the English, and delivered to the Grand Turk, as a spy. His life was saved by the friendly intervention of the ambassadors of Spain and Russia; but he was deprived of his freedom, and shut up in the cell of a fortress on the borders of the Black Sea, till the year 1801, when he was enlarged by the intervention of the first consul, and appointed to the consulship of Lisbon. He died at Nice, the same year, proceeding to the place of his destination.

In his voyage from Constantinople to

Trebisonde, he ascertained the geographical extent of the Black Sea, and the true situation of particular places. His narrative, which also contains useful information relating to commerce, is inserted, in an abridged form, in the second volume of the Memoirs on Egypt, printed by *Didot.*

BEAUJOUR (Félix), ex-tribune and ex-consul general in Greece, in Sweden, and in the United-States of America, is the author of an interesting work on the former country, entitled, *Tableau du Commerce de la Grèce,* 2 vol. in-8.°, 1800. He has likewise published two dissertations : *Du Traité de Lunéville,* 1801; *du Traité d'Amiens,* 1802.

During his residence at Philadelphia, he composed a statistical and financial account of the United-States, which has not yet appeared, under the title of *Apperçu des États-Unis au commencement du dix-neuvième siècle.*

BOSC (L. A. G.), member of the National Institute, inspector of the French national nurseries, and author of many articles on natural history, and particularly that of the

United-States, inserted in different works, was formerly French consul at Charleston, in South Carolina.

CHÉNIER, the father of the poet of this name, was, for many years, consul general at Morocco and at Constantinople. In 1767, he embarked for that country, at Brest, in company with Mr. Rochon, member of the National Institute. He was united in marriage with a Grecian lady of considerable literary talents. Some of her letters are inserted in the "*Voyage littéraire*," of Guys of Marseilles. Chenier was well versed in diplomatic affairs. He has left a history of Morocco, in three octavo volumes, entitled, *Recherches historiques sur les Maures* (Historical researches concerning the Moors), published in 1781.

CHOMPRÉ, one of the judges of the Council of Prizes, was formerly French consul in Spain. He translated the trigonometry of *Cagnoli*, of which a second edition was published in 1808.

CORANCEZ, formerly consul at Aleppo

and now at Bagdad, is well known as a mathematician. He has furnished the National Institute, of which he is a correspondent, with several interesting memoirs; the most curious of which relate to the Arabian tribe of Wahabis, of which he has described the origin and progress, as well as influence over the politics of the East.

COQUEBERT, *secretary general of the Ministry of Commerce and Manufactures*, distinguished by his researches in political economy, and by his labors in the formation of an uniform standard of weights and measures, was formerly French consul at Dublin and at Hamburgh.

CAUSINERY, lately appointed consul at Salonica, is one of the most ancient consuls of France. During his residence in Greece, he made a collection of medals, which is said to be estimated at 150,000 franks. The French Imperial Library proposed to puschase it, when the emperor of Austria, at the commencement of the last war, offered nearly the above amount.

CRÈVECŒUR, author of the *Lettres d'un Cul-*

tivateur Américain, and of another popular work, *Voyage dans la Haute Pensylvanie* (Travels in Upper Pensylvania), was formerly French consul at Boston, in the United-States.

D'ARVIEUX (Laurent), was consul at Aleppo, Algiers, Tripoli and other places. In 1668, in the quality of envoy extraordinary near the Sublime Porte, he negociated a treaty, by which he procured the release of three hundred and eighty French slaves; who, from sentiments of gratitude, offered him a sum of six hundred pistoles, which he refused to accept.

He was educated, in the Levant, by one of his relations, then consul at *Seyde.* Pope Innocent XI appointed him to the see of Babylon.

He furnished the earliest European account of the coffee plant, in a letter addressed to Dufour, in 1684. His works, entitled, *Mémoires*, in six volumes, in 12.°, were published, at Paris, in 1735, by Father Labat. He died in 1702, in the sixty-seventh year of his age.

Delile, physician and botanist, and one of the members of the Institute of Egypt, was lately vice-consul of France, at Wilmington, in North Carolina. He has published different memoirs on botany, and some very curious experiments on the poisonous effects of the *Upas-tree,* brought from Java by the naturalist *Lechenault.* His collections of natural history, made in Egypt and in the United States, are deposited in the Museum at Paris. M. Delile is now occupied with the botanical part of the great national work on Egypt, some numbers of which have already appeared.

D'Hauterive, counsellor of state, was formerly consul general at New-York. He is the author of several anonymous dissertations, and of a very interesting work, entitled, *De l'État de la France, à la fin de l'an* 8, which has been translated into several languages.

D'Hermand (le chevalier), chief of division of *Consulates,* at the department of Exterior Relations, was successively consul at Lisbon, Teneriffe and Cadiz, and consul general in Spain. When at Teneriffe, he published an interesting work on the *Guanchos.* His collection of medals is much admired.

De Maillet (Benoît), is author of the curious philosophical work, entitled, *Telliamed*, and of a description of Egypt, where he resided sixteen years, in the quality of French consul general. He was employed, by Lewis XIV, to open a correspondence with the princes of the interior of Africa, and this circumstance is supposed to have been the cause of *Du Roule's* death. In the *Telliamed,* which is his own name inverted, there are curious opinions concerning the nature of our globe, and the origin of the human race. In theory, he is a true *Neptunian;* for he supposes, that man originally belonged to the finny tribe.

His description of the Egyptian pyramids, is still considered as the most accurate that has yet appeared.

He descended from a noble family in *Lorraine,* where he was born, in 1659.

Du Roule was appointed consul for Abyssinia, and was assassinated on his way to that place. He is cited as a naturalist by *Linnœus;* and his labors are noticed in the Diary of the French Physician, *Lippi.* In the preface to Shaw's Travels we are informed, that a manuscript copy of the voyage of the embassy, which Lippi accompanied, exists in England.

Du Ryer (André), the translator of the Koran into the French language, resided many years as French consul general in Egypt, and afterwards at Constantinople. He was also author of a Turkish grammar, written in Latin, and he made a French version of the *Empire des Roses,* by *Saadi,* the celebrated Persian poet.

Fauvel, the present French consul at Athens, is the author of several interesting memoirs on the antiquities of Attica and Morea. He travelled in Egypt, in Greece and in all the islands of the Archipelago. He is better acquainted, perhaps, than any other person, with the geography and antiquities of *Peloponnesus* and *Attica.* One of his most important discoveries, concerning antiquities, is that of the Olympian Circus. Mr. Fauvel accompanied Mr. Choiseul Gouffier, in his first voyage into Greece, and returned with him to Constantinople, when he was appointed ambassador.

Fourcade, correspondent of the National Institute, and distinguished by his antiquarian researches, was formerly consul general at Salonica.

Giraud, French consul at Boston, is the author of several memoirs on literary subjects. He has translated into French, *Austin's Letters concerning England.*

Gondur, French consul at *Beiruth,* in 1788, published, at his own expense, an Arabian edition of the Acts of the National Council of the *Maronites,* which assembled at Mount-Liban, in 1706, in the monastery of *Mar Hannæ.*

"Gondur, consul Franciæ Beiruthensis, qui suâ munificentiâ effecit, ut liber typis describeretur, videtur illi esse, quem commemoravit Antonius arida Tripolitanus, Maronita in Arab."

Bibliotheca Arabica, etc. edidit Christ. Fred. de Schnurrer, in-8.° Halæ ad Salan, 1811, p. 317.

Guignes (de), ex-consul general in China, is author of the *Voyage à Pékin,* in three volumes, Paris, 1788.

Guys, distinguished by his erudition and researches concerning antiquity, was consul in Sardinia and at Tripoli, in Syria. He was the son of the classical Guys, author of the *Voyage Littéraire de la Grèce,* 1771.

L'Escalier, author of the *Marine Dictionary*, and other publications, and correspondant of the National Institute, is now consul general of France in the United-States.

Lesseps, the late consul general of France at Saint-Petersburg, and afterwards intendant of the province of Moscow, accompanied the celebrated navigator La Peyrouse in his voyage round the world.

Marbois (Barbé de), formerly intendant of Saint-Domingo, late minister of the Public

Treasury, and now senator and first president of the *Cour des Comptes,* was formerly consul general in the United-States. He is author of several anonymous Memoirs, and of a very interesting publication, entitled, *Voyage d'un Français aux Salines de Bavière et de Salzbourg, en 1776.*

MANGOURIT (de), ex-consul at Charleston, is the author of a work, entitled *Défense d'Ancône,* two volumes in-8.° with engravings, and of other publications.

NAUSEL (Alchasen), French consul at Beiruth, in 1756, is mentioned with distinction in the *Bibliotheca Arabica, p.* 318. " Qui patrum nominibus suum nomen adposuit, homo laicus Nausel al Chasen, consul Franciæ Beiruthi, avo ortus est qui a Drusorum principe Pakreddino rebus suis administrandis adhibitus, primus suæ familiæ *Chasen* opus est nomen paravit et patre, qui majorem etiam celebritatem et splendorem adoptus est,"—etc.

PEYSSONNEL (Charles), correspondent of the French Academy of Inscriptions, was consul general at Smyrna. In the quality of secretary to the French Legation at Constantinople, he contributed towards the formation of the articles of the treaty of Belgrade. He had applied himself to the study of geography and antiquity, and has left some treatises on commercial subjects; a dissertation on the kings of Bosphorus, another on *Coral*, and an eulogium on Marshal Villars.

PEYSSONNEL (N.) son of the former, was also consul at Smyrna. He was a correspondent of the Academy of *Belles Lettres*, and has left the following works:

1.° Historical observations concerning the barbarous tribes of the borders of the Danube and Pont Euxine.

2.° Observations on the memoirs of Baron de Tott.

3.° *Les Numéros.*

4.° A treatise on the commerce of the Black Sea, 1787.

5.° Remarks on Volney's considerations concerning the Turkish war.

6.° *Situation politique de la France.*

7.° *Discours sur l'alliance de la France avec les Suisses et les Grisons.*

He died in the year 1798, in the eightieth year of his age.

PERDRIAUX (Pierre Dietro), who died lately at Paris, in the ninety-first year of his age, was consul general of France in the Levant. He built a church at *Smyrna*, at his own expense, for the use of the catholics, and procured for them the protection of the *bachas*.

PERISTINIANI, a Venetian, distinguished for his antiquarian researches, was consul at Cyprus. Clarke, in his travels through Europe, Asia and Africa, informs us, that this gentleman dug up, in one spot of the Island of Cyprus, above thirty idols, supposed to belong to the most ancient mythology of the heathen world.

PICHON, lately counsellor of state to the king of Westphalia, lawyer of the Court of Common Pleas, at Paris, and author of Letters to William Pitt and of different memoirs, was formerly consul general of France in the United-States.[1]

[1] Mr. Pichon has lately printed a memoir *On the*

Poucqueville, author of *Voyage en Morée, à Constantinople, en Albanie, et dans plusieurs autres parties de l'empire Ottoman, pendant les années* 1798 *à* 1802, 3 vol. in-8.°, Paris, was formerly consul at *Janina,* in Epirus.

Rousseau, the present French consul at Aleppo, son of a former consul at Bagdad, is correspondent of the National Institute, and author of several memoirs on the *Wahabis.*

Savary, the author of letters on Egypt, *Voyage en Egypte,* resided for some time, as consul, in that country, of which he has given a poetical rather than a philosophical description. In the work of senator Volney, and also in the observations of the Egyptian Institute, the veracity of Savary was questioned; which circumstance preyed upon his mind, and is said to have occasioned his death.

judiciary functions of French consuls in foreign countries, which we received after our manuscript was given to the press.

SAINT-SAUVEUR (J. Grasset), formerly vice-consul in Hungary, is author of the work entitled l'*Antique Rome;* an historical and picturesque description of this city, ornamented with fifty engravings. He is also author of *Tableau des principaux peuples de l'Amérique, de l'Asie, de l'Europe et de l'Afrique.*—Engraved at Paris.

TOUSSARD (Louis de), a French colonel in the revolutionary war of the United-States, afterwards inspector of artillery, and author of the American Artillerist's Companion, two volumes in-8.°, is now vice-consul of France at New-Orleans.

English Consuls.

BARKER, now English consul at Aleppo, successfully introduced the art of vaccination there, in 1806. Bibliot. Britan. tome XXVII, n.os 394 and 400.

BEAWES (Wyndham), author of *Lex Mercatoria rediviva,* or a complete Code of Mercantile Law, was British consul at Seville and at Saint-Lucar.

Bruce (James), the celebrated traveller, was consul at Algiers; he died in 1794, in the sixty-fifth year of his age. His travels, in six volumes, in-4.°, embellished with charts and plates, were published in 1790.

Campbell (John), the author of the Political Survey of Great-Britain, published, in 1774, in two volumes, in-4.°, was consul, or agent, in Georgia, in the United-States.

Drummond, the author of Travels through Asia, published at London, in 1754, was some time English consul at Aleppo.

Eaton (Sir William), the author of the View of the Ottoman Empire, and of some other works, was consul, first in Russia and afterwards in Turkey.

Kerr (William), author of the Remarks on the Government of several parts of Germany, Denmark, Sweden, Hamburgh, Lubeck, the Hanseatic towns, and United-Provinces, was consul of the English nation at Amsterdam, where this work was published, in 1688. Sixteen years of the life of this gentleman were spent in travelling through different countries. He had the honor of accompanying king William into England, at the revolution; and of being interred, with his lady, in Westminster Abbey, where a monument was erected to his memory.

Mortimer (Thomas), who enlarged and improved the *Lex Mercatoria,* was British consul at Ostend.

Shaw (Thomas), had not the title of consul, though he acted as such in the quality of chaplain to the English Counting-house at Algiers, where he resided many years, and collected materials for his *Travels in Barbary and the Levant,* printed at Oxford, in one folio volume, in 1738. After his return to England, he received the title of Doctor, and was professor at Oxford. (See *Le Dictionnaire Historique de Prudhomme.* Article *Shaw.*)

Ricault (Paul), author of the *History of the Ottoman empire,* was English consul at

Smyrna, during eleven years. He died in 1708.

STROZZI (Lorenzo), consul of the English merchants at Florence, in 1485, is supposed to be the same person who wrote the life of his brother Filippo Strozzi, which is published along with *Benedetto Varchi's* History of Florence.[1]

FRAZER, English consul at Tripoli, and afterwards at Algiers, furnished his government, in 1767, with the *General State of the Commerce of Tripoli, by sea with the nations bordering on the Mediterranean, and by land with the natives of the interior parts of Africa.* In the year following, he drew up another report on the commerce of Algiers.[2]

Consuls of Russia.

BOREL (F.), consul general of Russia, at

[1] See Macpherson's Annals of Commerce, vol. I, p. 705.

[2] *Idem*, vol. III, p. 467.

the island of *Madeira,* was formerly, as announced in our preface, chief of division of the *Ministry of Commerce,* and assisting judge of the Imperial College of Saint Petersburg. He is author of the work already cited, *De l'Origine et des Fonctions des consuls.*

DASCHKOFF (Andrew de), the present minister plenipotentiary of Russia in the United-States, was, before this appointment, consul general in the same country. He has furnished his government with several memoirs on commercial and political subjects.

GUVREINOFF, who was appointed consul at Cadix, by Peter I, in 1723, was afterwards president of the College of Commerce.

Consuls of Spain.

COLOMBI (chevalier de), a direct descendant of Christopher Columbus, was commissary general of the armies of his Catholic majesty, and afterwards consul general in Russia.

VIRIO, consul in different countries, and lastly at Hamburgh, is author of a work entitled, *Datos sobre algunas leyes Inglesas que han contribuido al poder de la Gran Britaña an perjuicio de las demas naciones; con observáciones utiles a los que estudien la economia politica*, in 12.° Madrid, 1807. (Remarks on some English laws which have contributed to increase the power of Great Britain, to the prejudice of other nations; with observations useful to those who study political economy.)

Consul of Denmark.

SCHOUSBÆ, Danish consul at Tangers, member of the Royal Society of Copenhagen, has given a description of the vegetable productions of Morocco, in a work entitled, *Traité sur le règne végétale dans le pays de Maroc.* A Treatise on the vegetable productions of the country of Morocco.

Consul of Sweden.

Græberg de Hemso, vice-consul of Sweden, at Genoa, member of several learned societies, has published a volume on the ancient Scandinavian Bards, entitled, *Essai historique sur les Scaldes, ou les anciens poetes Scandinaves.*

FINIS.

www.ingramcontent.com/pod-product-compliance
Lightning Source LLC
LaVergne TN
LVHW101455200926
848483LV00001B/136

* 9 7 8 1 6 1 6 1 9 0 6 6 8 *